THIRD WORLD
AT THE
CROSSROADS

THIRD WORLD AT THE CROSSROADS

Edited by SHEIKH R. ALI

PRAEGER

New York
Westport, Connecticut
London

Library of Congress Cataloging-in-Publication Data

Third World at the crossroads / edited by Sheikh R. Ali.
    p.   cm.
  Bibliography: p.
  Includes index.
  ISBN 0-275-93057-2 (alk. paper)
  1. Developing countries—Economic policy. 2. Developing
countries—Economic conditions. 3. Developing countries—Politics
and government. I. Ali, Sheikh Rustum.
HC59.7.T444 1989
338.9'009172'4—dc 19   88-28834

Library of Congress Catalog Card Number: 88-28834
ISBN: 0-275-93057-2

First published in 1989

Praeger Publishers, One Madison Avenue, New York, NY 10010
A division of Greenwood Press, Inc.

Printed in the United States of America

The paper used in this book complies with the Permanent
Paper Standard issued by the National Information Standards
Organization (Z39.48—1984).

10 9 8 7 6 5 4 3 2 1

To my granddaughter, Jessica, whose birth
coincided with the completion of this book

Contents

1   Introduction
     Sheikh R. Ali   1

2   Third World Development: The Strategy Debate
     Jerry Kolo   13

3   Open Economies and Repressive Polities in the
     Third World
     Steven S. Sallie   25

4   Ethnocide: A State/Nation Interaction
     Marc Sills   37

5   The West and Third World Religion
     John G. Bitzes   47

6   A Typology of Islamic Revivalists
     Zohair Husain   57

7   Economic Impact of OPEC:
     Policies and Performances
     Shah M. Mehrabi   69

8   Human Capital: Untapped Resources in the Arab Gulf
     Amin M. Kazak   79

9   Vocational Training for Women of India
     Mary C. Muller   87

10   African-Americans and U.S. Foreign Policy in Africa
     Jacob U. Gordon   95

11   Political and Economic Origins of African Hunger
     Andrew Conteh   105

12   Nigerian Agricultural Crisis
     Pita O. Agbese   141

13   The Southern African Development Coordination
     Council
     Robert E. Clute   161

14   Nicaraguan Death Trip
     Thomas D. Lobe   183

15   The Third World Debt Crisis and U.S. Policy
     Sheikh R. Ali   193

Selected Bibliography   205

Index   213

About the Editor and Contributors   223

Introduction

Sheikh R. Ali

The end of World War II witnessed an upsurge of colonial peoples engaged in a desperate struggle to rid themselves of foreign rule. Throughout the length and breadth of Asia and Africa, nationalist movements generated among these populations a massive resistance to subjugation and an overwhelming determination to wrest freedom from alien hands. (Most Latin American countries had achieved independence much earlier.) The hold of colonial powers gradually began to weaken and finally gave way. As the march of the people started, the victorious echoes of their footsteps traveled from country to country and many nations began to emerge, holding high the banners of liberty and their own identities. Most of these new states became members of the United Nations, and many joined the nonaligned movement. Despite the desire of many nations forming what is called the Third World to think of themselves as a united bloc, they are beset by serious differences.

The appellation "Third World" refers to a noncohesive group of economically underdeveloped countries located in Asia, Africa, and Latin America; they are, however, considered to be united by common historical and political experiences. Most of the 125-plus countries in this category are struggling with problems of survival. At one extreme of the newly emerged nations are some of the new-rich oil countries—Kuwait, the United Arab Emirates, and Saudi Arabia. At the other extreme are impoverished nations—Ethiopia, Bangladesh, and Mali. The latter are so indigent they are often put in a separate category—the "Fourth World" countries, the poorest of the poor. In between the newly rich and the low-income countries are the newly industrialized nations of South Korea, Brazil, and India.

Slowly the gap between aspirations for technological development and the ties to traditional ways of life is widening and becoming a source of conflict. Many countries face the serious problem of defaulting on loans or of having them canceled. Such developments might deprive the Third World nations of future loans from the affluent countries—loans needed to sustain their growth.

What use the Third World countries make of their freedom will depend primarily on how they conduct themselves in the realm of thought, since it is ideas that generate action. Colonialism has bequeathed to them a formidable legacy of problems that they must face in order to resolve. This requires that they channel their emotional impulses into purposeful and constructive endeavors.

Years of toil and perseverance, of constraint and privation, lie ahead of them. The problems of poverty, hunger, disease, and illiteracy cannot be solved by the magic wand of freedom alone. The Third World must carry out a pragmatic study of its many social, economic, political, and religious problems, and find realistic answers. Each people has its own genius and destiny to fulfill, but there are certain human values and principles that are universal and that hold humanity together; these must be the bases for the new governments.

Many of the developing countries are nations only in a technical sense. Their cultures and civilizations date back to time immemorial and have in them good as well as bad elements, as do all human institutions. To these have been added both wholesome and unwholesome legacies left by foreign domination. Those countries that lay claim to ancient civilizations are sometimes under the illusion that the lure of Western development, based on science and technology, can be resisted by burying their heads in the sands of their past. But the speed with which men and ideas now travel makes it impossible to live in isolation; no country can remain aloof from world currents, and there is no reason why a modern nation should not, irrespective of the source, adopt outside ideas and technologies that work for its good, and reject whatever is unwholesome.

It would be to the advantage of many Third World countries to identify and retain the basic elements of their own culture and endeavor to synthesize them with the progressive elements offered by other civilizations. Only by effecting such a synthesis can they sustain their individuality and character, and still enter the age of science and technology that will enable them to consolidate their freedom, to raise the standard of living of their peoples, and to provide them with a full and satisfying life—free from physical want and mental stagnation.

It is easier to swing to the extreme than to attain the wise medium. Those who want to live in the past are often averse to the pain of adopting new ideas. On the other hand, those who shun the past completely perhaps do so because they do not wish to swim upstream; they find it easier to float with the current. Emerging nations must, therefore, think and act independently if they are to maintain their independent existence.

The strong desire of these developing nations to consolidate their independence, and to find their true places in the world community, cannot be realized unless there is a period of sustained peace. For it is only in an atmosphere of peace, free from conflict and the burden of arms and armies, that they can catch up with the time they have lost under alien rule.

Rising tensions between certain new nations and certain major powers, between small countries and their larger neighbors, continue to pose a serious threat to world peace. This threat is at once a challenge and an opportunity for the United Nations.

All of us are deeply concerned over the future of the United Nations as an institution designed to work for the lessening of tension in the world. In spite of its many limitations, the United Nations continues to serve as a forum for the expression of the views of the Third World nations as they seek to inform and influence world opinion. It is to be hoped that the United Nations will continue to provide this podium and to pursue even more effectively its original objective of maintaining world peace and goodwill. If the United Nations were to disintegrate, the developed nations might be able to adjust themselves to the new situation and continue their summit deliberations, but the voices of the Third World nations would be lost in the wilderness and in the silence.

This volume seeks to define, explain, and analyze the myriad issues and problems facing the Third World—a widely divergent group of states that defies sweeping generalizations. An intelligent examination of the Third World obviously demands an interdisciplinary approach—one that employs the analytical tools of the political scientist, historian, economist, and sociologist. Such matters as institutional stability, economic development, human rights, environmental protection, ethnic strife, regional cooperation, and national security require the breadth of a multifaceted perspective. Keeping these necessities in mind, we have therefore made selections for this volume that reflect the interdisciplinary nature of this scholarly exercise.

The Third World presents diverse and complex problems unlikely to be covered adequately in any single book. Still, we have attempted, wherever possible, to include chapters that treat, in a systematic and comprehensive way, many major questions about the tricontinental conjunction. One of the burning issues in the Third World is the political and economic crisis of hunger—especially starvation and death in Ethiopia and other African countries. In order to treat this topic adequately, we have chosen to include an exhaustive article (Chapter 11) on this increasingly global concern. Our primary goal has been to draw the reader into the great controversies and debates surrounding the future of the developing nations. To that end, our success lies in the hope that this collection will stimulate further creative thinking, and inspire subsequent study and discussion.

In Chapter 2 Jerry Kolo maintains that the development of the Third World constitutes a special challenge to all those directly or indirectly interested in the progress of this region. Part of the challenge for development planners and scholars continues to be the refinement of known development strategies, and/or the conceptualization of new ones, to suit Third World realities and help achieve sustainable development. The latest of the three major development strategies adopted in this region since independence is termed the people-oriented strategy. One of the many options of this strategy is institution building, that is, a process of (re)creating and blending indigenous and foreign action systems for problem solving. Kolo examines this option as well as the ramifications of its viability.

Chapter 3, by Steven S. Sallie, highlights the conceptual significance and analytical distinctiveness of national economic openness. He emphasizes an unacknowledged core position, within the debate, represented by mainstream and critical perspectives on both political and economic development issues. The paper also investigates (empirically) the relationship between economic openness and one potential political concomitant, government repression.

Sallie also analyzes a sample of 63 Third World nations during the 1960s, employing a cross-sectional design that uses aggregate data for broad-based indexes as variables. The statistical findings were contrary to those predicted by the mainstream view. They provided, rather, some substantiation for suppositions emerging from the critical sector perspective. Economic openness was discovered to be positively and significantly associated with government repression. In some repression equations, it was the most powerful determinant and best predictor of government repression.

In Chapter 4, Marc Sills gives a specific, operational definition of ethnocide. This definition is viewed as essential to the facilitation of the discussion of state behavior that may be destructive to both the existence and the character of indigenous nations. Use of this concept would make possible subsequent theoretical analyses of state/nation interaction, clarifying conditions under which ethnocide is likely to occur.

This chapter traces the ongoing effort of nongovernmental organizations to promulgate international legislation that would protect the right of indigenous nations to self-determination or "ethnodevelopment." Such an effort calls for clarification of key concepts, such as "ethnocide," as distinct from behavior that would be prohibited under international legislation. This clarification is necessitated by the consistent attempt of states to define conflicts with indigenous peoples as "internal problems," inherent to nation building (of states), rather than as power struggles endemic to most state/nation interactions. Correlation of a global excess of state/nation violence with ethnocidal dynamics demands the formulation of a working interaction theory that incorporates the concept of ethnocide.

Chapter 5, by John G. Bitzes, focuses on the adverse effects that religion has had on the foreign policy of the United States. He demonstrates how this has been largely caused by cultural differences, and by ignorance fostered by the educational systems and the information media of the United States and other Western democracies. Bitzes maintains that there are important changes to be made and new, more realistic attitudes to be developed that will be crucial to the establishment of a healthy relationship between the Western democracies and the Third World.

In Chapter 6, Zohair Husain identifies four major "ideal" types of Islamic revivalists: the Muslim fundamentalists, traditionalists, modernists and pragmatists. These four categories are subsequently compared in a typological way. They are described as follows: Fundamentalists are sometimes revolutionary and usually puritanical in their religiopolitical orientation. They often believe in *ijtihad* (inde-

pendent reasoning), condemn *taqlid* (blind emulation in legal interpretation), zealously promote the five *faraidh* (obligatory duties),
and struggle ceaselessly to establish an "Islamic state" based on the
comprehensive and rigorous application of the *shariah* (Islamic law).

Traditionalists often come from the ranks of the *ulama* (Islamic
scholars) and tend to adhere to the Islamic laws, customs, and traditions practiced in both the classical and the medieval periods of Islam.
The major hallmark of Sunni traditionalists is their rejection of *ijtihad*
and belief in *taqlid*. Though normally apolitical, passive, status-quo
oriented and tolerant of local customs, traditionalists do get involved
in politics when they perceive Islam and/or the *umma* (brotherhood
of Muslims) to be in danger.

Modernists are profoundly knowledgeable about Islam and are devout; they make a decided effort to reconcile the differences between
traditional religious doctrine and secular scientific rationalism, as
well as to close perceived gaps between unquestioned faith and reasoned logic. Like the fundamentalists, the modernists are vehement
critics of *taqlid* and persuasive advocates of *ijtihad*. However, unlike
the fundamentalists, the modernists advocate the incorporation of
far more contemporary ideas and emphasize the necessity for many
important revisions in Islamic laws.

Pragmatists are nonobservant Muslims who have been heavily influenced by both their formal and their informal secular education.
In fact, Husain points out that many in this group know more about
the Western intellectual process than the Islamic, and tend to view
the classical and medieval Islamic doctrines and practices as anachronistic. They often look to a broad spectrum of ages, philosophies, and
ideologies for their concepts and for models of political and socioeconomic progress. But despite their predominantly secular world
view, some in this group engage in the politics of Islam to enhance
their legitimacy, to integrate and unite their fragmented citizenry,
and, in fact, to inspire, mobilize, and galvanize the Muslim masses.

Husain's major conclusion is that Islamic revivals have not been led
by fundamentalists alone, as the mass media and scholarly preoccupation with Islamic fundamentalism suggests, but by traditionalists,
modernists, and pragmatists as well. In fact, the contemporary Islamic
resurgence results from the dynamic interaction of all four types of
Islamic revivalists.

In Chapter 7, Shah M. Mehrabi notes that every time the oil price
changes, the Organization of Petroleum Exporting Countries (OPEC)

is charged with provoking world economic crises by the escalation of oil prices. The subsequent price drop in the world market might then appear to be a fair rebuttal. But, according to the author of this chapter, oil price adjustments do not account for resultant inflation levels and recession in industrialized countries. Such developments are due to a laxity in supply/management policies in these countries and to soaring interest rates, which combine to delay the necessary structural adjustments in their economies.

This chapter cogently examines the nature and behavior of OPEC—specifically, it analyzes OPEC oil prices and the positive spillover effect. The first section discusses whether OPEC is a cartel, and whether Arab Gulf oil producers are engaged in a conspiracy to override the working of the free market system in the West. The second section deals with the supply, demand, and price of crude oil. The final section examines the oil revenues of the Arab Gulf states and their spillover effect.

Mehrabi maintains that the corpus of the economic literature that has been published in the West related to OPEC has been one-sided: it has concentrated mainly on the welfare of the Western economies while generally ignoring the economic welfare of the oil-producing states.

Chapter 8, by Amin M. Kazak, argues that oil syndrome analysis emphasizes the problem of asymmetry in relative rates of sectoral growth in the economy and the disappointing levels of the development policies of the oil-exporting developing countries. He points out that oil wealth has already enhanced national income and affected the social welfare of the capital-surplus oil-exporting countries of the Arab Gulf states. Yet those countries still have two principal constraints for balanced growth of their national economy: limited availability of productive agricultural land and limited supply of domestic labor.

The objective of Kazak's study is to emphasize the importance of educational investment in the process of economic and social transformation in the Arab Gulf states. Specifically, he demonstrates that the social and economic ills existing in the Arab Gulf oil-producing countries are not solely related to their inappropriate investment policies and patterns of public expenditures. The author identifies the main cause as the lack of an adequate policy of educational investment—one that will effect those positive changes in the domestic labor supply that are first priority for development.

In Chapter 9, Mary C. Muller develops an empirical analysis of a women's development program in India. In answer to recommendations of a report prepared by the Indian Commission on the Status of Women for the Decade for Women, the government of India embarked on an experimental project to train women for vocations that will enable them to participate more equitably in the labor force. Muller's descriptive report is based upon on-site observations, interviews, and discussions that are analyzed from the perspective of social change factors. The recommended project went through various phases before it became an official program of the Directorate General of Employment and Training of the Ministry of Labor. In this analysis, policy dialogue is given primary emphasis in order to discuss the salient features of social change factors.

Chapter 10, by Jacob U. Gordon, discusses the U.S. policy objectives in Africa. He raises some crucial questions: Are they compatible with the interests and aspirations of peoples of African descent in the United States? What has been the role of African-Americans in the making and implementation of U.S. foreign policy in Africa? Are there constraints and/or promises for African-Americans in U.S. foreign policy in general and U.S.–African foreign policy in particular?

Probing these questions, Gordon explains the historical roots of African-American involvement and/or the lack of it in U.S. foreign policy in general and U.S.–African foreign policy in particular. He highlights key issues in U.S. foreign policy in an increasingly revolutionary South Africa as symptomatic of U.S. policy toward Africa. Finally, he examines the historical patterns of limited African-American involvement in U.S. foreign affairs as a basis for exploring a model for effective African-American involvement in U.S. foreign policy.

Andrew Conteh, in Chapter 11, emphasizes that most sub-Saharan Africans are no better off today than their parents before them. And the next generation will be even worse off unless there is dramatic improvement in the region's economic development.

Sub-Saharan Africa captured the world's attention in 1984–1985 when a devastating drought and poor government policies triggered a famine in the region, costing thousands of lives and putting 30 million others at imminent risk of starvation.

Famines have occurred throughout history, some of them worse than those of the early and mid 1970s. Yet, due to progress in communications, in the late 1970s the world began paying far more attention to hunger. Now it has become a global concern.

Political scientists have generally been preoccupied with international aid efforts, and with assessments of the varying strategies adopted by donor countries and international and national agencies. A common theme in much of this analysis has been a familiar refrain of "too little, too late," as if any amount of assistance could ever have been enough and on time.

Conteh does not criticize the sociological or the anthropological approaches to the problem of African hunger, but calls attention to one area of analysis that is overlooked. Despite the wide range of disciplinary and ideological viewpoints, the perspective on African hunger has one basic premise: it treats the issue of diminishing food supply primarily in terms of natural calamity. In so doing, analysts have foregone an opportunity to broaden their understanding of the causes of the current predicament to include political and economic factors—a matter of no minor importance. Policies of development for the food-starved areas of Africa can be improved only by an expanded understanding of the political and economic roots of the continuing crisis.

Furthermore, Conteh says, policy prescriptions that are formed by a predominantly nonpolitical view of the world tend, generally, to consist of technical and administrative recommendations. They stress, for example, the need for irrigation programs, for more modern and weather-resistant agricultural practices, and for the introduction of newer high-yield varieties of seed. Donor countries have been urged to create grain banks and to set aside a certain proportion of their produce to be sold to poorer nations at below world-market prices. However desirable and worthwhile such policies might be, they in no way impact upon the political and economic arrangements that, far more than changes in climate and rainfall, are at the base of human suffering and deprivation. In Africa, political and economic arrangements have converted a problem of climatic unpredictability into an immense human catastrophe.

Chapter 12, by Pita O. Agbese, deals with the current agricultural crisis in Africa that has forced many African states to reappraise their agricultural policies. The new policies being implemented include generous incentives to the private sector, the establishment of large-scale agricultural enterprises, the granting of loans for agricultural development, and the institutionalization of land reform programs. Agbese analyzes the magnitude of the food crisis in Nigeria and the various policies that have been devised to solve the crisis. He suggests that these programs are unlikely to resolve the situation in Nigeria. On the contrary, the present policies are likely to aggravate the food crisis, as they are liable to increase the dependence of the economy on the global system.

In his presentation (Chapter 13) Robert E. Clute looks at the nine states of southern Africa that formed the Southern African Development Coordination Council (SADCC) in 1980, in the hope of developing the area and reducing its dependence on South Africa. The SADCC has been relatively successful in achieving a greater degree of independence in the areas of energy, communications, and transportation. It has been less successful in the sectors of agriculture and of mineral and industrial development—due to divergent national policies, the lack of regional policies, and a dearth of funds. South Africa's destabilization efforts through harassment of SADCC transportation, military incursions into SADCC states, and the support of guerrilla activities in Angola and Mozambique have greatly damaged SADCC gains. The Reagan administration was rather parsimonious in its economic aid to SADCC and did not give the military aid requested by the group to defend itself. Unless SADCC receives increased economic and military aid, it may go down in history as a noble but failed experiment.

Chapter 14, by Thomas D. Lobe, describes Nicaragua's revolutionary experiences since the late 1970s. Three separate, though interrelated, issues have caused the downward spiral in the revolutionary movement of Nicaragua toward apathy, cynicism, and undirected anger.

First, Lobe explains that the nature of socialist revolution in an impoverished peasant country creates enormous difficulties; the vanguard party generally has few technical resources to transform society. The Sandinistas were not a mass party and did not possess great talent with which to handle the details of rebuilding and developing a socialist Nicaragua. Moreover, the new government was unable to persuade the vast majority of professionals, managers, and bourgeoisie to participate in the revolutionary process. Manpower demands in such social service areas as health, education, housing, and jobs were multiplied, due to the promises and ideological nature of the Sandinista party. The gap between expertise and delivery of services has widened—leading to economic mismanagement, social frustration, dependence on foreign advisers, and financial indebtedness.

Second, the long-term influence of the United States determined the conditions within which the Sandinistas must operate. Ever since the U.S. Marines occupied Nicaragua (1912–1933) and helped shape its values and expectations, much of Nicaragua has looked north for leadership, education, financial assistance, and cultural sustenance. This resultant exposure to cultural imperialism means that many city dwellers quickly learn English, expatriation continues, cynicism among bureaucrats is the norm, and black-marketing, speculation, and private trading are now rampant. Developing a committed and talented revolutionary professional group, when confronted with the deep roots of Yankee values, has proven painfully difficult.

Third, U.S. hostility and economic and military aggression against the Nicaraguan revolution compound the task of reconstruction and create further social contradictions. Economic embargoes and lack of trade and investment opportunities diminish the economic options available to the overworked Sandinistas. Moreover, against Contra attacks and fears of U.S. invasion, Nicaraguan defense efforts constantly necessitate shifts in budgetary and manpower calculations; social service delivery and economic performance are secondary to survival. Two contrasting ramifications develop from this matrix. As the economy falters, the willingness of many Nicaraguans to oppose the Sandinistas increases, and the U.S. government's readiness to offer leadership, training, and financial assistance further exacerbates this social tension. Also, the needs of Nicaraguan defense and security forces multiply, resulting in the recruitment of the most talented and energetic young Nicaraguans. It is this cadre of promising young leaders and professionals, including those in the militia, who are the most supportive of the government. They are the first to be killed in Contra attacks.

Thus a revolution that is thin on basic talent, is imbued with implicit and endless social ambitions, and faces unmitigated imperial hostility allied with outside social and cultural forces. The revolution must direct its few resources to survival. Its leadership faces painful choices that often contradict the revolutionary goals and purpose; low-intensity warfare is the utilization of such information so that revolutionary success can be translated as the failure of an unsuccessful, unpopular government to keep its promises.

In the last chapter, Sheikh R. Ali investigates the political and economic dynamics of the Third World debt crisis and its implications for U.S. foreign policy. The developing countries owe over $1 trillion to the governments and banks of the developed world. Most political scientists and economists say that this debt crisis constitutes a potential powder keg—a crisis that threatens to wreak massive political and economic instability upon the developing nations. The United States is particularly concerned about the strain that the debt problem places on friendly countries. It is therefore important to examine the impact of the debt crisis on the world financial system and to consider the proposal of former U.S. Treasury Secretary James Baker, for sustained economic growth in the Third World.

In sum, the authors of this volume have presented an encompassing analysis of many of the major developments in the Third World. It is hoped that this volume will serve as an aid to understanding the highly complex nature of Third World nationalism. The new nations cannot be the political and economic equals of the developed nations in the First and Second Worlds. Painfully aware of their actual weaknesses, the overriding assumption of the Third World leaders, of whatever political persuasion, is to preserve themselves from foreign encroachment. They have a desire not to become dependent on any single country for economic aid or for political and military support.

2

Third World Development: The Strategy Debate

Jerry Kolo

At no place and time in modern history has the issue of development seemed so contentious as it is in the developing nations today. This is especially true of the U.N.-classified 37 least-developed countries (LDCs), 24 of which are in Africa. Neither has there been any time when the concern of the global community about the problems and prospects of Third World development has been surpassed. Four decades of development planning in the Third World has left local and international development scholars and practitioners theorizing about the development problems and prospects of this region. This period has witnessed three major development strategies: the economic growth strategy of the postindependence era of the 1950s to mid 1960s; the Cold War-tainted modernization strategy of the mid 1960s to mid 1970s; and the people-oriented strategy since the late 1970s. The key components of this extant strategy include popular participation, environmental conservation, self-reliance, demilitarization, and fundamental human rights.

THE ECONOMIC GROWTH STRATEGY

The catastrophe that befell the economic growth strategy in the Third World is attributable to several factors:

a. The generally unsuitable economic atmosphere of the Third World for the workability of the strategy—for example, lack of investment capital, lack of skilled manpower, inadequate development data, lack of commodity markets, and lack of infrastructure and services for promoting the kinds of economic activities assumed by the strategy

b. A shallow grasp, by Third World political neophytes and development administrators, of the workings and intricacies of the strategy, and their resulting reliance on foreign development tutors

c. The lack of fit between the growth model and the development histories and experiences of the Third World

d. The socioeconomic and political instability of the Third World since independence, sometimes induced by imperialism, resulting in the constant preoccupation of most Third World leaders with the legitimization of their administrations rather than with the welfare of their fellow citizens.

THE MODERNIZATION STRATEGY

The failure of the modernization strategy (a package of projects such as family planning, community development, and the green revolution) is attributable to its intent, which was clearly ideological, and to the ethnocentrism of its proponent, the United States. The strategy was equated with Westernization, an ideal and ultimate state of development, epitomized by the United States, to which the developing nations ought to aspire. The strategy was used by the United States during the Cold War to lure these nations away from the Soviet Union, and not for their genuine and sustainable development.

THE PEOPLE-ORIENTED STRATEGY

The growth and modernization strategies came under severe criticisms in the mid 1960s, intensifying the quest for a more appropriate and feasible development strategy for the Third World. The criticisms emanated mainly from the dependency theorists, who posited that the unequal relations between the developed and developing nations result in a form of global politics that has a causal relationship with the internal structure, politics, and problems of the Third World. The dependency theory was the first substantive contribution by Third World scholars to debates on Third World development theory. Although it fell short of proposing an alternative Third World development strategy, it triggered some self-criticism and rethinking among

Western social scientists. It also fueled Third World resentment of imported development paradigms, leading to what Howard J. Wiarda described as a Third World global chorus with the theme and cry of "Let us do it our own way." He stated: "The Third World is increasingly inclined to reject the models and recommendations imposed as suggested by the West and is more and more searching for and asserting indigenous models and institutional arrangements more attuned to their own preferences, histories, and ways of doing things."[1]

From this "rethinking era" there emerged a new breed of development theorists, best termed neo-institutionalists, concerned with institutional transformations that will make people the centerpiece of development planning. It is only fair to say, at this juncture, that the people-oriented strategy advocated by these theorists, and also by the United Nations, is still in the experimental stage in most of the Third World. However, its effects are becoming increasingly evident, especially in Asia, where the nations are rapidly graduating from Third World status to that of newly industrializing nations.

Elsewhere, especially in the LDCs, certain institutional, structural, political, economic, and ecological factors continue to thwart development efforts. As part of the search for development strategies for the twenty-first century, these factors must be analyzed and comprehended within the present and future contexts of these nations, and in light of any development strategy proposed for the future. A brief look at some of these factors in their present state is undertaken below.

The Family Unit and Population Growth

Two observations are pertinent here. First, the family unit in the Third World has gone from biological reproduction to biological breeding. It has also retrogressed from an economically productive and self-reliant unit to a consumptive and dependent one. These changes have resulted from and/or led to a population growth rate that exceeds the economic growth rate, and is threatening to effective development. This threat is echoed by current Third World population and economic forecasts. For example, India's population, now growing at 2.1 percent per annum, compared with China's 1.3 percent, will be the largest in the world by the year 2048. Sub-Saharan Africa's and North Africa's rates have skyrocketed from 2.4 percent per annum in the 1960s to between 3 and 5 percent in the 1980s. By 2008, Africa's population is projected to reach 1.1 billion, with a work force of 510.3 million, 44.7 million of which will be unemployed.[2] From all indications, these figures will only exacerbate the economic decline or stagnation already plaguing these regions.

Centralized Governments and Bureaucracies

Among the key prerequisites for effective Third World development are the deconcentration of development structures, the devolution of development powers, and the division of development responsibilities. These measures are not very appealing to the growing one-party, military, dictatorial, and lifetime governments in the Third World because they do not shelter such unpopular or undemocratic governments from the wrath and people power of Third World citizens, who are becoming increasingly disgruntled with their venal governments. Experience has shown that these governments often pay lip service to these measures, especially when international donors stipulate the measures as conditions for aid.

Stupendous Foreign Debts

Most Third World development has been heavily import-oriented for investment, for sustaining production facilities, and for providing both basic and consumer goods. This has led to constant and large-scale borrowing to support investment programs and to avoid reducing imports. Sub-Saharan Africa's case is most serious, next only to South America's. As of 1986, for example, the former's total foreign debt was about $100 billion, including arrears. The annual debt service ratio was about 58 percent, and much higher for the LDCs. Scheduled annual debt servicing in 1986–1987 exceeded $11 billion.[3]

Dependence on External Aid

The prayer "Give us this day our daily aid" seems to have become a common method for financing capital investment projects and development programs in many developing nations. This addiction to aid is again exemplified in sub-Saharan Africa, where dependence on aid increased 2.5 times in the 1970s. In the 1980s, aid provides over

10 percent of the region's combined GNP.[4] Undoubtedly, these nations must strive to break out of this aid dependency syndrome if they are ever to achieve sustainable development.

A Destitute Agricultural System

While most Asian countries approach self-reliance in food supply, other Third World nations grapple with deteriorating food situations, both quantitatively and qualitatively. No sadder example of a destitute agriculture exists in recent history than that of Africa today, one that until the late 1960s produced surplus food for both domestic and external markets. Given the current Third World food scenario, agriculture can be pinpointed as the key priority area for the immediate and foreseeable future.

A DEVELOPMENT STRATEGY FOR THE TWENTY-FIRST CENTURY: SOME CONSIDERATIONS

Any Third World development strategy for the twenty-first century must acknowledge the spillover of the influence of the factors identified above into future decades. In addition to these factors there will continue to be the influence of global factors on Third World development. Some of these factors are reviewed below.

1. First, and quite crucial for Third World development, is the "aid fatigue" now being expressed directly or indirectly by international donors. In 1986/1987, for example, the United Nations, backed by its rich member nations of the North, as well as the Organization for Economic and Cooperative Development (OECD), flatly rejected two major requests by the Organization of African Unity (OAU) for a U.N. special session and for an international conference on debt. And as late as March 1988, U.S. Treasury Secretary James Baker told a Senate appropriations subcommittee that he strongly disagrees with proposals to forgive some of the Third World's debt, which now exceeds $1 trillion. Indeed, some Third World leaders are guilty of aid abuse. However, the developed nations cannot justifiably exonerate themselves from the historical processes that put the Third World in this predicament, nor from the political maneuvers that make them condone such an abuse.

   The declining aid flow from the North to the South is attributable to, among other factors, the fact that the North has to spend substantial portions of its resources on the welfare of its own citizens and to fight the adverse effects of overdevelopment, such as drug abuse, homelessness, and environmental pollution. Essentially, the cost of keeping development in check in the North is rising so fast that the aid the North can spare for the South is decreasing rapidly.

2. The disbursement of aid will be increasingly predicated on the subscription of the aid recipients to the terms, conditions, and, most important, the ideology of the donors. The fear of using aid to pursue ideological ambitions is likely to increase dramatically, especially as Western leaderships veer steadily to the far right. The backlash effect of tied aid on both poor and rich nations or economies is now leading many Western scholars to advocate a strictly ethical approach to the aid issue in future decades. While this issue is being debated in the West, it will be in the long-term interest of the Third World to start working out some measures for economic recovery, however hard or cruel these measures may be in the interim. The crucial thing is for these nations to cultivate the political and moral will to resist tied aid, to strive to align their population and economic growth rates to maximize the use of their limited resources, and to combat environmental abuse.

3. The global politicoeconomic game will only get more complex, and player-nations will need to operate from positions of strength. That is, they must have some leverage that will make them forces to be reckoned with, however relatively, instead of spectators to be towed along by the key players. The economic reforms currently being vigorously pursued by the Soviet Union's Mikhail Gorbachev, and advocated for the socialist world, attest to the growing reality that any nation that seeks to compete effectively in the capitalist-powered global economy must do so from a position of reasonable economic strength, in addition to the military strength needed to protect national territories. For the Third World, especially the LDCs, this will mean coming up with development strategies that will help them, primarily, to achieve self-reliance in food and housing, as well as guaranteed productive employment and fundamental human rights.

In light of the above, the twenty-first century will require a strategy that will bring about significant and widespread social change in the action systems by which development is undertaken in the Third World. The strategy must bring forth and utilize the initiatives of those whose living conditions need to be improved through development planning. Over 85 percent of these people reside in the rural areas of the Third World.

Given the tenacity with which most Third World leaders cling to power, and the lengths to which they will go to monopolize power, the strategy proposed for change must be one that will not exacerbate the already fuzzy political and development situation in these nations. It must be less dramatic and more incremental in order to achieve extensive and lasting change.

INSTITUTION BUILDING: A PROPOSED
STRATEGY AND AN ANALYSIS

In light of the conditions identified above, this chapter proposes the institution building (IB) strategy for Third World development in the twenty-first century. In the IB model institutions are perceived not solely as the structures and mechanisms for action, but basically as systems of action that comprehend structures such as organizations or agencies. The structures furnish the capacity and support for action. Institutions are "entities arising from collective action intended to influence individual behavior."[5] They are "the forms in which people organize their affairs in relationship with each other."[6] Siffin stated that the term "institution" refers to both the "normative qualities of an organization" and "a set of continuing patterns of action that encompass both the organization and its transactional relations with its environment."[7]

IB is one of the various approaches to social change. Change is the leitmotif of IB, which is a guidance system or activity for purposive change. IB seeks to bring about change through innovations or the development of new technologies that lead to substantive and qualitative changes in the norms of the change-inducing system or organization, in its interactional and behavior patterns, in the perception of its goals and means, and ultimately in its problem-solving capacity.

Briefly conceived, an innovation or a technology is "a reliable body of practical knowledge" that can be scientific (synonymous with Western knowledge), pragmatic (conceivable as indigenous knowledge), or a mixture of both.[8] An incisive analysis of the concept of indigenous or pragmatic knowledge was undertaken by Banpasirichote. She advocated that development should, wherever feasible, be anchored in pragmatic knowledge. Innovations are expected to ensue from organizations that are quite responsive to societal needs, that seek to solve societal problems, and, as a result, become "valued" or "institutionalized" in the society.[9]

The IB model underscores the importance of organizations in introducing and developing new technologies. A dynamic, change-inducing organization is supposed to deviate in many ways from the initial circumstances of its environment. Relative to extant organizations and the status quo, it is supposed to function or operate unconventionally, since its object is to produce new values within its environment—that is, to exert strong influences on the world views and value orientations of the people in its environment through some form of brainwashing. To do this effectively, an organization must have something valuable to offer, and it must have mechanisms for transmitting, remembering, and relearning its value orientations. These are the conditions by which the organization becomes institutionalized in society.

Institutionalization implies that the organization and its innovations are valued, accepted, and supported by the society or larger environment. Depending on the effectiveness of its problem-solving capacity, it is able to attain recognition in this environment; it is highly esteemed by other institutions; and it gets those other institutions to adapt its innovations, technologies, norms, or methods.[10] The need to be accepted by other organizations makes institutionalization a reciprocal process entailing normative, functional, and power linkages.[11]

The underlying process of IB is essentially heuristic and political rather than coercive. Through this process, an organization induces and guides innovations and also mobilizes the resources and interorganizational support for sustaining these (and inducing more) innovations.[12] The essence of IB, therefore, is to engender indigenous and long-run innovations that will enable practical problem solving in the society. For the developing nations, especially the LDCs, this implies digging into their rich histories for practical, effective, and comprehensible institutions or action systems for addressing community needs and problems. These institutions should then be "refrozen" within reorganized development structures.

Development and social science research must aim increasingly at exploring the unique characteristics of indigenous institutions and their impacts on the Third World environment under certain conditions. The research should provide development planners with more insight into potential or normative strategies of social change, ones that will respect and not disrupt familiar norms and practices but will reorganize them where necessary. Herein lies another advantage of the IB strategy. It implies a relatively stable, nonrevolutionary environment.[13]

CONCLUSION

The lack of fit between the Western-structured and Western-suited institutions transferred to the largely traditional societies and loosely organized governments of the developing nations has thwarted development efforts in these nations over the years. These imported institutions introduced predetermined solutions and inhibited the development of analytical and innovative skills among Third World planners and citizens, respectively, to address the unique problems of their nations.

It can be learned from history that indigenous innovations or technologies guaranteed the self-reliance of Third World nations in meeting their basic needs before the advent of Westernization with its monetized economy and structured bureaucracy. The proposal in this chapter is not to re-create the development wheel in the Third World, a proposal that clearly denies reality. However, the case is made for a realignment of the wheel to Third World realities, and for decentralized development structures that will accommodate indigenous action systems and broaden the people's capacity for self-reliant and sustainable development. It is proposed that some basic human needs (preventive health care, housing, food/agriculture, and elementary and adult education) should be provided through indigenous action systems comprehended by structures and mechanisms decentralized to the grass roots. That would leave the macrogovernmental structures—the existing bureaucratic agencies with tasks related to foreign affairs, national defense, external trade, national budgeting, and energy. This division of labor is a feature of the IB strategy that seeks to boost the people's sense of responsibility and achievement.

From the analysis thus far, it can be said that the IB paradigm has enormous potential for implementing people-oriented development effectively in the Third World. The organizational framework for operationalizing this paradigm must be designed by Third World planners to suit the circumstances surrounding or unique to development planning in their nations. Kulshrestha, Ariyo, and Kolo each attempted such a framework, albeit a conceptual one, for Nigeria.[14] Some aspects of their models may be said to have universal applicability in the Third World—contingent, of course, on appropriate adjustments to local realities.

The implications of, or conditions for, operationalizing the IB model effectively in any developing nation cannot be overlooked. Concisely, these include the following:

a. The political will of Third World leaders to institute a genuine process of change through, and by legitimizing, IB

b. Decentralization of developmental structures and deconcentration of development powers

c. Responsive and accountable organizational leadership

d. Surveys and research on development conditions

e. Skilled manpower in all institutions

f. Resources to train and remunerate manpower, to fund research, and to disseminate information.

NOTES

1. Howard J. Wiarda, "Ethnocentrism and Third World Development," *Society* 24, no. 6 (1987): 55, 63.

2. U.N. Economic Commission for Africa, *ECA and Africa's Development, 1983-2008: A Preliminary Perspective Study* (Addis Ababa, Ethiopia: ECA, April 1983), p. 21.

3. M. J. Williams, "African Debt and Economic Recovery: Required Adjustments by the IMF and Donor Governments," *Development* 2/3 (1987): 7.

4. Ibid.

5. G. H. Honadle et al., "Dealing with Institutional and Organizational Realities," in *Implementing Rural Development Projects: Lessons from A.I.D. and World Bank Experiences*, edited by E. R. Moss and D. D. Gow (Boulder, Colo.: Westview Press, 1985), p. 42.

6. G. F. Gant, *Development Administration: Concepts, Goals, Methods* (Madison: University of Wisconsin Press, 1979), p. 13.

7. William J. Siffin, "The Institution Building Perspective: Properties, Problems, and Promise," in *Institution Building: A Model for Applied Social Change*, edited by D. W. Thomas et al. (Cambridge, Mass.: Schenkman, 1972), p. 114.

8. Ibid., p. 123.

9. Chantana Banpasirichote, "Indigenous Knowledge and Development Theory," *New Asian Vision* 3, no. 2 (1986): 38-59.

10. G. S. Cheema, "Introduction," in *Institutional Dimensions of Regional Development*, edited by G. S. Cheema (Singapore: Maruzen Asia for the United Nations Centre for Regional Development, 1981), p. 4.

11. Harry R. Potter, "Criteria of Institutional Change as Guildelines for Assessing Project Maturation," in *Institution Building: A Model for Applied Social Change*, edited by D. W. Thomas et al. (Cambridge, Mass.: Schenkman, 1972), p. 154.

12. Milton J. Esman, "Some Aspects in Institution Building Theory," in *Institution Building: A Model for Applied Social Change*, edited by D. W. Thomas et al. (Cambridge, Mass.: Schenkman, 1972), 67.

13. Ibid., p. 82.

14. Joseph A. Ariyo, "National Development Planning and Regional Policy: The Nigerian Case," unpublished Ph.D. dissertation, University of Waterloo (Ontario), 1983; Jerry Kolo, "Institutional Design for Community Planning in

Nigeria: A Conceptual Model," unpublished Ph.D. dissertation, University of Waterloo (Ontario), 1986; and S. K. Kulshrestha, "A Proposed Concept of Polarized Activity Centers for Spatio-Economic Development," unpublished Ph.D. dissertation, Department of Urban and Regional Planning, Ahmadu Bello University, (Zaira, Nigeria), 1980.

3

Open Economies and Repressive Polities in the Third World

Steven S. Sallie

The less-developed countries (LDCs) of the Third World continue to experience, as commonly perceived, much more political violence and coercion than do the more-developed countries (MDCs) of the First World. In particular, government repression has been a seemingly dominant political characteristic in most of these nations since at least their independence in the 1950s and 1960s. Government repression includes a wide array of coercive activities sponsored and supported by the state: censorship of the mass media; restrictions on opposition parties; declarations of martial law; the institution of curfews; the arrest and jailing of political opponents; the exile and deportation of political persons; the use of torture and beatings; threats to use physical force; and an intimidating physical presence, visible or otherwise.

Which environment, the domestic or the international, is the main causal reservoir of these afflictions? Whereas traditional social science theories of political violence and coercion have emphasized internal causes within the domestic environment, so-called radical theories have postulated external determinants within the international system. The endogenous versus exogenous debate on both political and economic development issues centers unequivocally on the utility and, ultimately, on the desirability of national economic openness to world market forces and external actors, including multinational corporations (MNCs).

This chapter attempts to highlight the conceptual significance of economic openness; emphasize its often unacknowledged position within the debate by presentation of competing analytical perspectives on development; and investigate empirically the relationship between economic openness and government repression within LDCs during the 1960s, by means of a quantitative cross-national analysis.

ECONOMIC OPENNESS

In this study, economic openness is underscored as the central concept to be used within almost any model linking systemic and national levels, and in uncovering how world market forces are transmitted to nations to generate or induce economic conditions and political behavior. Economic openness, as a national attribute, is considered to be logically prior to, and analytically distinct from, both a syndrome of conditions defined as dependency and the sensitivity or vulnerability effects experienced within a network of interdependence. The tautological arguments stemming from these theoretical frameworks—that the conditions inherent in underdevelopment equal dependency or that the interactive stimulus-response effects correspond to interdependence—should be circumvented by national economic openness. In addition, an understanding of economic openness as an attribute permits the testing of hypothesized relationships relating it to the conditions and effects drawn from these theoretical frameworks. In this instance, the focus is on the hypothesized political concomitants and consequences of economic openness.

CONTENDING THEORETICAL PERSPECTIVES ON DEVELOPMENT

The LDCs are selected for analysis because of the perception that they tend to experience more government repression than do the MNCs. Such a selection necessitates a discussion of economic openness within the historical, though on-going, controversy over development and underdevelopment issues.

Mainstream Perspective

Conventional social science theories on economic development and modernization, as advocated by North American scholars during the 1950s and 1960s, postulated that all nations would eventually become developed by proceeding through a series of evolutionary stages.[1] The progression of economic stages was to have beneficial political concomitants and consequences for the newly emerging nations and was posited to be synchronized to the stages of political development.[2] The political instability, violence, and repression so apparent and widespread within LDCs were to be replaced with political development (peaceful change, stability, and democracy)— from the perspective of liberal capitalism.[3]

The major causes of economic problems such as poverty and stagnation, including obstacles to political democracy, were thought to lie primarily within the society. Mass and elite political instability, as well as government repression, were deemed to be remnants or products of an earlier precapitalist stage when LDC societies were largely agrarian, feudalistic, and closed. Conversely, the theory and practice of liberal capitalist development, both political and economic, suggested that the solutions could be derived from, or alleviations could be facilitated by, increased contact with the MDCs, MNCs, and international financial institutions (IFIs). Emulation of Western societal values and increased participation in the world economy not only provided sizable economic gains but also cultivated political benefits. Thus, openness to foreign trade, foreign capital, and foreign aid meant increased opportunities to import ideas and mentalities conducive to the promotion of desirable political behaviors. Indirectly, economic openness was expected to lead to the adoption of such attendant attributes as instrumental rationality and competitiveness, coupled with the embracing of such value-oriented goals as the promotion of self-interest and profits. These traits were assumed to have strong capabilities to foster peaceful, legitimate political competition within the process of democratization.

In the 1950s an important extension to this logic, which rested on the mechanistic classical and neoclassical nineteenth-century theories of free trade and comparative advantage, pervaded much of the Third World. The "invisible hand" of an increasingly open market economy was to forge conscious political attitudes and behaviors that produced a rational and stable democracy. Or increased economic openness was to lead to higher levels of economic development, which, in turn, would create a middle class determined to push for democratization. Hence, all preferable changes, such as economic development, social modernization, and political democratization, were thought to occur together in some natural and unified fashion.

By the 1960s, these ideas reflected the merging of an instrumental rationality in the economic realm and a value-laden ethnocentrism in the political sphere. Such a meshing of ideas could be viewed as a more modern and disguised version of the "white man's burden," coupled with an idealized version of a benevolent liberal capitalism. The integration of these ideas had established, arguably, the theoretical and normative foundation for a liberal capitalist paradigm of political and economic development that emphasized, either directly or indirectly, the beneficial and desirable aspects of economic openness.

Critical Perspective

After initial critiques by structuralist and imperialist schools, the more contemporary challenges to mainstream theories of political and economic development have been posed by dependency theory and world-systems analysis. These critical frameworks locate the problems of political and economic underdevelopment and instability within the context of colonialism, imperialism, and dependency. Their essential argument is that Third World economies and polities have been negatively influenced by the world economy and intrusive external actors. The coercive and manipulative ways in which most LDCs have been incorporated into and conditioned by the world division of labor have made them extremely susceptible both to the vicissitudes of world market forces and to the instruments of exploitation employed by MDCs, MNCs, and IFIs through mechanisms of unequal exchange.[4] Besides the negative economic consequences of these processes, political concomitants have been alleged as well: hyperinflation as a form of socioeconomic conflict; mass and elite political instability; elite control and corporatism; creation of technologically advanced, bureaucratic-authoritarian regimes; and government repression.[5]

Although economic openness is not a direct, explicit, or highly noticeable component of either dependency theory or world-systems analysis per se, such a dimension or measure may be inferred from James Caporaso's interpretation of dependency: ". . . dependency requires us to aggregate all external reliances, or at least all those that are capitalist together."[6] The suggestion that dependency requires the aggregation of all external reliances for its measurement seems to make a broad-based concept, such as economic openness, theoretically important for the critical perspective.

Economic openness also should be a potentially useful empirical referent for social scientists who use cross-national designs, aggregate data, and linear statistical techniques to investigate issues of develop/underdevelopment. This study finds social science methodology useful in making well-grounded assessments concerning the relative plausibility of these two divergent analytical views on the political concomitants of economic openness. We now move closer to an empirical examination of the mainstream and critical positions on the relationship between economic openness and government repression in LDCs during the 1960s.

RESEARCH DESIGN AND MEASUREMENT

This study employed a cross-sectional design for a sample of 63 LDCs during the 1960s. Variables were first measured over a span of years, next weighted, then standardized via z-score transformations, and ultimately combined to form indexes intended to encompass many highly related phenomena. Multiple regression analysis was used to assess the relative explanatory power of economic openness for government repression when controlling for other independent variables. Data for the political variables were drawn from studies by Taylor and Jodice[7] and by Banks.[8] Data for the economic variables were selected from the World Bank[9] and Reuber's OECD study.[10] All of the following variables were transformed into z-scores.

Index of Repression, 1960–1967

This index, the main dependent variable, consisted of the sum of z-scores for the number of government sanctions and political executions from 1960 through 1967 per capita, and the number of internal security forces per 1,000 working-age population in 1966. The first component is an indicator of the repressive behavior of the state. The second represents the coercive potential of the state to repress the population. Although sometimes the state may carry out forms of repression through violent means, at other times it may only threaten repressive acts through an intimidating presence, visible or otherwise.

The combination of these two measures seems to capture more accurately the level of repression in a nation than just the use of behaviors, since so much of repression is psychologically threatening rather than continually demonstrated through behaviors. Furthermore, an effectively repressive state can make a population docile through the coercive potential at its disposal and may not need to demonstrate a repressive act. Such repression has not shown up in data used in previous studies. Seemingly repressive states such as Brazil, Chile, Nicaragua, Turkey, and South Vietnam have tended to be ranked much lower in any scale of repression than one might intuitively expect. The index partially remedies this problem.

Political Instability, 1958-1967

This indicator of rebellion controls for the normally expected response by the state to a certain level of threat or disorder. It consists of the number of protest demonstrations, strikes, and riots per capita.

Past Repression, 1955-1959

This variable is included in the analysis to assess the propensity of the state to practice repression at a later period. It contains the number of government sanctions and political executions per capita.

Index of State Strength, 1965

This index is used as a proxy for past repression in some equations. It is built by adding the separate z-scores of general government consumption as a percentage of gross domestic product (GDP) in the 1960s and military forces of 1,000-working age population in 1965. A state with greater consumption and larger military forces should be able to pay for a more costly repressive apparatus. Estimates for consumption were made for Afghanistan, Burma, Cambodia, Haiti, Jordan, Laos, Lebanon, Nepal, and South Vietnam. Estimates on military personnel were created for Pakistan and South Vietnam.

Index of Economic Openness, 1960s

This main index consisted of the sum of separate z-scores for foreign aid per capita, foreign trade as a proportion of GDP, and foreign capital investment per capita. It provided a more comprehensive measure of the overall relationship between global and national economies. The mainstream view is that foreign aid, trade, and direct investment have faciliated the process of political development (democracy and stability). They have been seen as useful sources in generating national income, allowing the regime to supply some of the basic needs or expanded wants of the population, thereby working as safety valves releasing pressures to satisfy mass demands and reducing the likelihood of political violence and the need for government repression to restore order. The critical view has argued that these processes produce economic stagnation, unemployment, inflation, and inequality. Wide-scale dissatisfaction, frustration, discomfort, and fear caused by these economic conditions can produce the mass political instability that stimulates repression. The few economic benefits to be gained from these processes are often spent by the regime to purchase the hardware, technology, and training used to repress.

Economic Growth and Development

Energy consumption per capita in 1965 was used as a measure of development, and the average annual growth rate of GDP was employed as an indicator of growth. Estimates for these control variables were made for Jordan and South Vietnam.

DATA ANALYSIS AND FINDINGS

If the question is posed as "Do nations that have more open economies also tend to possess more repressive polities?" the answer is "Yes," according to the findings of this study. All indicators of economic openness have positive, moderate-size, and statistically significant correlations with the index of government repression. The associations range from .43 to .66, and all are significant at the .001 level. All null or negatively directed hypotheses are clearly rejected.

An examination of these relationships by use of multiple regression analysis allows for an assessment of the combined effect of the independent variables and their relative importance to explaining government repression within the LDCs. The findings are summarized in Table 3.1. Equation 1 in this table indicates that 56 percent of the total variance in government repression is explained by the combination of state strength, collective protest, and economic openness. Economic openness, as reflected by the relative size of its beta weight (.43 versus .30 and .23), is clearly the best predictor of the level of repression within LDCs. The beta weights indicate how much change

Table 3.1

Regression Equations for the Large Sample and the Regional Subsample of Third World Nations in the 1960s
(large sample = 63; subsample = 44)

Dependent Variable:

Government Repression, 1960-67

Independent Variables:	(n=63) Eq. 1	(n=63) Eq. 2	(n=44) Eq. 3	(n=44) Eq. 4
State Strength 1960s	.25 .09 .23 .0076		.25 .09 .27 .0058	.16 .10 .18 .0965
Political Instability 1958-67	.48 .16 .30 .0032		.41 .20 .20 .0507	
Economic Openness 1960-67	.23 .05 .43 .0001		.31 .05 .59 .0001	.25 .06 .47 .0001
Economic Development 1968		.22 .15 .17 .1446		.06 .15 .04 .7008
Past Repression 1955-59		.07 .02 .41 .0005		
Economic Growth 1960s		.10 .06 .19 .0914		.07 .04 .15 .0968
constant	.06	-1.94	-10.77	-.81
F	27.09	9.58	35.01	20.00
R	.76	.57	.85	.88
R^2	.58	.32	.74	.77
adj. R^2	.56	.29	.70	.73

Entries are unstandardized slope, standard error of slope, standardized beta, and the significance of t. The regional subsample includes LDCs in Africa, Asia, and the Middle East, but not any nations in Latin America.

in repression is produced by a standardized unit change in each of the independent variables when the effects of the others are controlled. These coefficients suggest that when the influence of the other variables is taken into consideration, economic openness is the most important variable accounting for the level of repression. This interpretation of comparative beta weights is permitted because the variables were transformed into z-scores prior to their entrance into the regression equations. Even after the control variables have been entered into the equation first, to allow them to explain as much as possible of the variation in repression, economic openness is still able to explain an additional increment of 19 percent of the variance.

Equation 2 contains three "control" variables. As expected, past repression is the best predictor in the model, allowing one to infer that prior repression leads to more repression. Economic development and economic growth do poorly with repression. The model explains only 29 percent of the variance.

The next stage in the analysis consists of dividing the sample of 63 LDCs along regional lines. After running separate regressions for each region, it was discovered that the main model did very well in explaining the variance in repression for LDCs in Africa, Asia, and the Middle East, but not in Latin America. This unexpected finding runs contrary to the critical view relating foreign economic influence to forms of repression, which is deemed to be especially evident in Latin America. Only political instability explains much of the variance in repression.

Equation 3 reveals the findings for 44 non-Latin American LDCs of the Third World. A sizable portion of the variance in repression (70 percent) is explained by the main model. Once again, economic openness is easily the best predictor of government repression. In order more fully to assess the impact of economic openness on government repression, the five control variables are entered into equation 4 prior to that of economic openness. After this, it is still able to explain an additional increment of 15 percent of the variance in repression. Hence, economic openness can be considered a powerful variable in the analysis. In fact, its strength rivals the combined effects of past repression, state strength, and political instability. Whether economic openness is either a necessary or a sufficient factor, however, cannot be determined here.

CONCLUSION

The major finding of this study is that economic openness is a salient determinant and the best predictor of government repression for LDCs in the 1960s. As such, it buttresses the critical perspective's

Table 3.2
Indexes of Repression and Economic Openness

sample:	Index of Repression 1960-67 (Z1+Z2)	Index of Openness 1960s (Z1+Z2+Z3)
Afghanistan	-1.19	-2.69
Algeria (1962)	1.78	1.61
Argentina	-1.03	-2.56
Boliva	.23	- .87
Brazil	-1.06	-3.04
Burma	-1.64	-2.64
Cambodia	- .29	-2.50
Cameroon	- .75	- .09
Chad (1960)	-1.43	.25
Chile	.03	-1.44
Columbia	- .58	-1.92
Congo	3.90	5.96
Costa Rica	-1.34	.84
Dominican Republic	4.92	- .52
Ecuador	.22	-1.87
Egypt	.50	-1.54
Ethiopia	-1.28	-2.86
Ghana (1957)	.62	- .74
Guatemala	- .58	-1.72
Guinea	-1.34	-1.48
Haiti	.83	-2.07
Honduras	- .72	.35
India	-1.40	-3.55
Indonesia	-1.10	-2.60
Iran	- .93	-1.61
Iraq	1.26	- .40
Israel	1.25	4.72
Jamaica (1962)	.58	4.14
Jordon	3.14	4.00
Kenya (1963)	- .06	.34
Korea, South	- .72	-1.39
Lebanon	1.69	2.41
Liberia	2.60	8.55
Libya	4.11	5.65
Malawi (1964)	- .97	- .24
Malaysia (1957)	.49	2.08
Mali (1960)	-1.96	-1.56
Mexico	-1.20	-2.70
Morocco (1956)	- .38	-1.05
Nicaragua	.60	.42
Nigeria	-1.77	-2.01
Pakistan	-1.15	-2.53
Panama	2.50	7.82
Paraguay	2.17	-1.87
Peru	- .79	-1.01
Philippines	-1.90	-1.92
Senegal (1960)	- .63	2.10
Sierre Leone	-.20	.19
Singapore	2.48	9.93
Somalia	- .28	.95
Sri Lanka	-1.19	- .95
Sudan (1956)	-1.22	-2.55
Syria	1.03	-1.36
Tanzania (1961)	-1.69	- .68
Togo	- .52	- .13
Tunisia (1956)	.01	1.02
Turkey	- .22	-2.87
Uganda (1962)	- .96	-1.09
Upper Volta (1960)	-1.96	-1.93
Uruguay	- .70	-2.70
Venezuela	1.03	2.65
Vietnam, South	2.69	3.12
Zambia (1964)	.84	- .25

In the first column, the higher the score, the greater the level of political repression. In the second column, the higher the score, the greater the degree of economic openness.

assertion that forms of economic openness are related to repression in Third World nations. Economic openness appears to have played a role either in the generation or in the maintenance of repression in Third World LDCs outside of Latin America. Although no effort has been made here to extend the findings beyond either the present sample of LDCs or the time period, they clearly raise sufficient doubt as to the validity of the mainstream position on the relationship between economic openness and political development. The implication is that economic openness did not necessarily promote political stability and nonrepressive polities in the 1960s. To the contrary, the evidence suggests that LDCs with more open economies also had more repressive polities. A conclusion such as this disputes conventional postulates found in the social science literature of the 1950s and early 1960s—many ideas of which are strongly advocated in the 1980s.

NOTES

1. Walt W. Rostow, *The Stages of Economic Development: A Non-Communist Manifesto* (Cambridge: Cambridge University Press, 1960), pp. 307–331.

2. A. F. K. Organski, *The Stages of Political Development* (New York: Alfred A. Knopf, 1965), pp. 5–17.

3. Samuel P. Huntington, *Political Order in Changing Societies* (New Haven: Yale University Press, 1968), pp. 1–78, 397–432.

4. Immanuel Wallerstein, *The Capitalist World-Economy* (Cambridge: Cambridge University Press, 1979), pp. 66–76.

5. Guillermo A. O'Donnell, *Modernization and Bureaucratic Authoritarianism* (Berkeley: University of California Press, 1979), pp. 51–111.

6. James A. Caporaso, "Dependence, Dependency, and Power in the Global System: A Structural and Behavioral Analysis," *International Organization* 32 (Winter 1978): 24.

7. Charles Lewis Taylor and David A. Jodice, *World Handbook of Political and Social Indicators*, 3rd ed., vol. 2 (New Haven: Yale University Press, 1983), pp. 16–77.

8. Arthur S. Banks, *Cross-Polity Time Series Data* (Cambridge, Mass.: MIT Press, 1971), segment 1.

9. World Bank, *World Tables 1980* (Baltimore: Johns Hopkins University Press, 1980), pp. 30–227.

10. Grant L. Reuber, *Private Foreign Investment in Development* (Oxford: Clarendon Press, 1973), pp. 290–293.

4

Ethnocide: A State/Nation Interaction

Marc Sills

Since the first efforts of Jaulin, "ethnocide" has increasingly appeared in the discussion of the apparent cultural destruction of indigenous peoples.[1] Indigenous peoples are those "ethnic" or "national" groups that inhabited particular territories as viable social entities before states appeared and claimed control of those territories. Many of these peoples continue to assert their autonomous existence apart from the states in which they are found. "Ethnocide" has been used to call attention to the fact that such peoples are apparently dying out, or at least are undergoing rapid and chaotic culture changes that have very unpredictable outcomes.

Most of the literature in which ethnocide is mentioned is the work of either "activist" anthropologists or "indigenists," or the indigenous peoples themselves; many members of this community of writers are at present attempting to promulgate international norms and legislation that would outlaw the acts that may be interpreted as ethnocide, just as acts of genocide have been outlawed.[2] It is evident that this community of writers understands the meaning of the word, because they use it quite frequently. However, at present there is no common meaning, especially one that is accepted throughout the social sciences.

Although "ethnocide" appears in no major dictionary or social science encyclopedia, the word seems to describe a social phenomenon that is very real but only partially understood. Current working theories of anthropology, sociology, and political science have all explained different aspects of ethnocide, but because the phenomenon appears in the theoretical interstices of the disciplines, none have adequately described it so that the meaning carries across the boundaries of the disciplines.

In this chapter, I have tried to treat the concept of ethnocide as the basis on which to build a synthetic, multidisciplinary operational theory that is amenable to "reality testing," comparative analysis of unrelated situations, and quantifiability along a common scale. And, I hope, it will assist the process of promulgating the protective international norms mentioned above.

THE PROBLEM OF DEFINITION

"Ethnocide" has often been used as a negative "buzz word" to describe, in alarmist and polemical terms, a variety of distinct behaviors and situations. It has achieved currency as an instrumental concept in the victimology, as well as the anthropology, of native peoples. "Ethnocide" has been used to refer to military actions, state legislation, resource extraction, economic development, flood control, and a variety of other activities or products of various actors, including development agencies, multinational corporations, missionaries, state governments, and particular individuals. It has been used to talk about both the process and the accomplishment of imposed change in every aspect of "culture" (a system of attributes) from language to legal procedure and from nutrition to national identity.

Ethnocide, or "cultural genocide," is a concept that is taken from genocide, which connotes acts made evident by body counts, forced prevention of births, or forced removal of children. In ethnocide, there are often no bodies to count, as people are usually allowed to go on living, although they disappear as a distinct culture (a people with particular attributes). Hence, ethnocide is easier to see in retrospect, and harder to see as a present or possible occurrence, as it is not completely evident until a culture actually disappears.

In one of the most recent and coherent definitions of ethnocide, Stavenhagen holds it to be "the process whereby a cultural distinct people (usually termed an ethnie or ethnic group) loses its identity due to policies designed to erode its land and resource base, the use of its language, its own social and political institutions as well as its traditions, art forms, religious practices, and cultural values."[3]

But Stavenhagen is somewhat equivocal, adding: "When the process occurs due to the more impersonal forces of economic development, cultural change and modernization, yet not guided by any specific government policy, it is still ethnocidal as to its effect but may be labeled, in sociological or anthropological terms, simply social change or acculturation."[4]

This qualification is confusing, especially when coupled with a subsequent limitation of the definition that eliminates "intercultural influences and diffusion" as ethnocide. "Economic ethnocide," because it is not intended by policy to achieve cultural destruction but, rather, economic development, becomes impossible to distinguish from the "universal processes" of acculturation and cultural diffusion. Ethnocide may appear to be nothing more than "natural" culture change, unless it is explicitly directed, but toward a goal that has yet to be defined. How much and what aspects of culture must change, in order for the change to qualify as ethnocide?

The word root "-cide" implies that someone or something is killed, as in "homicide." But how is ethnocide to be distinguished from "natural" cultural death? Just as people die natural deaths, so, presumably, do peoples. History is replete with examples of cultures, peoples, and nations that are no more, and not all because someone or something killed them. And whereas it is clear how to determine whether a person is dead, how can we certify that a culture is dead? More to the point, how can we certify that a culture is going to die, in order to prevent it, if possible? At what point do we know if we have prolonged or saved a victim's life?

There is, as yet, no method for distinguishing ethnocide from acculturation, nor is there any particular way to determine the effects of past ethnocidal processes (for instance, during colonial periods) from those of the present. And the fact that, despite the enormous pressures of deliberate or incidental ethnocidal behavior, indigenous peoples continue to assert their separate identities imparts the additional possibility that active resistance prevents ethnocide. But does this mean that ethnocide does not occur because nobody or nothing "dies," because of resistance to the process?

"Homicide" is understood to be a crime having several possible contexts that determine the seriousness of particular acts. There are intentional, nonintentional, and incidental degrees of homicide, as well as several kinds of lesser acts against individuals, such as assault with intent to kill, assault and battery, and simple assault. Does ethnocide have similar contexts and interpretations? Homicide implies the roles of distinct, identifiable actors. Does ethnocide imply such clear distinctions? Who commits the acts? Can cultures be viewed as actors?

The "ethno-" root of "ethnocide" seems to imply the death of culture, which can mean both attributes and a people that is identified by particular attributes. Even after centuries of experience of massive and profound changes (many of them imposed), indigenous peoples continue to distinguish their cultures from those of dominant societies. Does this assertion of identity seem to imply that ethnocidal assaults are not directed at culture in the sense of attributes (because they are both mutable and persistent), but rather at culture in the sense of "peopleness," which implies the possession of the power that determines cultural attributes?

If power is the object of ethnocidal assault, does this not imply a power struggle between entities capable of possessing power? Can cultures possess power? To possess the power to determine one's own cultural destiny implies sovereignty, a concept of political science and not of anthropology, which conceives of cultures. Historically, indigenous peoples have been viewed as legitimate sovereign powers.[5]

IDENTIFYING THE ACTORS

To identify power-possessing actors, we turn first to the dominant actor, which, clearly, is the state. The state (the modern, European-model state) is a reified actor, identified by its territory and by the machinery of the centralized governmental control that is continuous throughout that territory. It is identified, over the course of time, by a succession of administrations that serve to define and enforce its particular version of social, economic, and political order by means of its monopolization of legitimized violence.

The state is part of a system of other states, all of which follow, more or less, the European model, although they may come to it via different histories. Since the Treaty of Westphalia in 1648, the state form of social organization has literally taken over the world. There is no inhabitable territory left unclaimed by some state. The system of this form of organization has proliferated especially rapidly in the twentieth century. The population of the system has grown to 168 states since the end of World War II, when the population was 46. But this expansion is by no means complete, nor are the assertions of state sovereignty automatically established in fact across the territories that are claimed.

The state is recognized as the dominant actor in ethnocide, as it alone is capable of generating the monopolized legitimacy of sanctions and other instruments employed to coerce the subordinate actor. Such sanctions, including the use of armed force, are not available to other actors, such as corporations, missionaries, or "dominant cultures." These lesser actors rely upon the state to act in their behalf. Although ethnocide may seem to benefit or even to be the product of lesser actors, it is the state that ultimately holds responsibility. The state remains the actor over the long term, whereas particular governments or administrations command the state over the short term.

The dominated or subordinate actor is problematic in its nature, because it does not follow a consistent or definite model. Indigenous peoples, ethnies, or cultures (all concepts from anthropology) may qualify as nations (a concept of sociology), especially where the social entities follow traditions of extensive confederation of smaller entities; but even when they are organized on a level only as extensive as a village or community, their nationality or "peopleness" is not necessarily diminished.[6]

Whatever their size or tradition, the people may be viewed as possessors of the power to determine their own cultural attributes and the reproduction of those attributes. The word "nation" implies this power of self-determination, so it is used; but in some cases "peoples" may be more readily understood. In any case, both "peoples" and "nations" are commonly considered the subjects of the right of self-determination;[7] this may help to explain the common disposition of states to diminish indigenous nations and peoples to the level of "ethnic groups" or "minorities," which presumably have no power or right to self-determination.

The state's integrity and national identity are threatened by competition from within that asserts the power to define a separate identity and a reality apart from the state. Likewise, the indigenous nation is threatened by absorption, assimilation, and other forms of domination, including exploitation of land, resources, and labor. For both state and indigenous nation, the idea of the nation relies on the common history, experience, and perceived destiny of the people. People may be organized in a variety of forms, including the state and indigenous national configurations.

Like states, nations are abstract concepts brought to life by the existence of people in real and distinct social organizations. The existence of the state form of organization does not automatically negate preexisting national organizations. In fact, it may never do so.

THE PHENOMENON OF ETHNOCIDE

In a model of state/nation interaction, determination of the phenomenon of ethnocide (which should be regarded both as a process and as a final accomplishment, though made specific by those who use the word) would require the identification of several distinct elements that affect the scope of culture of the indigenous people. Scope includes national self-identity, the control of territory and resources, the form of economy and political organization, the definition of individual rights and obligations, and cultural traits, such as language, religion, diet, healing practices, and costume.

The relative importance of these items of scope apparently has not been tested. Some have suggested that control of territory and retention of language are key elements, but clearly the most important item is national identity. Ethnocide must be considered final when the state has subsumed the identity of the people, as indicated by the fact that individuals identify themselves with the state rather than the indigenous nationality.

The elements of state/nation interaction that affect the scope of culture are locus of decision, content of state decisions, intent of the state, the effect of attempted ethnocide, and indigenous resistance.

The state must be seen to have usurped the locus of determination of any one or any combination of the indigenous attributes, within the scope of their culture. This might be established through review of the decision locus for any item of the scope.

The usurpation of locus of decision must be accompanied by a concomitant content that describes the item of scope in terms that are not consonant with those which would have been chosen by the indigenous people if the locus of decision had not been usurped. Such content is made evident by analysis of both declared and enforced state policy.

Together, locus and content, across the scope of culture, describe the intent of the state as one of the following possibilities: (1) the attempted elimination of some or all of the indigenous culture complex, (2) the unintentional effect of state conflict with the indigenous nation, (3) the incidental effect of extraneous (such as economic) policies of the state, (4) assault without intent to destroy, or (5) the acceptance of the autonomous determination of attributes by the indigenous people themselves. Possibly intent will be ambiguous.

The effect of the state's intentions, in order for ethnocide to be evident, must be the replacement of indigenous cultural attributes with those of the state culture. But one possible effect is that the attempted ethnocide will produce resistance, which may take many forms, ranging from low intensity (including passive compliance, minimal cooperation, and secret participation in prohibited religious ritual or clandestine use of the native tongue) to high intensity (including demonstrations, marches, and violent acts or armed confrontation with state authority). A typology of global conflict indicates that high-intensity resistance of indigenous nations to domination by states clearly surpasses all other forms of organized violent conflict: 72 percent (86) of the 120 wars presently in progress around the globe.[8] Of these wars, most are occurring in states of the Third World. Although he gives no clear analysis of social relations between states and nations, either preceding or in the aftermath of this violence, Nietschmann does consider indigenous nations to be geographically recognizable social organizations, like states. Resistance to ethnocide must be examined as an interpretation of this excess of violence.

Evaluation of any given state/nation interaction requires the summarization of elements. To the degree that ethnocidal intent (indicated by locus and content of decisions of cultural self-determination) is established, and to the degree that the action is successful (which is a function of both state practice and indigenous national resistance), we may conclude that ethnocide occurs. To the degree that ethnocide involves the full range of the scope of culture, the seriousness of the crime increases.

If there is intent without effect, ethnocide must be considered "attempted" (a lesser crime). If there is effect without intent, such as the concomitant of the economic development or nation-building attempts of the state, then ethnocide must be viewed as unintentional or incidental (also lesser crimes), depending on extenuating circumstances. If there is neither intent nor effect, then culture change of the indigenous people must be autonomous, that is, acculturation.

When the state has clearly intended and achieved elimination of any one or any combination of the attributes of the indigenous nation, ethnocide should be considered unequivocally intentional and pre-meditated, and deserving of the maximum opprobrium and punish-ment that can be mustered among other states and indigenous nations.

RELATIVITY OF THE DEFINITION

Ethnocide, in summary, should be defined as the attempted and/or successful elimination of the competitive control and the competi-tive claims for the control of territory, resources, economy, political organization, individual rights and obligations, cultural attributes (in-cluding language, religion, diet, and costume), and, above all else, the national identity of indigenous people. It is an act of the state against indigenous nations or peoples.

The phenomenon is not conceptualized in black and white but as the process of the destruction of any aspect or any combination of aspects of the culture complex, and the diminution of the ability of the indigenous nation to determine its own attributes. What to one particular state/nation interaction is ethnocide may not be ethnocide to the next interaction. Therefore, ethnocide must be considered a relative process. Comparison of unlike cases requires a common terminology and analytical base, provided by the interac-tion model.

Interaction of the state and the nation is also viewed as a relation-ship that is identified along a continuum between extremes of ethno-cide and autonomy (or ethnodevelopment) of the indigenous nation. Over the course of time, the interaction may display changes along this continuum that may correlate with variation in global economic conditions, modernization of technology, or other factors that may generate one of the configurations of internal colonialism, which has often been taken by itself as the equivalent of ethnocide.

The interaction might also be characterized in complementary terms of nation building of the state. Processes of consolidation of state legitimacy, penetration of internal colonies, or actualization of the nation-state all might describe the other side of the coin.

Following elements of locus, content, intent, effect, and resistance, a state/nation interaction analysis model permits comparative analy-sis, both in time series and across separate and divergent interactions. The building of a data base incorporating these elements of interac-tion presumably would permit quantification of the process, which

in turn would permit correlations of samples of state/nation relationships with independent variables, such as economic development,
population growth, and technological modernization, which have
been suggested as important factors in ethnocidal dynamics.

SUMMARY

Because of the nature of the global system, which is dominated by
the state form of organization, any international legislation that
would protect indigenous peoples must be the product of agreement
among states. No matter what form of political, social, and economic
organization is promoted, all states share the reciprocal recognition
of territorial integrity and will resist any agreement that seems to
threaten maintenance of this mutual objective. States will be reluctant to recognize even the existence of indigenous nations, much less
to consider proposals for autonomy that are based on vague and
polemical accusations of cultural destruction.

To the degree that it is established that indigenous nations do
control the determination of attributes of their own cultures, their
existence as coherent social entities becomes harder to negate. To the
degree that it can be shown, in specific detail, that states have usurped
the locus of control of indigenous cultural attributes and replaced
them with others that are destructive to the continuity of indigenous
culture, the evidence of the actual dynamics of ethnocide becomes
harder to dismiss as rhetoric. Where it is made evident that these
dynamics are the source of violent resistance, states must see that it
is in their interest to come to terms with indigenous peoples' aspirations to exist according to their own precepts.

That states should understand their own conflicts realistically is
not an impossible goal. If the ethnocide of indigenous nations is at
the root of the prevailing form of global conflict, then understanding
ethnocide is essential to the resolution of those conflicts.

NOTES

1. Robert Jaulin, *El ethnocidio a través de las Américas*. 2nd ed. (Mexico City:
Siglo XXI, 1972, 1976), and *La decivilization: Politique et pratique de l'ethnocide* (Brussels: Editions Complexe, 1974).

2. United Nations, *Charter of the United Nations and Statute of the International Court of Justice* (New York: United Nations). United Nations, *Conven-
tion on the Prevention and Punishment of the Crime of Genocide* (New York:

United Nations, General Assembly 260A III, 1948); United Nations Working Group on Indigenous Populations, *Declaration of Principles Concerning the Rights of Indigenous Peoples* (New York: United Nations, 1985).

3. Rodolfo Stavenhagen, "Ethnocide or Ethnodevelopment," *Development* 1 (1987): 74–78.

4. Ibid., p. 75.

5. See Glenn T. Morris, "In Support of the Right of Self-Determination for Indigenous Peoples Under International Law," *German Yearbook of International Law* 29 (1986): 277–316.

6. Anthony D. Smith, *The Ethnic Origins of Nations* (Oxford: Basil Blackwell, 1986); T. Morris, "In Support of the Right of Self-Determination. . . ."

7. United Nations, *Charter of the United Nations and Statute of the International Court of Justice* (New York: United Nations, n.d.).

8. Bernard Nietschmann, "The Third World War," *Cultural Survival Quarterly* 2, no. 3 (1987): 1–15.

5

The West and Third World Religion

John G. Bitzes

Weaknesses in the educational system and the news and information media of the United States have had a limiting and debilitating effect on the substance, course, and success of U.S. foreign policy. This is particularly true in regard to religion as it concerns the developing nations of the Third World.

Since the middle of the nineteenth century, the West has been undergoing a series of subtle changes moving it closer and closer to complete secularization of its cultures. Today, particularly in the United States, with its doctrine of separation of church and state, religious values usually exist on the periphery of thought, education, aspirations, and daily living. This may be understandable, and perhaps even acceptable, within the context of the Western experience. When, however, education and the news and information media ignore the roles that Buddhism, Islam, Christianity, Judaism, and other religions play in non-Western cultures, the door is open to dangers arising from ignorance.

If, for instance, the American people are to exercise their democratic right to help determine the substance and course of U.S. foreign policy, they first must be formally educated for the responsibility, and then the media must continue to supplement their education thereafter. Unfortunately, this has not been the case.

The "activist," the demagogue, the "yellow press," and the unscrupulous who covet a high rating no matter what the cost have all preyed on the American public's ignorance. This was very apparent during the Vietnam war and is obvious in today's relations with the Islamic countries, particularly Iran.

In both instances the U.S. media blindly followed the nation's leadership and exhibited little, if any, understanding or knowledge of the role of religion in determining policy and the course of events. Obviously, most of the nation's educational institutions were so shallow in their knowledge of the Vietnamese and Iranian cultures that, more often than not, educators were nothing more than extensions of the media and reflections of their ignorance, biases, and political or ideological persuasions.

As early as the Korean War (1950–1953), a knowledge gap was apparent between makers of U.S. foreign policy and the media and educators. The Sino-Korean invasion of South Korea not only exposed the weaknesses of the United Nations as a peacekeeper but also caused some important questions to be raised regarding the United States as the leader of the free world. First, did the media, leadership, people, and educational system of the United States have the knowledge and the psychological preparation for such a role of leadership? Were the American people willing to surrender their wealth and young people to implement a policy opposing the totalitarian forces in the world, be they fascist or Communist?

The answers to both questions seemed illusive and highly subjective, but some information should have been taken seriously and acted upon. One thing is certain: the Korean experience proved costly, if not embarrassing, for the United Nations and the United States. Further, in February 1956, Major William E. Mayer, a U.S. Army psychiatrist, reported some disturbing facts after studying captured Chinese Communist military and interrogation reports and interviewing returning U.S. prisoners of war. The Chinese had concluded that the American prisoner of war had "weak loyalties" toward his family, his community, his religion, and even his fellow soldiers. He was "ignorant of social values, tensions and conflicts." Even among university graduates, there was a paucity of knowledge or understanding of U.S. history, values, strengths, and weaknesses. The American soldier was described as "exceedingly insular and provincial, with little or no idea of the problems and the aims of what he describes as 'foreigners' and their countries." What Mayer had found was not enemy propaganda or a state secret. His findings were published and available to all Americans.[1] And obviously the facts pointed to the conclusion that U.S. education and the news and information media had not adjusted well to the significance of the United States as a world power. Yet the U.S. role was, and is, vital to the survival of the West.

In light of this role, it is mind-boggling to know that there were, and are, educators and school board members who shared, and share, the feeling that world history should not be a required subject in the schools of the United States. If anything, there is the tendency to believe that world history should be diluted and/or circumvented by some illusive course such as "international relations," using "relevence" as an excuse for the blind to lead the blind. Moreover, history at the high school level was, and is, too often relegated to teachers who consider the subject to be their secondary, if not tertiary, interest. Thus, it is not surprising that the 1956 Mayer report fell largely on deaf ears. Also, in 1957 the United States was too busy recovering from "Sputnik shock" and chastizing its educational system for being weak in languages, mathematics, and science.

Can a democracy and a world leader afford to allow an endemic ignorance to cloud its people's minds with regard to the nature and purpose of the nation's foreign policy? Today there is little doubt that the domestic crisis the United States experienced during the Vietnam War in the 1960s had resulted largely from unbridled license disguised as free speech, on the one hand, and from political and military leadership on the other. Soul searching and hindsight tell us that most of the positions taken were based on an unconvincing, crippling, and alarming ignorance at all levels of U.S. culture.

When the dust settled, the media were severely criticized from all sides for their limited, biased, and irresponsible reporting. More than ever before in the history of the United States, there surfaced a widespread awareness of the power of the media to affect issues, to redistribute power, to manipulate and isolate, to promote ignorance, and to "foment discontent among the public."[2]

Specifically, in 1968 the Tet offensive by the Viet Cong laid bare the inadequacies of the media and the U.S. political leadership in dealing with the situation in Vietnam. "The first casualty," David Halberstam states in his *The Powers That Be*, "of the battle was Washington propaganda machinery."[3] It was the Tet offensive that "changed the country," "forced the beginning of the end of the American combat participation," and "changed Walter Cronkite," who up to that time was a member of the Johnson-Westmoreland-

McNamara team.[4] Johnson no longer had the backing of Cronkite's credibility.[5]

Earlier, however, Vietnam had exposed still another weakness in U.S. policy: the failure to understand and appreciate the role religion played in the goals and aspirations of the Vietnamese people. This was particularly true in dealing with the Buddhist-Roman Catholic rivalry in South Vietnam and the resulting Buddhist[6] opposition to the Diem regime. Reading Jean Lacouture's *Vietnam: Between Two Truces*, one cannot help noting a parallel between the role of religion in the struggle of the Buddhist monks against Ngo Dinh Diem's family regime and the struggle of the Shi'ite clerics against Shah Reza Pahlevi's family and its determination to force an alien culture on the Iranian people.

Lacouture wrote that the contest between the aristocratic Catholic Diem regime and the Buddhists began on May 8, 1963, when "a large mass of people assembled before the governmental house of the old imperial capital of Hue to protest Diem's decision to forbid a public ceremony in honor of Buddha's anniversary." Diem had earlier permitted huge processions to celebrate the installation of two Catholic bishops and the anniversary of Monsignor Thuc, the archbishop of Saigon and Diem's older brother. The police got out of hand and attacked the Buddhist protesters. "Eight dead were counted, among them three women. Two children had been decapitated by shells."[7] It was not long before protesting Buddhist monks were turning themselves into living torches and engaging in other acts of self-mortification.

Buddhist martyrdom created a festering sore and set in motion cycles of violence that included the sacking by Diem fanatics of pagodas in Saigon. Lacouture wrote, "Rarely have 'moral forces' and those 'imponderables,' of which Bismarck used to complain that they were uncontrollable, played so powerfully against a regime."[8] Later, in August 1963, the first lady of a nation that was overwhelmingly Buddhist, Madame Nhu, when asked to comment on the sacking of the pagodas, said: "'I would clap hands at seeing another monk barbecue show....'"[9] Within weeks, the husband of this Roman Catholic woman died of a coup-inspired "suicide," and within a decade South Vietnam was lost to the Communist north. The United States, which continued to grope with a problem and culture it could not fathom, suffered its greatest humiliation as a world power. In closing his book, Lacouture offered some good advice: Build a popular base to support a government that reflects the will of the majority, which is Buddhist and is proud of its heritage. In 1966, the advice may have been too late for Vietnam, but it is just as true today in dealing with Third World countries.

Meanwhile, in the United States, defeat and humiliation were followed by recrimination after recrimination and book after book in an effort to explain away the Vietnamese nightmare. It seems, however, that no one has been willing to admit that there was a basic and pervasive U.S. ignorance concerning Vietnamese culture, and that the lessons of the Korean War had gone unheeded.

Today U.S. education, the media, and the people they serve, with some notable exceptions, are still not doing the job demanded of them by their democratic ethos. The Iranian crisis is the most important recent case in point.

In spite of some progress and innovations since the 1960s, one must report, regretfully, that the news and information media of the United States did a very poor and shallow job of reporting the Iranian crisis (1978–1980). The reporting reflected an inexcusable and basic ignorance relative to the history and the nature of the Islamic revolution. There seemed to be little effort or sensitivity in conveying the facts, let alone the underlying causes of the Islamic revolution, to the American people. The history of the events leading up to the revolution and its emphasis could have served to temper the emotions of the American people during and after the hostage crisis.

The loss of Iran as an ally, and the respect and friendship of her people, was, and continues to be, a tragedy of the first magnitude. Iran was, and is, vital to the survival of the West as a viable obstacle to Soviet expansion. Iran is important in the struggle for the right of the world's peoples to seek their own destiny and to change that destiny as time and experience permit and direct.

Ever since 1962, when the shah declared his Shah-People Revolution, the U.S. press with few exceptions blindly supported the shah's line, reflecting his unappeasable determination to drag his people into the West's twentieth century and to make Iran a major world power. Iran's internal problems, which included bloody rioting, political murders, gross violations of human rights, and the persecution and the humiliation of Shi'ite leaders, were explained away as the results of the excesses of religious extremists who opposed the shah's progressive programs. Most U.S. press accounts seemed to suggest that such behavior was to be expected of an uncivilized and basically illiterate people.

An examination of the historical facts, however, reveals that the Islamic revolution resulted from an affliction, the symptoms of which first appeared in the early 1950s and eventually spread throughout every facet of Iranian culture. Ayatollah Khomeini merely prepared and chose the right time to administer what he and his followers considered would be the cure the Iranian people wanted and their faith demanded. Their fear of cultural captivity by the West was, and is, real. For them, they are the true "People of the Book," and the West is religiously shallow and opportunistic. It is possessed by an insatiable materialism, which has produced a rootless society of divorce, drug addiction, alcoholism, self-indulgence, racism, and "plastic people." The leaders of the revolution are not ignorant and reactionary religious fanatics, but well-educated men with a proud heritage who are dedicated to Islam. They are jealous of their role in Iranian culture and in the daily lives of their people.

Thus, it should not have been a surprise when the shah's "revolution" was immediately challenged by Ayatollah Khomeini, who quickly gained a reputation in the Western press for his antifeminism and anti-Semitism. His arrest in 1963 caused bloody riots that took the lives of hundreds, perhaps thousands.[10] On June 15, 1963, the ayatollah delivered a "crushing speech against the Shah, the United States, Israel, imperialism and predicted the Shah's end." That day is considered a watershed in the history of Iran.[11] Khomeini was released, only to be arrested and sent into exile on November 4, 1964, when he attacked the Extraterritoriality Bill passed by the Majlis under pressure from the shah. The bill was designed to exempt foreign nationals from prosecution in Iranian courts.[12]

In the West's view, another meddling cleric was put in his place. What the West, especially the United States, did not seem to realize was that Khomeini was following the teachings of the Prophet, that is, in pursuit of social justice one may justifiably oppose civil authority. For the shah, the victory was ephemeral and a temporary illusion.

The ayatollah, first from Iraq and then from Paris, where he moved in October 1978, used couriers to carry his fight to the shah until his Islamic revolution became a reality. This effort cost him the life of his son. What is most disturbing is what has happened since February

1, 1979, when Ayatollah Khomeini triumphantly entered Tehran. The hostage crisis plagued the Carter administration and probably gave the White House to the Republicans in 1980. More recently, the United States, perhaps with the baiting of Iran, has become dangerously entangled in the affairs of the Middle East and of Latin America. The results of these involvements are not promising. They do convey the clear message, however, that it is time for some serious introspection. Some substantive changes are in order. To improve the U.S. role as a world leader, the merits of the following suggestions must be examined and evaluated.

First, the U.S. State Department should add a separate category for "Education" to its *Traffic Analysis by Geography and Subject Index* for implementing Executive Order 11652 of President Nixon, "Classification and Declassification of National Security Information and Material," dated March 8, 1972.[13] What are other nations teaching their people through their schools and the media? At present, education seems to play a very limited role in the information-gathering process of the State Department.

Second, much of the information gathered by U.S. agencies at home and abroad should be declassified quickly and made available to educators and the media.

Third, the U.S. Information Centers and their libraries abroad must be discontinued as dated intrusions.

Fourth, the federal government should subsidize the salaries of teachers in public and private schools. This subsidy would go primarily, if not entirely, to teachers of U.S. and world history, the language arts, science, and mathematics. Teachers wishing the subsidy would qualify by passing a comprehensive subjective and objective test in their teaching area. The yearly subsidy, renewable every five years, must be at least $5,000 per year.

Fifth, and very important, teachers who are not qualified to teach in the above areas should not be hired. Too often, an applicant's coaching ability in a sport rather than his/her teaching qualifications in an academic subject takes precedence in school board hiring policies.

Sixth, the media, educators, and leaders need to exercise more caution in their comments and statements. Insensitive and shallow remarks regarding Iran, Israel, the Soviet Union, the Contras, the Sandinistas, and others should be avoided. Also, reporting events out of historical or cultural context is not fair or wise.

Seventh, schools of journalism and colleges of education should raise the standards for awarding degrees, especially in humanities, science, and mathematics. They should have five-year programs.

Eighth, *The Ugly American*, by William J. Lederer and Eugene Burdick, should be must reading for all young Americans. As a people who cherish freedom of choice and the sanctity of the individual, Americans should avoid judging the world by their values, which are not always identifiable.

Ninth, ever present in any Western evaluation or decision relative to the Near and Middle Eastern questions, for instance, should be the fact that without the Holocaust, the state of Israel likely would not have materialized in 1948. Western guilt created Israel, which has earned the right to exist. Unfortunately, the people of Islam have been forced to pay the price for that existence. That is to say, Cain is trying to slay Abel while the West looks on with an arrogant and condescending attitude.

Tenth, all must recognize the decisive role religion plays in some nations. In Latin America, for instance, the Roman Catholic faith must be considered and supported as one of the forces of the people against the tyranny of fascism and Communism.

Finally, the people of the United States especially must realize that the Third World is at a crossroads, a pivot point, in history, and that its chosen direction is bound to have a profound affect on the future of the free world.

NOTES

1. William E. Mayer, "Why Did Many GI Captives Cave In? *U.S. News & World Report* 40 (1956): 56–66, 69, 72.

2. David L. Paletz, *Media Power Politics* (New York: Free Press, 1981), p. 6.

3. David Halberstram, *The Powers That Be* (New York: Alfred A. Knopf, 1979), p. 511.

4. Ibid., pp. 511–512.

5. Ibid., p. 50.

6. Unlike the West's institutionalized forms of religion, east Asian religion is an amalgam of Buddhist, Confucianist, Taoist, and animist principles and practices. The weight of each in any given combination is determined largely by individual and/or family practice. Buddhist monks, however, are accorded respect by almost all.

7. Jean Lacouture, *Vietnam: Between Two Truces* (New York: Random House, 1966), p. 76.

8. Ibid.

9. Ibid., p. 80.

10. The Shi'ite branch of Islam forbids the arrest of an ayatollah of the sixth rank.

11. *Tehran Times*, June 16, 1983.

12. William H. Sullivan, *Mission to Iran* (New York: W. W. Norton, 1981), p. 91.

13. U.S. State Department, *Traffic Analysis by Geography and Subject Index* (Washington, D.C.: U.S. State Department, 1976), pp. 3, 40.

6

A Typology of Islamic Revivalists

Zohair Husain

The individuals, groups, and movements that have led Islamic revivals fall into four ideal-typical categories: fundamentalists, traditionalists, modernists, and pragmatists. While they all speak about defending and promoting the "true" Islam, the style and substance of their approaches differ. Some Islamic revivalists may be considered as having affinity with one or other of the four categories, depending on the principal thrust of the beliefs of the actors and the issues involved, but they do not fall under one heading.

The term "Islamic revivalist" has been used generically in the literature on Islamic revivalism to refer to any participant in an Islamic revival. However, for purposes of this chapter, revivalists are those individuals who make significant (if localized) contributions to bringing about an Islamic revival at a crucial moment in history. In disseminating their perception of the true form of Islam, Islamic revivalists frequently promote the creation of an Islamic state by teaching, preaching, writing, and, on rare occasions, force of arms. The four major types of Islamic revivalists, mentioned above, will be discussed briefly in this chapter.

MUSLIM FUNDAMENTALISTS

The first major category of Islamic revivalists, the Muslim fundamentalists, are also referred to in the popular and scholarly literature as scripturalists, legalists, literalists, restorationists, restitutionists, and puritans.

Muslim fundamentalists are extremely devout and very knowledgeable about Islam. They believe in literally interpreting and rigorously adhering to the fundamentals of their original faith embodied in the Quran (Islam's Holy Book) and the Sunnah (prophet Muhammad's words and deeds). The majority of them are often exceedingly political and revolutionary in their orientation, and believe in zealously crusading to impose the *shariah* (Islamic law) on society at large, and to purge all influences that they feel take Muslims away from the fundamentals of their faith.

While all Muslims believe in the doctrine of *tawhid* (oneness of God) because it is the central premise of Islam, the fundamentalists are often obsessed with its importance. Many Sunni fundamentalists, for instance, have such a literal, rigid, and narrow interpretation of *tawhid* that they denounce any mediatory agent between man and Allah as *shirk* (polytheism), because in their eyes it undermines and compromises the dominant principle of *tawhid*. Therefore, in their puritanical zeal they condemn such traditions as the veneration of the prophet Muhammad, imams, saints, martyrs and *pirs* (spiritual guides); the offering of prayers for assistance at their tombs or at shrines built in their honor; the sacrifice of animals, lighting of candles, sanctification of water, deposit of money, and distribution of food in honor of those venerated with expectation of special favors; the wearing of *taweezes* (amulets) with verses from the Quran to ward off evil or to bring good luck; and excessive displays of mourning in the form of weeping, *maatam* (breast-beating), and *taziyah* (mourning) processions during the Islamic month of Moharram (first month of the Islamic calendar) to commemorate the martyrdom of Imam Husain (prophet Muhammad's grandson). The fundamentalists reject the church-state dichotomy that non-Muslims and Muslim pragmatists encourage, and that twentieth-century modernists and traditionalists tolerate in varying degrees. While the traditionalists and modernists also often talk about the fusion of church and state, and how separating the two would deprive the government of ethical and spiritual foundations, the fundamentalists assertively and even aggressively crusade against such separation.

The fundamentalists, like the traditionalists and modernists, believe that the most important function of the Islamic state is to maintain and enforce the *shariah*. However, unlike the modernists, who wish to revise and modernize it, and unlike the traditionalists, who accept it in its entirety but do not actively crusade for it, the fundamentalists consider it their duty to struggle ceaselessly to implement the *shariah* in its entirety.

Most fundamentalists are far more aggressive than the traditionalists and modernists in their crusade for the obligatory practice of the five *faraidh* (duties) as well as against prostitution, pornography, the selling or use of alcohol and drugs, gambling, Western music, singing, and dancing.

Virtually all fundamentalists, like all modernists and pragmatists, and unlike all traditionalists, reject the dogma of *taqlid* and embrace its antithesis, the dynamic notion of *ijtihad*. *Taqlid* entails blind and unquestioning adherence to the legal rulings (of one or more schools of Islamic jurisprudence) of the learned, competent, and renowned theologian-jurists of the medieval Islamic era. *Ijtihad*, on the other hand, means to strive or exert oneself intellectually to the utmost (researching, analyzing, and reasoning) in order to draw independent conclusions and judgments on legal or other issues with the assistance of the Quran and the *Sunnah*. Fundamentalists often limit the right of *ijtihad* to those knowledgeable about and competent in Islamic theology and law.

While all traditionalists and many modernists also claim to oppose secular nationalism, they display less vehemence in their opposition than do the fundamentalists. They aggressively oppose nationalism because they strongly believe in "Islamic universalism" as mentioned in the Quran and the *Sunnah*, and are bitterly opposed to the alien, secular, and territorial nature of nationalism—which, they are convinced, would divide and weaken the *umma* (brotherhood of Muslims) because national interests would then come to prevail over global Islamic interests.

Muslim fundamentalists in the late twentieth century, unlike their predecessors and traditionalists, are willing to embrace what they perceive as beneficial modern values that conform to the basic tenets of Islam. For example, although they wish to follow the revered body of *shariah* strictly, they are willing to interpret the letter of the law more broadly than in the past. Many fundamentalists, for instance, have come to accept the Western notions of democracy. However, in order to ascertain that no legislation is passed or decisions made that are not in keeping with the Quran or *Sunnah*, the fundamentalists insist that competent fundamentalist *ulama* (Islamic scholars) ought to play an important role in advising the democratically elected representatives of the people and in ratifying all legislation.

MUSLIM TRADITIONALISTS

The second major category of Islamic revivalists is the Muslim traditionalists. They are generally the products of traditional Islamic education and come exclusively from the ranks of the devout and learned *ulama.*

As their name implies, the traditionalists often tend to conserve and preserve not only the beliefs, customs, and traditions practiced in the classical period of Islam but also those of subsequent Islamic periods. They are tolerant of Sufism, mysticism, and numerous local or regional customs and traditions commonly referred to as "folk Islam" or "popular Islam." They justify this on the premise that Islam is not merely a set of abstract and utopian principles, but a comprehensive and living belief system that interacts with historical and cultural traditions of those who call themselves devout Muslims. To suppress all these values, therefore, would be to weaken the popular form of devotion among the Muslim majority. These are the practices referred to as "accretions" and "innovations" by revolutionary and puritanical Muslim fundamentalists committed to eradicating all but the practices prevalent during the classical period.

Unlike the fundamentalists, who, when not at the apex of power, often play an aggressive oppositional role in the political arena, the traditionalists are generally apolitical and detached scholars and teachers of religion. In disengaging themselves from active politics and the worldly temptations of power and wealth, they sincerely believe that they are protecting the integrity and cherished ideals of Islam from being tarnished. Thus, they have ended up tolerating the de facto separation of religion and politics where none really exists in Islamic theory. However, whenever they have perceived Islam or the *umma*—whether local, regional, or subsystemic—to be in imminent danger, they have asserted themselves in the political arena. The traditionalist *ulama* of the Indian subcontinent, for instance, launched the Khilafat movement in 1918 to pressure the British to stop dismantling the Ottoman Empire and threatening the survival of the sultan of Turkey. This was because many Muslim traditionalists regarded the sultan of Turkey as a symbol of unity for the Millat-e Islam (Nation of Islam).

Another major hallmark of the Sunni traditionalists that separates them from the other three categories of Muslims is their rejection of *ijtihad* and firm belief in the dogma of *taqlid*, for "to alter the decision that has been accepted for ages would be to deny the eternal immutability of God's law and to admit that earlier jurists erred would be to destroy the idea of the continuity of the divine guidance of the Muslim community."[1]

Nevertheless, these scholarly and respectable gentlemen do have serious limitations when they are viewed in a contemporary light. They are often naive, if not ignorant, about the modern natural and social sciences. At times even the modern scientific theories—if read— are examined and either accepted or rejected in the light of the Quran and *Sunnah*. They are generally oblivious to the complexities, institutions, and processes of modern governments and the conduct of international relations in an interdependent world. They are not perturbed about their shortcomings because they are convinced that the all-embracing and perfect religion of Islam, in which they are well versed, reveals all truths and can help to resolve all internal crises and external threats facing Muslim societies around the world.[2]

The traditionalists, like the fundamentalists and even most modernists, are profoundly concerned about the increasing secularization of the critically important educational, legal, economic, and social spheres of their Muslim societies. Secularization, to them, is tantamount to the elimination of the *shariah*, and eventually will erode the very foundations of the Muslim community. In the educational sphere, the traditionalists, like the fundamentalists, demand the generous funding of *madrassahs* (Islamic schools); advocate syllabi that comprise mainly Islamic disciplines and few, if any, of the modern Western sciences; and promote the segregation of the sexes in educational institutions and extreme modesty in dress. In the legal sphere, the traditionalists want to adhere rigidly to their respective schools of *fiqh* (Islamic jurisprudence). They demand an Islamic constitution that draws heavily upon the Quran, *Sunnah*, and *shariah*. They believe in the establishment or strengthening of Islamic law courts presided over by *qadhis* (Islamic judges) and the implementation of the *shariah*. In the economic sphere, they would like to see the institution of the *zakat* (2.5 percent of one's wealth given annually in alms to the poor) and *ushr* (10 percent tax on irrigated farmland, payable by each landholder to the poor), as well as the prohibition of *riba* (usury). Unlike the fundamentalists, however, the traditionalists do not engage in a sustained crusade for the aforementioned beliefs in the political arena.

The detached attitude of the traditionalists is manifested in their reluctance to adapt Islamic viewpoints to contemporary eras. Modernists, pragmatists, and even some fundamentalists excoriate the detachment and reluctance of the traditionalists to change, and attribute this fatal flaw in their world view to the loss of dynamism and the stagnation of the Muslim world, as well as to the impotence of the *umma* on the world stage. The traditionalists forcefully reply that Islam has not changed, cannot change, and never should change, for it is founded on the divine comprehensiveness and immutability of Allah's words and laws. Consequently, immutability is not the cause of the Muslim world's stagnation and Muslim power's decline on the world stage. Rather self-righteously, they argue that the problem arises from the Muslim world's inherent imperfections, and from the fact that Muslims have not steadfastly followed the letter and spirit of the religion.

MUSLIM MODERNISTS

Muslim modernists, also referred to as "adaptationists," "apologists," "syncretists," and even "revisionists," are extremely devout Muslims who are very knowledgeable about Islam. The Central Institute of Islamic Research in Pakistan—created by President Muhammad Ayub Khan in 1960—succinctly revealed the modernist position as twofold: first, "to define Islam by bringing out the fundamentals in a rational and liberal manner and to emphasize, among others, the basic ideals of Islamic brotherhood, tolerance and social justice," and second, to interpret the teachings of Islam in such a way as to bring out its dynamic character in the context of the intellectual and scientific progress of the modern world.[3]

In contradistinction to the traditionalists, who are concerned with maintaining the status quo, and the puritanical fundamentalists, the modernists believe that they are making a sincere and dedicated effort to reconcile the differences between traditional religious doctrine and secular scientific rationalism; between unquestioning faith and reasoned logic; and between the continuity of Islamic tradition and the unpredictability of change.

Modernists, like fundamentalists, vehemently disagree with the Sunni traditionalists who believe in the dogma of *taqlid*, which implies the unquestioning and rigid adherence to one of the four schools of Sunni *fiqh* developed in the postclassical period. The modernists often argue that the main reason for the decline of Islam is the inhibition of independent, creative, and critical thought, as well as the lack of vigorous discussion and debate about Islamic laws and issues that resulted from the closure of "the gates of *ijtihad*" a millenium earlier. Instead, the modernists are convinced that Islam is a progressive, dynamic, and rational religion in which there is no place for the inhibiting dogma of *taqlid*. Consequently, their solution is an unconditional reopening of "the gates of *ijtihad*," which will facilitate the reinterpretation and reformulation of Islamic laws in the light of modern thought and contemporary times. Modernists reinforce their appeal for the restoration and exercise of *ijtihad* by quoting from the Quran: "And to those who exert we show the Path."[4] Additional evidence comes from Quranic verses that say: ". . . God would never change His favor that He conferred on a people until they changed what was within themselves"[5] and "Verily, God changes not what is in a people until they change what is in themselves."[6] The net effect of these Quranic verses, according to the modernists, is that Islam is not a confining and inhibiting force, but an inspiration and spur to progress. Indeed, dynamic change in Islam not only is possible, but is based upon the authority of Allah. Therefore, according to most modernists, Islamic laws have to be carefully revised so that they have the built-in flexibility and adaptability to take into account modern political, economic, social, cultural, and legal conditions.

In addition to being very knowledgeable about Islam, modernists have been exposed to modern non-Islamic (especially Western) ideas in their formal and/or informal education at home or abroad. Most Muslim modernists, after exposure to the West, are filled with new ideas and insights that they are eager to introduce into their societies. In this respect, they have lived up to Iqbal's belief: "The West's typhoon turned a Muslim into a true Muslim . . . [in the] way waves of the ocean nourish a pearl in the oyster."[7] Consequently, unlike the fundamentalists and traditionalists, the modernists do not fear or dislike Western ideas and practices. On the contrary, they welcome all non-Islamic ideas and practices they consider beneficial to the progress and prosperity of Muslim societies. The resultant amalgamation of Islamic and Western ideas is then creatively and harmoniously synthesized to produce a pragmatic reinterpretation of Islamic thought noted for enlightened cosmopolitan, liberal, and realistic perspectives. This approach represents a tolerance for diversity and a willingness to adjust relatively rapidly to a changing environment, and thereby contributes to the emancipation of the individual Muslim and to the progress of Muslim societies.

One of many examples of a Western idea being presented in an Islamic framework is Muhammad Iqbal's recommendation to expand the scope and authority of *ijma* (consensus) to encompass not only the *ulama* but also the legislative assembly—comprising the elected representatives of the people—of the nation-state.

Modernists are generally so agitated by the divisions and frictions between the various *madhabs* (Islamic schools of jurisprudence) that they expend a great deal of time and effort advocating reconciliation and unity of all Muslims.

Finally, the Modernists have tried to bridge the extremely wide divergence between the fundamentalists and the Muslim pragmatists while concurring with them in renouncing the traditionalists' *taqlid*-based world view. Conversely, they have differed from the fundamentalists in advocating the incorporation of far more "modern-day" ideas while emphasizing far more revisions in Islamic laws. However, their desire to retain Islamic laws in a revised form separates them from the pragmatists. The modernists have, therefore, struggled to reappraise and reform a comprehensive religion revealed to mankind nearly 1,400 years ago, so that constructive and feasible solutions to the new problems of a dramatically changed socioeconomic and political environment can be found. This extended and difficult task (invariably speeded up during the periodic Islamic revivals) has often been at the cost of much that has been cherished in past times as well as in the face of unrelenting opposition from the traditionalists and fundamentalists. Finding innovative insights into the Islamic scriptures, or emphasizing and elaborating ideas that may have been dormant in the substantive body of Islamic scripture, is bound to continue indefinitely while yielding dividends for the entire *umma.*[8]

MUSLIM PRAGMATISTS

Comprising the fourth category of Islamic revivalists, and perhaps the least religious of them, are the Muslim pragmatists. They are generally Muslims by name and birth, have had some religious socialization in childhood, cherish Islamic ideals and values, identify with the

Muslim community and culture, and are perceived as Muslims by non-Muslims.

While faithful to their Islamic allegiance—albeit sometimes without much theological grasp of its details—and fully aware of the basic tenets of their faith, Muslim pragmatists often do not observe the ritual obligations incumbent on all Muslims: performance of *salat* (prayers), observance of *sawm* (fasting) during the month of Ramadan, payment of the annual *zakat*, and performance of the *hajj* (pilgrimage to Mecca) at least once in a lifetime. Despite their nonchalant attitude toward the faithful adherence to and dutiful observance of their religion, they fall back on it in moments of personal crisis or when they find it necessary to conform to the social or political pressure of their brethren.

This group can be considered nonpracticing and nominal Muslims with a veneer of a liberal and eclectic version of Islam. Frequently their Islam boils down to various basic ethical, moral, and spiritual principles emphasized by Islam: equality, justice, liberty, freedom, honesty, integrity, brotherhood, tolerance, peace, and other such attributes. While they leave it up to Allah and their conscience to pass judgment on their thoughts and deeds based on ethical, moral, and spiritual principles inculcated through early socialization, their liberal and lax approach to Islam is not appreciated by devout Muslims, who consider them "wayward souls" at best and "unbelievers" at worst.

Many in this group have been exposed to secular Western education in their homeland or in the West, and often know more about Western intellectual thought than about Islamic intellectual thought. In fact, due to their formal and informal Western educational experiences, they view the classical and medieval Islamic doctrines and practices as anachronistic, reactionary, and impractical in the modern age. If accused of acquiring non-Islamic Western knowledge and training, they, like many Muslim modernists, could easily quote the popular saying of prophet Muhammad: "Seek knowledge even if you have to go to China." China was not only a distant foreign land in those days of very slow transportation and communication, but was inhabited by non-Muslim foreigners who had their own distinct culture. Therefore, instead of looking back with nostalgia, as the fundamentalists and traditionalists do, to the "Islamic state" of prophet Muhammad and the Khulafa-e-Rashidin as the golden age of Islam, the Muslim pragmatists emulate Western capitalist and socialist ideologies to modernize their societies on the basis of secular capitalism or socialism, or some combination of those systems. Understandably, they believe not only in the inevitability of secularization but also in its desirability, appreciating that devout Muslims see it as "un-Islamic" and "anti-Islamic," and a threat to Muslim societies.

Though a minority in all Muslim societies, the Muslim pragmatists hold a disproportionate amount of wealth and power because they enjoy leadership positions in the influential institutions of their countries. They are in the upper echelons of their governments' civil services and armed forces. They are heavily represented in the mass media, educational institutions, business communities, and landlords and many professions. They have an appreciation of what is happening in their country and the world at large. They are also the most assertive and vocal segment of their societies.

The pragmatists are pleased that Islam does not give a privileged status to the *ulama* in the governance of Muslim societies, and reiterate the view that there is no institutionalized clergy in Islam; all Muslims are responsible to Allah for their thoughts and deeds. They base this conclusion on the views of many Islamic scholars. Further, they point to Islam's emphasis on equality and aversion to the formation of any privileged class, including a priestly one, that fosters elitism and encourages differentiation between men. According to the pragmatists, the *ulama* are experts in the Islamic religion per se, and are therefore fully entitled to give their invaluable religious guidance in the affairs of the state. However, in economic, political, technical, and international and non-Islamic legal matters, the *ulama* cannot claim to impose their viewpoint on the nation.

Ironically, the pragmatists often find it expedient to use traditional Islamic rhetoric and symbolism to capture the support of the Muslim masses despite their essentially secular world view and a firm conviction that religion is a personal affair between man and God, whereas the state links man and man. More specifically, their use of Islamic rhetoric and symbolism allows them to gain or enhance their legitimacy; integrate and unite their fragmented Muslim societies; and inspire, mobilize, and galvanize the Muslim masses.

In summary, the pragmatists are influenced by their formal and informal secular education and often are only nominally Muslims, not practicing even the obligatory duties. They look to a broad spectrum of ages and philosophies for their models of political and socioeconomic progress. In their search for the ideal system, they adopt con cepts and ideologies from both capitalist and socialist countries, adapting them to their indigenous environment. They are concerned with the dynamic modernization of their societies and interested in addressing practical realities in a rational manner. Though at times pressured by the fundamentalists and traditionalists to promote and defend the faith, they often prefer a secular state with secularism as its guiding principle. They also believe that competent lay Muslim politicians and statesmen ought to govern modern-day nation-states instead of the *ulama*, who ought to keep to their professional religious duties.

The Islamic revival of the 1980s has not been led by Muslim fundamentalists alone, as mass media and scholarly preoccupation with Islamic fundamentalism suggests, but by Muslim traditionalists, modernists, and pragmatists as well. In fact, the most recent Islamic revival resulted from the dynamic interaction of all four types of Islamic revivalists.

NOTES

1. Leonard Binder, *Religion and Politics in Pakistan* (Berkeley: University of California Press, 1963), pp. 20, 24, 26, 42–43, 74; Freeland Abbott, *Islam and Pakistan* (Ithaca, N.Y.: Cornell University Press, 1966), pp. 89, 225.

2. S. Alam Khundmiri, "A Critical Examination of Islamic Traditionalism," *Islam and the Modern Age* 2, no. 2 (May 1979): 11.

3. *Muslim World* 50, no. 2 (April 1960): 155. Also cited in Donald Eugene Smith, ed., "Emerging Patterns of Religion and Politics," in *South Asian Politics and Religion* (Princeton: Princeton University Press, 1966), pp. 32–33.

4. Quran, 29:69.

5. Ibid., 8:53.

6. Ibid., 22:10.

7. Hafeez Malik, *Sir Sayed Ahmad Khan and Muslim Modernism in India and Pakistan* (New York: Columbia University Press, 1980), p. 99.

8. Abbott, *Islam and Pakistan*, p. 23.

7

Economic Impact of OPEC: Policies and Performances

Shah M. Mehrabi

It is generally agreed that the 1973 crude oil price increases effected by the member countries of the Organization of Petroleum Exporting Countries (OPEC) constitute one of the more important landmarks in the petroleum history of the world. Although OPEC has been in existence since 1960, it was not until the October and December price increases of 1973 that OPEC found itself the subject of analysis. What is OPEC? How was it formed? And how has it functioned?

The seeds of OPEC were sown when the Arab League held its first meeting in 1945. Almost from the beginning, the Arab League considered the possibility of forming an organization of Arab oil-exporting countries. However, the representatives recognized the desirability of including the large non-Arab oil exporters as well, notably Venezuela and Iran, and plans were postponed. Then, in February 1959, the major oil companies reduced posted prices unilaterally, without consulting the producing countries. This set off a series of events that led to the first formal meeting of OPEC.

In April 1959 the Arab League sponsored the first Arab Petroleum Congress in Cairo, with representatives of Venezuela and Iran invited as observers. The formal agenda included only matters of interest to Arab countries, but informal meetings between Sheikh Abdullah Tariki of Saudi Arabia and Perez Alfonzo of Venezuela resulted in a "gentleman's agreement" for the establishment of a formal organization of petroleum-exporting countries. Having reached an agreement in principle, the two leaders made a joint declaration in May 1960, urging the producing countries to adopt a common policy in defense of their interests. The atmosphere for cooperation improved when posted prices were again unilaterally reduced in August 1960—once more without consultation with the producing countries. This led directly to the establishment of OPEC.

On September 6, 1960, representatives of the governments of Iran, Iraq, Kuwait, Saudi Arabia, and Venezuela met in Baghdad, Iraq. On September 14, they reached an agreement providing for a permanent intergovernmental federation to be known as the Organization of Petroleum Exporting Countries.

OPEC has 13 full members. To be eligible for membership, a country must be a "substantial net exporter" and show that its petroleum interests are similar to those of other members. The current members are Algeria, Ecuador, Gabon, Indonesia, Iran, Iraq, Kuwait, Libya, Nigeria, Qatar, Saudi Arabia, the United Arab Emirates, and Venezuela.

The organization of OPEC is important, and will remain so, because its member nations have sovereign control over two-thirds of the world's most accessible petroleum reserves. Since 1973, OPEC has probably influenced the material well-being of more people worldwide than any other international organization.

The corpus of economic literature published in the West that is related to energy, and specifically to OPEC, has been one-sided; every time the oil price rises, OPEC is blamed for provoking a world economic crisis through exorbitant oil prices. Furthermore, most of the literature has concentrated mainly on the welfare of the Western economies while ignoring the oil-producing states' economic welfare in general.

The purpose of this chapter is to do the following: to examine the validity of two allegations that have evolved in the West against OPEC and the Arab Gulf states (AGS); to evaluate the existing supply, demand, and price of crude oil and what could be an alternative method of establishing payments for crude oil; and to examine the positive spillover effect of the AGS oil revenues on Western and non-Western economies during the 1980s.

THE TWO MYTHS IN THE WEST

The myths that have originated in the West about OPEC and AGS since 1973 are numerous; an attempt will be made to examine the validity of two of them: (1) OPEC is a cartel; (2) Arab Gulf oil producers are engaged in a conspiracy launched in 1973 to override the working of the free market system in the West.

The first myth is misleading and inapplicable to OPEC because of several conditions that prevail in the world oil market. First, new oil discoveries around the world from 1970 through the 1980s—in the North Sea, Alaska, Mexico, China, and the Soviet Union—have increased the world supply of oil.

Second, OPEC's supply of crude oil to the world market has been decreasing since 1979. Statistics cited in the *OPEC Bulletin* in 1988 indicate that the OPEC share of the world oil supply decreased from 30.5 million barrels in 1979 to 17.5 million barrels daily in the first quarter of 1988.

The quantity of crude oil supplied by non-OPEC countries has increased steadily from 14 million barrels in 1976 to 28 million barrels daily in 1988. The impact of new oil supplies is evident in the statistics: non-OPEC producers of oil have more power over the supply than does OPEC. At present, OPEC produces 32.5 percent of the world oil supply, while non-OPEC countries produce 67.5 percent. According to the *OPEC Bulletin*, any reference to OPEC as a cartel displays sheer ignorance about the economic characteristics of a cartel.[1]

Third, the $19 per barrel decrease in the price of crude oil since the first quarter of 1983, which could be followed by other cuts in price, provides strong evidence of OPEC's decreasing power over the price. The spot price of oil had fallen to less than $15 per barrel in 1986 from an official price of $34 per barrel in 1982–1983.

Fourth, conservation and energy switching, as well as increases in the availability of nuclear power, have reduced oil consumption in the West in the 1980s. There is a huge effort in many Western nations and industries to conserve energy. Aircraft, cars, air conditioners, and refrigerators are more energy efficient. Housing is better insulated, large buildings are more economically heated by computer-controlled systems, and heavy industries from cement to steel have learned to cut energy consumption. The 24 Western countries of the Organization for Economic Cooperation and Development—which include the United States, Japan, and Western Europe—have reduced their energy consumption by 20 percent since 1972, according to the Paris-based International Energy Agency. That is the equivalent of 1 billion tons of oil a year, the current production in the United States and Western Europe.

Fifth, extensive stockpiling of crude oil in the West—especially in the United States—has distorted world supply and added extra costs in the form of upkeep of the storage facilities. This extra cost is transformed into an additional burden on the taxpayers.

Furthermore, economic theory defines a cartel as an arrangement under which output is restricted and there exists a common price and market-sharing arrangement. The purpose of any cartel is to maximize profit by eliminating competitive selling and to regulate entry. None of the above elements can be found in OPEC. If OPEC market-sharing arrangements are examined, it becomes evident that OPEC does not have such an arrangement. Oil is produced either directly or through service contracts, and is available for sale to a large number of buyers.

As for output, the evidence is also overwhelmingly convincing: OPEC member countries are without any centralized arrangements to limit each member's output. There are several reasons for this. First, each member's national sovereignty interferes with the need to cooperate to achieve output restriction. Second, the extreme diversity of per capita output and petroleum reserves that characterizes the OPEC membership is a continual impediment to the achievement of cooperation in output restriction. Third, market conditions are such that output restriction is not needed because it is generally agreed that the combined output of the OPEC countries tends to exceed the level needed to finance ordinary budget and capital investments.

As for pricing, it is accurate to state that OPEC has always been deeply divided over what price will maximize profits for the group. OPEC is a shell organization for 13 sovereign, competitive governments: 6 in the Middle East, 2 in northern Africa, 2 in southwestern Africa, 2 in South America, and 1 in Southeast Asia. The OPEC countries' diversity of economic and political goals makes it impossible to adhere to a rigid system of pricing. In addition, OPEC has always reacted to market conditions with a time lag. In other words, it has always adjusted posted prices after market prices had overtaken them. Demand for OPEC crude oil is determined by two factors: (1) the demand for oil products, which in turn is determined by economic conditions in consuming countries; (2) oil-consuming countries' tendency to meet their needs from indigenous sources before they resort to OPEC oil.

The point here is that OPEC does not act in a manner intended to raise prices for the purpose of profit maximization. As a matter of fact, there is a general agreement that most member countries are producing at higher rates than is necessary. Saudi Arabia chose to increase its output, either to keep prices from going up or to force them down. A cartel is supposed to benefit from the higher price, and the price leader is supposed to maximize profit. In the case of OPEC, the major producing member not only was not trying to raise prices, but was trying to lower prices by increasing its output.

The second myth that has surfaced in the West since 1973 is without foundation because 80 percent of the Arab oil-producing states' investment, long- and short-term, is placed in Western bond and equity markets. Many public agencies in the Gulf have been heavily involved in the purchase of U.S. and Western European government bonds since the late 1970s; they also have increased their contributions to the World Bank and the International Monetary Fund.

The myth that the AGS seek to destroy the working of the free market system in the West exists only in the minds of Western politicians who want to find scapegoats for their failure to contain inflation and unemployment during the period 1979–1982. The real challenge facing OPEC, industrial nations, and Third World states is how world supply and demand interact and what the established level of prices should be.

SUPPLY, DEMAND, AND PRICE OF CRUDE OIL

From the 1940s to the early 1970s, the supply of crude oil was directly under the influence of Western companies and Western governments with their extensive domestic regulations, especially in the United States. W. W. Riddick maintains that from the 1940s through the 1960s, Western oil companies, assisted by their governments, were able to buy crude oil at a fraction of the cost of any alternative source of energy. The same Western companies were successful in keeping the world oil price low in comparison with an increasing demand for oil from the 1950s to the early 1960s.[2]

Throughout the period, oil producers were unable to control the operations of oil exploration, production, pricing, shipping, refining, and marketing of the final product even in their own states. Therefore, the price adjustment that was implemented by OPEC in 1973 was a by-product of poor-quality and low-priced crude oil that the West had forced upon the world oil market since the 1940s. OPEC was able to control oil prices from 1973 through 1977, when it was producing about 45 percent of the total world supply. However, since 1978 its share of world oil supply has decreased to about 32.5 percent, a situation that makes it difficult to control prices.

Oil supply and prices on the world level have never been left free to fluctuate according to market forces, but the West had the upper hand in this area until 1973. Western governments were unable to find scapegoats and blamed OPEC whenever their economies were facing domestic problems such as inflation, unemployment, currency instability, trade deficits, or recession. Michael R. Darby points out that it became common in the West to blame OPEC for any ills facing a Western economy.[3]

This unsettled state of affairs in the world oil market calls for the establishment of an equilibrium in which the concerned parties' welfare is considered. Jeffrey Sachs asserts that the West needs to abandon all forms of interference in the market that have been established since the 1970s, especially in the United States, while allowing the AGS and other OPEC members to decide on production levels that coincide with the world's demand.[4]

In order to avoid instability in the price level, payments for crude oil could be settled by International Monetary Fund (IMF) special drawing rights (SDR). SDR is a reserve of assets for use in the international payments created by the IMF in the early 1970s and allocated to its members. This means of payment could eliminate the currency instability that affects the price of oil if the U.S. dollar or the British pound appreciates or depreciates vis-à-vis other world currencies. (The U.S. dollar and the British pound are the two means of payment for oil sales on a worldwide basis.) The acceptance of such a payment system needs the agreement by all concerned trading partners: non-OPEC, OPEC, industrial, and Third World states. This form of payment system will eliminate allegations and counterallegations by Western states and OPEC about who is damaging world trade and slowing economic growth and development.

OIL REVENUES OF THE AGS
AND THEIR SPILLOVER EFFECT

The most commonly ignored topic related to OPEC revenues or surpluses since 1973 is the failure of Western scholars to examine the positive spillover effect that the oil revenues have on OPEC trading partners' economies and the effect of the capital transfer made by workers and businesses to their home economies. But since the late 1970s, not all OPEC members have enjoyed surpluses in the balance of payments. There are high absorbers, such as Nigeria and Indonesia, and low absorbers, such as the AGS.

This section will center on the AGS, which are enjoying surpluses in their balance of payments and are also low absorbers. These states are Saudi Arabia, Kuwait, the United Arab Emirates, and Qatar. A multiplier will be used as a tool to measure the size of the oil payment spent by these states and the magnitude that would be generated by Western states, Southeast Asian states, and certain Arab economies. *The Balance of Payments—Statistics Year Book* (1982) shows that the largest exporters to the Gulf region are the United States, Canada, Germany, Italy, the United Kingdom, Japan, and France.

The two major factors that play vital and positive roles in the economies of the AGS are oil revenues and government budgets. The budgets and the fiscal policies are the important elements that governments utilize to influence their economies, and there is little room for monetary policy. For example, when governments increase their spending, all economic activities will be stimulated, while the reverse is true when government spending is reduced.

Three assumptions are made relative to public and private spending, saving, and the magnitude of the positive spillover to non-AGS economies: (1) 80 percent of the gross domestic product (GDP) is allocated to spending on overhead capital such as roads, airports, health care, education, public utilities, defense, amenities, and other public goods and services that central governments provide fully or in a subsidized form for their people; (2) 20 percent of government revenue is invested in the West, where the positive spillover accrues to Western economies; and (3) 20 percent of the amount spent by all levels of governments is saved by income receivers, wage earners, and the business community.

The GDP of Saudi Arabia in 1981 was $113.24 billion; that of the United Arab Emirates, $18.76 billion; of Kuwait, $14.92 billion; and of Qatar, $5.32 billion. Taking 20 percent of the GDP of all four of these countries ($152.24 billion) yields $30.45 billion. Therefore, $30.45 billion is the sum invested by all levels of government overseas. The private marginal propensity to save (MPS) is 20 percent of the $121.80 billion ($24.36 billion). The value of the multiplier is $5(1/1 - MPC = 1/1 - 0.80 = 5)$, and its generating capacity is $487.20 billion. The generating factor for 1981 oil revenues to other non-AGS is (1) 121.80 – 24.36 = $97.44 billion; and (2) 5 × $97.44 = $487.20 billion.

The GDP of the four above-mentioned oil-producing states in 1982 amounted to $107.82 billion. The GDP of Saudi Arabia was $77.24 billion; of the United Arab Emirates, $15.35 billion; of Kuwait, $11.00 billion; and of Qatar, $4.23 billion. Again, 20 percent of the GDPs for 1982 ($107.82 billion) amounts to $21.56 billion of the total AGS revenues. Therefore, $21.56 billion is the sum invested by all levels of government overseas. The MPS is 20 percent of $86.26 billion dollars ($107.82 – $21.56 = $86.26 billion), which amounts to $17.25 billion. The value of the multiplier is 5, and its generating capacity is $345 billion. The generating factor for 1982 oil revenues to other non-AGS is (1) $107.82 – $21.56 = $86.26 billion; (2) $86.26 – $17.25 = $69.01 billion; and (3) $69 × 5 = $345 billion.

The generating factor of $487.20 billion for 1981 generated economic activities in the exporters' economies. AGS imports from the West and Japan are machinery, equipment, and durable and nondurable goods. But for their labor supply, they are heavily dependent on India, Pakistan, Philippines, certain Arab states, and Korea. At the same time, the positive spillover affects the economies that are heavy exporters to the AGS and are involved in the construction sectors. Normally, construction companies import the labor force needed for a project from their own nation. Therefore, the amount of income transfers by the labor force and businesses to their home countries is vital to the labor-exporting states. These capital transfers benefit the workers' home economies rather than the domestic Gulf economies. But there is certain financial benefit derived by local citizens, since, according to domestic laws, foreign companies and businesses operating in the domestic markets need local partners before being allowed to operate.

Since in 1982 the generating factor was less than in 1981, because of the reduction of oil revenues, the economies of nations that depend heavily on exports to the AGS were affected adversely. There is a direct relationship between reduction of oil revenues and imports of AGS. In 1988, all AGS revenues will be decreased due to the reduction of oil prices and the decrease in their output; this will be reflected in a further reduction of the positive spillover on the trading economies.

CONCLUSION

This chapter has analyzed the issue of whether OPEC is a cartel. The analysis indicates that OPEC is not a cartel, because it does not possess the necessary conditions that would qualify it to be a cartel. The concept of sovereignty plays an important role in the decisions of OPEC member countries with respect to output and prices. It is also clear from this analysis that, given the diversity of the political, economic, and social orientation of OPEC member countries, it is difficult to see how oil policies can be relegated to an intergovernmental organization.

It is also important to note that any future Western analytical studies pertaining to OPEC need to take into consideration the positive spillover effect that OPEC revenues generate to Western and non-Western economies. The West needs to abandon the strategy of blaming OPEC for causing all types of economic ills that are facing the world community. Supply, demand, and price of crude oil need to be freed from political whims and chauvinistic gestures that occur from time to time in the West. A new medium of payments for crude oil could enhance price and market stability in the future. More specific studies are needed on the positive spillover of AGS spending.

NOTES

1. OPEC Secretariat, Statistics Unit, "OPEC and the World Crude Oil Trade," *OPEC Bulletin* 12, no. 1 (1981): 10–31.

2. W. W. Riddick, "The Nature of the Petroleum Industry," *Proceedings of the Academy of Political Science* (1973): 152.

3. Michael R. Darby, "The Price of Oil and World Inflation and Recession," *American Economic Review* 72, no. 4 (1982): 738–751.

4. Jeffrey Sachs, "Stabilization Policies in the World Economy: Scope and Skepticism," ibid., pp. 56–61.

8

Human Capital: Untapped Resources in the Arab Gulf

Amin M. Kazak

While the tremendous increase in oil revenues in the 1970s produced explosive wealth and set off a spurt of economic growth in the countries of oil-export-led economies in the Arabian Peninsula, oil syndrome analysis raises two important issues concerning a primarily export-led economy: first, it emphasizes the problems of asymmetry in relative rates of sectoral growth in the economy of the oil-exporting countries; second, it contends that the instability of dependence on export of a single commodity—oil—might deteriorate the productive capacity of other sectors of the economy, because oil revenues are subject to large price fluctuations. In short, revenues from an oil-export-led economy can be a mixed blessing.

Given this element of oil-export-led economies, transition to less oil-oriented economies has become more of an immediate policy objective in oil-exporting countries of the Arabian Peninsula, and the pressure to speed up diversification of their economies into nonoil sectors has increased. In these countries, diversification has always been defined as the longer-term strategy for the economy. Yet diversification is no longer a remote goal, and its ultimate objective of reducing dependence on oil should be achieved through the tremendous task of creating a new structural basis for stable future growth.

The critical issue is whether the nonoil sector can be developed rapidly enough to command an increasing share of the gross domestic product (GDP) of the countries under discussion. The efforts in this direction have ramifications in the policies of diversification that have been embraced by the Arab Gulf states. Diversification, though a lofty policy, is difficult to implement successfully, as policymakers in these countries have come to realize, because economic diversification based on widespread expansion of industry is inevitably dependent on foreign expertise and investment in Western enterprise, both of which render these states subject to fluctuations and change beyond their control.

Undoubtedly the policy objective for structural change and diversification in the economies of oil-producing countries of the Arab Gulf will increase the dependence upon and demand for a more professional and skilled labor force at all levels. Thus, the core argument of this discussion will contend that diversification of the economy and the growth objectives for nonoil sectors in these states can be met with the increase and development of indigenous human resources and the productivity of the local work force. This means the maximization and efficient utilization of the knowledge and skills of the society, and the release of the energies, participation, and capabilities of all the people in the process of socioeconomic transformation.[1] The real development is not just the growth of GNP (Gross National Product), but a transformation of the economy that is likely to include changes in attitudes, habits, values, and, above all, knowledge, skills, and methods of work of the whole society.

PROBLEMS AND POLICY OPTIONS

The Predicaments

The capital-surplus oil-producing countries of the Arab Gulf share the same socioeconomic features, and the problems that confront them are similar. The striking features of the economic structure of this group of countries are a high per capita income, a substantial capital surplus, a high savings ratio, an abundance of oil and gas reserves, and a comprehensive welfare system that offers free social and health services. On the other hand, these countries share economic conditions and a number of social factors that constraint their economic and social development.

The oil-producing Arab countries of the Gulf lack a sizable agricultural sector; a strong base of indigenous, sufficiently skilled manpower; and have low participation in the work force among young educated men and women in certain occupations. Also lacking is the scientific and technological experience, the necessary ingredient in the process of socioeconomic transformation. These predicaments create three major vulnerabilities:

1. A high level of dependence on foreign expatriates
2. A heavy reliance on a single depletable resource (oil)
3. A relatively low agricultural input in national production.

These vulnerabilities, either individually or together, present policy makers and planners in these countries with few choices.

To sum up, although oil revenues practically eliminated the financial constraints to economic growth, the mere abundance of funds cannot in itself offer the oil-producing countries in the Gulf a panacea for all their economic and social ills. Therefore, the challenge facing policymakers in these countries is not only to develop a consistent and coherent package of government policies that will aim at diversifying the economy and at the same time reduce the magnitude of the vulnerabilities mentioned above, but also to make these policies compatible with the difficult task of mobilizing other factors of production: the development of human resources.

Policymakers in surplus-capital Arab countries of the Gulf have considered the problem of how they can reduce their dependence on just one resource, and of how they can link the oil and the nonoil sectors. Undoubtedly the oil sector has positively influenced the rest of the economy of these countries through financial linkages, increases in aggregate demand, and expanded imports.

Serious imbalances exist in their economies, however, as a result of an inadequate resource base. The imbalances have prevented the emergence of sufficient linkages between the oil and nonoil sectors. Thus, these countries have realized that the future of their economic development depends on their success in transforming some of the ephemeral oil revenues into productive and reproducible assets. So what are the policy options for these surplus-capital countries? Because oil will remain dominant in their economies for many years to come, one important issue in probing this situation is to identify the best way of handling capital surplus and to select the most efficient investment policy to remedy the economic imbalances by making qualitative changes in the development of other subsectors.

The Appropriate Investment Policy

A vast literature on development has emphasized the need for a substantial investment effort to break the vicious cycle of underdevelopment in Third World countries, and thus to make the effort worthwhile. Whether it is called the "big push," "balanced growth," "takeoff," or "trickle down," the message is always the same.[2] One of these growth models that has been a traditional part of the analysis of economic problems of development in Third World countries is the growth of capital stock. The growth of capital stock or capital accumulation became the centerpiece of the early economic development theories and analysis, and has maintained a major position in the literature of economic development. According to conventional wisdom, the simplified notion is that the key to the problems of development in Third World countries is to increase available capital by producing enough domestic savings. The implication is that a country that cannot generate enough savings to finance the target growth has to make up its capital shortages through inflow of funds from external resources, thus setting the basis for transfer of physical capital from advanced countries to poor countries. Indeed, the historical role that physical capital has played in advanced Western nations is emphasized, forming the framework for identifying the stages of development that all nations must follow.[3]

With the emergence of surplus capital in the oil-producing countries of the Arabian Peninsula, however, a new issue has reemphasized the crucial role of inputs other than the accumulation of capital. These surplus-capital countries have demonstrated that it is not the growth of physical capital, but the growth of human capital, which is the principal source of economic progress. The development of human capital is singled out as the most effective way to increase the contributions of capital in the economic and social development of these countries. In this connection, a number of questions might be raised within the context of allocation of resources in the development process in the countries of the Gulf. What is the appropriate investment policy to achieve the objectives of growth and diversification of the economy? How do we rank the priorities and needs in an appropriate investment policy?

In principle, it would seem that any government, when it decides to allocate the necessary resources for its development budget, should take into consideration the social and economic return to the whole society and all sectors in the country, whether rural or urban, on the basis of priorities. The selection of priorities and needs should be within the context of social, cultural, economic, and political benefits to all segments of the society.

That decision in a nation's development budget should go beyond the analysis of a single statistic of aggregate growth. Accordingly, the study of the characteristics of a society is a base for determining its needs as well as its present and future priorities. Identifying these needs and priorities helps to form a vivid and comprehensible picture of the objective and policy targets of economic and social development.

In general, there is no agreement as to the objectives of a particular society and its rating or priority scale. Security, equity, and growth are common objectives in most societies of the Third World, including the oil-producing Arab countries of the Gulf. While the traditional goals of development, such as increasing national income, reducing unemployment, adjusting the balance of payments, and coping with foreign exchange scarcity, are familiar policy targets in most countries, in the oil-producing countries of the Arabian Peninsula the overwhelming concerns and needs seem to be different and such policy objectives are not of primary importance to this group of nations. Because of their peculiar set of socioeconomic conditions, and the endowment that distinguishes them from other societies, new types of needs have inspired these societies. Education is considered one of the most important elements and factors that help to meet the needs and goals of progress and development. As Adam Smith points out, education and culture are not only the foundation of an efficient state system but also the elements upon which the state is based on economic matters and development. It is now generally recognized that the development of a country's human resources is essential to its prosperity and growth, and to the effective use of its physical capital. It follows that educational investment is now regarded as a vital complement to physical investment. Investment in physical capital and infrastructure in surplus-capital oil-producing Arab countries of the Gulf will not achieve their full potential without investment in the people who are ultimately responsible for the successful operation of the infrastrucutre of the economy.

At this point, the availability of capital from the inflow of large oil revenues has offered the Arab Gulf states unique options to translate capital surpluses into development in order to achieve greater sectoral balance and diversification, and to maximize a skilled and motivated labor force. Unfortunately, for two major reasons abundance of capital and funding have not been adequate to solve their predicaments. First, despite the rapid strides that educational development has made in these countries, many observers and scholars will argue that educational systems in the Arab Gulf states have undergone considerable change, but the changes in most cases have been quantitative, without alteration of the structure and quality.[4] Second, although human resource development has been a major theme in the developmental planning process in these countries, to date no effort has addressed the question of what manpower needs would be in the countries' self-interest. Some observers contend that the diffused definitions of specific manpower training needs have delayed the response time of the educational and vocational institutions charged with developing appropriate curricula to train skilled personnel.[5] For the most part, development plans in Arab oil-exporting countries in the Gulf have not adequately addressed the problem of manpower and educational policies.

CONCLUSION

It is clear that the quantitative nature of the educational systems and the overall manpower policies in the Arab oil-exporting countries cannot bring, in a true sense, the desired vigorous development of human resources. For the Gulf states, the following factors can help in formulating and evaluating a strenuous approach to human resources development and manpower policy planning. First, a gradual shift of the educational structure toward more emphasis on vocational and technical education, in response to labor-market requirements, will prove more beneficial. Second, comprehensive labor force planning is a prerequisite in any policy that attempts the Saudization or Kuwaitization of the labor market. Third, development and modernization can not be pursued when most of the native population is not involved in the process of socioeconomic transformation. The development of a fully mobilized population capable of effecting political and social changes in the process of modernization is a vital and imperative policy. Fourth, to overcome the immediate difficulties in human resource development, greater economic integration is needed by the Arab Gulf states. This includes coordinated programs for vocational and professional training and rehabilitation at all levels and stages. Clearly, the cooperation of the Arab Gulf states in joint actions with the rest of the Arab countries in a Pan-Arab system of human resource development represents a more rewarding policy in the process of economic transformation.

NOTES

1. Nader Fergany, "Manpower Problems and Projections in the Gulf," in M. S. El-Azhary, ed., *The Impact of Oil Revenues on Arab Gulf Development* (Boulder, Colo.: Westview Press, 1984), p. 156.

2. Rosentein-Rodan's "big push" theory showed that a huge increase in investments was needed to break through the lower per capita income equilibrium. The Harrod-Domar model of "balanced growth" was used to demonstrate that poor countries remained poor because they were not able to invest enough, wheras Rostow's "takeoff" theory demonstrated the importance of the rise in the rate of productive investment for the stage of growth.

3. For more details about balanced growth and capital formation, see G. M. Meier, *Leading Issues in Economic Development*, 4th ed. (New York: Oxford University Press, 1984), pp. 215–233.

4. Mohammed A. Rasheed, "Education as an Investment of Progress in the Arab Gulf States," in El-Azhary, ed., *The Impact of Oil Revenues*, p. 176.

5. J. W. Viola, *Human Resources Development in Saudi Arabia: Multinational and Saudization* (Boston: International Human Resource Development Corporation, 1986), p. 160.

9

Vocational Training for Women of India

Mary C. Muller

The period 1975–1985 was designated by the United Nations as the Decade for Women. During this decade the expectations of women worldwide were raised once again in anticipation of social changes that would guarantee economic equity in their lifetimes. At the end of the decade questions were asked to evaluate the extent of positive change and progress. Had ten years as a designated priority achieved the goals women desired? Had the crossroads been reached, or were they still ahead?

A vocational training program for women in India is an example of an effort made during the Decade for Women to alleviate economic inequities. The Ministry of Labor of the government of India studied recommendations made by the Indian Commission on the Status of Women and decided to embark on a special vocational training project. The major goal of the project was to make vocational training for women an integral part of the national plan for growth and development.

India, with a population of over 750 million, ranks among the top industrialized nations and has the third largest reservoir of highly skilled technical and scientific labor.[1] In charge of a vast nationwide training program is the Directorate General of Employment and Training of the Ministry of Labor, which oversees 850 industrial training institutes with a capacity of over 200,000 students.

Though not denied entry, women have been severely underrepresented in those institutes because they have had to cope with grossly inferior facilities, limited resources, lack of employment opportunities, and very little encouragement in acquiring occupational skills. As pointed out in the report of the Commission on the Status of Women in India, as in the rest of Asia, women are actively discriminated against in their search for vocational training:

Women share a common experience of sub-ordination, lack of property rights, insignificant recognition of their roles, undervaluation of their work and often acquiescence in inferiority, which affect their participation at every level. The sense of inferiority is intensified by the ever widening gap between the sexes in knowledge, information resources, opportunities, power and authority, both inside and outside the household.[2]

Women have a very limited access to knowledge, training, and information, which consistently constrains their attempts to achieve individual economic development. Success is defined by giving birth to males.

In order to offer an opportunity to improve this situation, the Directorate General of Employment and Training initiated a women's vocational training program. With financial assistance from the Swedish International Development Authority and technical assistance from the International Labor Organization, three training institutes were established exclusively for women in the cities of Bombay, Bangalore, and New Delhi. To be eligible to attend the institutes organized by the project, young women had to be between 18 and 25 years of age and have a secondary school certificate. In India, as in much of Asia, these women are a privileged group and are not representative of the total population. The majority of women in India—about 80 percent of them—live in rural areas, and of these about 90 percent drop out of school in the primary grades. However, in order to include the institutes for women within the Directorate General training organization, it was necessary to comply with existing regulations.[3]

As in the rest of the world, women workers in India hold jobs with low pay, low status, and little opportunity for advancement. The curriculum of studies for the women's training institutes did little to improve this situation. The vocational areas that were chosen were dressmaking, secretarial skills, beauty care, and electronics, all considered to be sex-stereotyped work. In India, however, there are some differences from the tradition of Europe and the Americas. For instance, dressmaking is a relatively recent export industry, because saris continue to be the preferred attire. It requires only the most basic sewing skills, because the patterns are cut in Europe and the United States. Beauty care is gradually becoming a commercial enterprise in shopping malls of major cities as traditional ways are changing. And, unlike many other parts of the world, secretaries are predominantly males.

Also, it is important to recognize that for these young women who were not poverty stricken, work outside the home was just becoming generally acceptable. Therefore, a curriculum of studies was necessary in order to have the tangible elements upon which to develop a program. If an approach was used that was considered so innovative as to be radical, a women's program would never have been started by the government.

TRAINING POLICY

Introducing "change factors" is more realistic when there is something to change. Since there was virtually no vocational training for women prior to the project, the first step was to get the Ministry of Labor involved. "Emerging from the shadow—entering new occupations with new opportunities" was the slogan adopted by the women's vocational training program. Women have always participated in productive activities in society, but their output has seldom been counted and measured, and their work generally has not been considered as economic activity. Therefore, emerging from the shadow meant becoming recognized contributors to economic growth with a goal of self-sufficiency. Dependence upon male members of the household has been a cultural burden Indian women have often found unbearable.

After five years of an experimental project, over 2,000 young women had been trained and the project became an active part of the Ministry of Labor's program. In addition, the special Women's Unit was established by the Ministry of Labor to act as a catalyst and to coordinate all women's vocational training activities at the national and the state levels.

The principal concern of the Women's Unit is training policy. During the experimental period many policy issues were raised that had not been given sufficient attention by the original planners. Do the skills acquired by the young women lead to employment that

warrants the investment in training? Is mere skill acquisition sufficient for a women's vocational training program, or are support
structures equally important? What type of help is available to cope
with problems of travel, hostel accommodation, child care, and loss
of income from the lack of participation in customary daily activities?
What decision-making powers does a young woman have in her vocational training course of study? After training, what control, if any,
can the young woman expect over the fruit of her labors?

The relationship between training and employment can be very
exploitive unless the members of a well-trained labor force have
opportunities and options to use their training to improve their
quality of life. Usually women who are well trained have fewer opportunities and fewer options than men. Unfortunately, the alternative for most women is unemployment, so they are often overtrained,
overskilled, and underemployed.

The expedient components of a vocational training policy for
women are (1) skills training, (2) training designed to maintain the
economic viability of work, and (3) training that includes how to
organize support structures. Skill acquisition—that is, how to perform the skills on the job—should be in growth industries, where
competition with men could be minimized. In India the abundance
of unemployed male carpenters and plumbers eliminated such trades;
and tailoring, an all-male preserve, made dressmaking risky. The skills
being taught to women should require incremental levels of competence that would build a hierarchy of skills enabling them to get beyond the assembly line. And certain generic skills, such as selling,
needed to be included in the skill acquisition component because
they can be applied to a wide range of job opportunities.

In terms of economic viability, a training program has to concen-
trate on the marketability of the skills being learned. The conventional approach of a needs assessment for certain skills is inappropriate because discrimination against women in the work place negates
a concept of need. It is necessary to train women in areas where their
ability overshadows the attitude toward women workers. Therefore,
work in new technologies offers potential opportunities. In addition
to the marketability of skills, the economic viability of training is
enhanced in a pragmatic work setting. The training should be coupled
with production centers developed in conjunction with subcontracting industries and credit institutions.

Organizational support structures are necessary for equitable employment. Women are not ordinarily union members in India, making up only about 16 percent of unionized labor. Thus it is important to include alternative support systems, such as the formation of cooperatives, in the vocational training. In this way emphasis can be placed on entrepreneurial skills, management skills, and marketing skills.

POLICY DIALOGUE TO CONFRONT REALITY

Since independence, India has made enormous strides in the face of enormous problems. It has taken major steps to improve agricultural output, as seen in the "green revolution," and its industries have extended to the point where India is one of the top ten industrial powers in the world. But problems of obsolescence, a concentration on heavy industry, and limited use of "leapfrog technology" left India behind its Asian neighbors in the field of electronics in the early 1980s.

It is generally accepted that women both have found employment and have been exploited in the electronics industry around the world. In light of this, the electronics industry was chosen as the target industry for the women's vocational training program, with the aim of changing employment practices. There were three reasons for this choice: (1) because of the industry's crucial role and its strong growth potential; (2) because women were already being employed (albeit as the lowest, unskilled labor) and therefore were less likely to be perceived as a threat by displacing men; (3) because the government's need for future-oriented planning encouraged acceptance of social change.

In designing vocational training for women who have had great difficulty gaining access to the wage labor market, it is necessary to address issues of exploitation and discrimination. Policy dialogue is the strategy development planners use when such sensitive issues interfere with a program's goals because it can be the key to effective institution building. Through interpersonal communication, the principal participants in a development activity identify problem areas of public policy issues and conduct factor analysis for the negotiation of possible conflict resolution. The functions of communication in a policy dialogue are mutual understanding, consensus, and ultimately collective action.

The first three institutes implementing this new program had received over $1 million worth of state-of-the-art electronics training equipment from the Swedish International Development Authority, to be used exclusively by the women trainees. The equipment was superior in many respects to what was being used in the electronics plants at that time. Thus, a crucial economic question was raised: Can women with high-level skills in electronics find employment commensurate with the investment in their training?

Policy dialogue to address these issues was conducted through economic conferences. Bombay was the site of the first conference. After a survey of the electronics industry to identify the existing production conditions, key respondents were invited to participate in the conference with government officers from the ministries of Labor, Industry, and Social Welfare, as well as managers of training institutes, representatives of economic planning agencies and credit institutions, and feminists.

At the conference the industrial leaders presented views of the consumer electronics sector as well as of defense and communications. Economic planners from the industrial sites around Bombay presented their views on the export orientation of the industry, density and impact constraints, and the need for diversification. The trainees said they were looking for work other than as assemblers and packers. Women activists, supporting social development, insisted that training include counseling, adequate boarding facilities, clean and safe classrooms, and responsible treatment. This dynamic needs assessment analyzed the situation from several perspectives: the needs of industry as seen by employers and economic planners, the needs of trainees as potential workers seeking equitable conditions, and the needs of training institutes to develop appropriate courses of study.

Due to endemic underemployment in India, the government offers support to persons who can become small-scale entrepreneurs, offering very special credit terms at very low interest rates. Representatives from banking and credit institutes were invited to the conference to explain and discuss their financial plans. Though these people thought that they could encourage young women to start small businesses, such as electronics repair shops, this was not very realistic at that stage of the program. On the other hand, cooperatives were considered a possible option, and several women social workers with subcontracting cooperatives discussed their experiences.

In the jargon of development projects, the term "target population" or "client population" is used to identify the group toward which a project is directed. In the policy dialogue strategy the two groups were differentiated, one as the target population and another as the client population. The client population was made up of all women interested in promoting and participating in vocational training. The target population was made up of decision makers, both national and international, many of whom held misconceptions regarding training for women. During the conference the atmosphere was relaxed but structured. The positive argument for women's vocational training was built by stressing competence in job skills and dedication in work habits. Positive role models were featured, and persons holding controversial views were not harassed. The presentations were objective and without emotional pleas. Credibility was achieved by avoiding unrealistic aspirations, admitting social and cultural constraints, and focusing on the economic viability and equity of the vocational program.

After Bombay the series of conferences continued throughout the country in Bangalore, Madras, New Delhi, and Mysore. They became the impetus for planning a policy for vocational training in terms of realistic and economically viable options. The Directorate General of Employment and Training began to realize that it needed to ensure the marketability of skills and that curriculum planning needed to include the study of income-generating activities outside of wage employment. This meant that changes had to be made, and a course of study would have to include how to develop leadership skills, how to run a small business, how to organize a cooperative, and how to market skills and services. The participants at these conferences represented the human resources that could be tapped to prepare a new curriculum of study.

POLICY AS A FIRST STEP

Needless to say, the conferences represented only the first step toward change. The initiation of a policy dialogue opened the doors for vested interests to present divergent views. Although it is not possible to recount resounding success, the fact that issues of equitable opportunities for women were discussed by decision makers must be counted as an achievement. As in so many social change programs, the magnitude of the problem often overwhelms the first signs of improvement.

The Women's Unit of the Directorate General of Employment and Training is weak and must continually struggle for survival, but it has an identity and a structure. The unit can work through established training institutes that serve one growing, dynamic sector of the economy, as well as others that are more traditional. The road ahead for the staff of the Women's Unit is an arduous one with many new challenges. Continuity and perseverance are the arrows at the cross-roads that indicate the road already paved; but ahead the arrows point to equity and opportunity through a morass of jungle growth as yet untamed.

The Women's Vocational Training Program of the Ministry of Labor is part of an international movement for social development of women seeking equity in the world of work. It is part of a process that is multidimensional and can be appreciated only over a prolonged period of time. As women seek more equitable participation in economic development, there are both positive and negative reactions. Though women's rights are not denied, the forces of change pose threats to some who are too confortable with the status quo. The environment of social change is fragile, and it needs to be nurtured and supported with a tolerance for the unexpected.

In a message to the International Conference on Women and Development, Indira Gandhi summarized the situation thus:

No country can claim to have insured complete equality—but, society as a whole has begun to respond. More and more women are adopting careers and finding fulfillment as individuals while contributing to the building of happy homes. But the fact is that women, whether in traditional or modern situations, have to work harder than men and bear more burdens. The attitudes of minds of women as well as men must change. Both are partners in life's struggle.[4]

NOTES

1. *Far Eastern Economic Review* (Hong Kong), August 20, 1987.

2. Z. Ahmed, "Technology, Production Linkage and Women's Employment," *International Labor Review* 126, no. 1 (1987): 136.

3. *Report of Women's Vocational Training Project* (New Delhi: International Labor Office, 1983).

4. Indira Gandhi, Message to International Conference on Women and Development, New Delhi, 1984.

10

African-Americans and U.S. Foreign Policy in Africa

Jacob U. Gordon

The present U.S. awareness of Africa, more widespread than it has ever been in the past, dates back no further than World War II, when strategy, politics, and economics combined to force the United States to pay attention to a part of the world it had hitherto largely ignored. Of the earlier links with Africa little need be said, since for the most part they do not give much of a clue to the nature of the contemporary U.S. foreign policy interest. By far the greatest of them, in terms of its consequences, was the slave trade, which provided the United States with the ancestors of nearly 13 percent of its present population. There was a long series of tangles with the Barbary State at the end of the eighteenth and the beginning of the nineteenth centuries. The founding of Liberia in 1822, itself deriving from the slavery issue, established one spot on the African coast to which the United States had a special attachment. U.S. delegates participated in the Berlin Conference of 1884–1885, which laid down some of the ground rules for the already active scramble for Africa.

These and similar contacts, including continuous trade relations, indicate how slight and episodic U.S. contact with Africa has usually been. It should be noted, however, that developments in world politics since 1945 have hammered home the lesson that U.S. supplies of raw materials are far from inexhaustible, thus forcing reliance on other parts of the world. For both its agricultural and its mineral resources, Africa has come to occupy a new place in U.S. calculations on how to keep raw material supply and demand in equilibrium. Similarly, like it or not, Americans, especially African-Americans, must reconcile themselves to the realization that what goes on in Africa may have a decisive influence on the future direction of their lives.

The role of black Americans in U.S. foreign policy toward Africa has been well documented by many scholars. Jake Miller's *The Black Presence in American Foreign Affairs* examines both the historical and the contemporary contributions of black Americans to U.S. foreign policy. His analysis of individual and organizational contributions to U.S. foreign policy brings together a useful body of knowledge.[1] "The Influence of Black Americans on U.S. Foreign Policy Toward Africa," by Herschell Challenor, documents the persistence of African-American interest in African nations. The paper suggests reasons for the escalation of interest in African affairs since 1960, and examines the constraints and opportunities of a black impact on U.S. foreign policy. Challenor suggests three principal reasons why black Americans have not significantly influenced policy toward their ancestral continent: (1) the historical absence of black political power as a result of disenfranchisement in the South and the neutralization of the black vote in the North; (2) the low esteem accorded to blacks and to Africa; (3) official attempts to discourage close, effective links between Africans and African-Americans.[2]

John Davis, professor of political science and editor of *African Forum: A Quarterly Journal of Contemporary Affairs*, has addressed the subject from a different perspective. In his essay "Black Americans and United States Policy Toward Africa," he discusses the involvement of black Americans in U.S. foreign policy as early as 1788, when African-Americans in Newport, Rhode Island, wrote to the Free African Society in Philadelphia, proposing a plan of emigration to Africa. Davis's hope for black American impact on U.S. foreign policy on Africa is based on two factors: (1) African-content education for black youth and (2) the rise of black urban politicians who will inherit the black nationalist movement in the United States.[3]

Other scholarly works include Milton Morris's essay "Black Americans and the Foreign Policy Process: The Case of Africa"; "The African-American Manifesto on Southern Africa," a ten-point document adopted at a conference of organization leaders convened by the Congressional Black Caucus in 1976;[4] "The Afro-American Response to the Occupation of Haiti: 1915–34," by Brenda Plummer;[5] "American Negroes and U.S. Foreign Policy: 1937–1967," by Alfred Hero;[6] and numerous essays written by W. E. B. DuBois, beginning with his publication of "The Suppression of the African Slave Trade in the United States of America, 1638–1870," in 1896. The list includes the unpublished works of Locksley Edmondson and the publications of the Joint Center for Political Studies in Washington, D.C.[7] A few U.S. black diplomats, especially Donald McHenry, have documented the black American role in U.S. foreign policy. These works have dispelled the notion that African-Americans have shown no interest and have not been involved in U.S. foreign policy, especially in the Third World.[8]

Many urban black politicians have attempted to make Davis's dream come true. Perhaps the most outspoken individual in this endeavor is former Representative Charles C. Diggs, Jr. The record shows that this Michigan congressman has led the fight to get a fair shake for black Africa. He argues that the destinies of African-Americans in the United States and of Africans in Africa are inextricably linked. Diggs sees two major areas of policy toward Africa; (1) ending white racist rule in South Africa and (2) accelerating economic development throughout the African continent. To influence U.S. policy toward Africa in these areas, Diggs suggests, among other things, that blacks in the United States must follow foreign policy developments diligently, demonstrate their displeasure through voting, put effective pressure on their elected representatives in Washington, and use their $50 billion purchasing power to exert leverage. These are sound ideas, except that they have not been translated into reality. Africa continues to remain the unchallenged occupant of the bottom rung of U.S. foreign policy priorities. How do we explain U.S. interest in Africa and the apparent lack of effective policy? First, let's reexamine U.S. interest in Africa.

In a speech by Secretary of State George Shultz at the World Affairs Council in Boston, on February 15, 1984, the secretary pointed out four major interest areas:

First, we have a significant geopolitical stake in the security of the continent and the seas surrounding it. Off its shores lie important trade routes, including those carrying most of the energy resources needed by our European allies. We are affected when Soviets, Cubans, and Libyans seek to expand their influence on the continent by force, to the detriment of both African independence and Western interests.

Second, Africa is part of the global economic system. If Africa's economies are in trouble, the reverberations are felt here. Our exports to Africa have dropped by 50% in the last 3 years; American financial institutions have felt the pinch of African inability to repay loans. And Africa is a major source of raw materials crucial to the world economy.

Third, Africa is important to us politically because the nations of Africa are now major players in world diplomacy. They comprise nearly one-third of the membership of the United Nations, where they form the most cohesive voting bloc in the General Assembly.

Finally, Africa is important to us, most of all, in human terms. Eleven percent of America's population traces its roots to Africa; all of us live in a society profoundly influenced by this human and cultural heritage. The revolution of Africa's independence coincided with the civil rights revolution in this country. Perhaps it was not a coincidence. Both were among the great moral events of this century: a rebirth of freedom, summoning all of us to a recognition of our common humanity. Just as the continued progress of civil rights is important to the moral well-being of this country, so too the human drama of Africa—its political and economic future—is important to the kind of world we want our children and grandchildren to inherit.[9]

Although Africa is taking on increasing importance in several respects, many Americans, according to Secretary Shultz, have images of Africa that are anachronistic, partial, and often inaccurate. He went on to say, "The perception of Africa that most of us grew up with—unknown lands somehow exotic and divorced from the rest of the world—has unfortunately persisted in some quarters despite the last 25 years of Africa's independence and increasing presence on the world stage. It is a misperception that ignores compelling realities." The compelling realities were probably better explained by Vice-President George Bush during his 1982 tour of Africa. In his speech to the Kenya Chamber of Commerce in Nairobi on November 19, 1982, the vice-president indicated U.S. interest in what he called "constructive change in southern Africa" when he said:

We will not ignore or disguise our strong belief in the importance of justice and equality before the law. Apartheid is wrong. It is legally entrenched racism—inimical to the fundamental ideals of the United States. America's history and America's future can only be understood in terms of our commitment to a multiracial democracy in which all citizens participate and from which all benefit. Will Black Americans play a role in meeting this commitment? Are these constraints and/or promises for Black Americans in developing more aggressive and productive American foreign policy toward Africa? Is race an issue in U.S. policy toward Africa? What theoretical model should we explore for African-American effective involvement in American foreign policy issues, particularly in Africa?[10]

An important aspect of black history since the 1960s is the increased interest of black Americans in Africa and African affairs. This is not to suggest that they had no interest in Africa until the 1960s. On the contrary, black Americans have always been interested in their roots in Africa. The difference now, it seems to me, is that they are more aware than ever of the bonds that link them to the continent of their origin. This new awakening may represent a new hope as the United States continues to experiment with "constructive engagement" with South Africa and goodwill tours to the rest of Africa. But first we must begin to create a better understanding of some of the major issues raised in this chapter.

Institutionalization of interest is a critical measure of these developing orientations. The founding in 1962 of the American Negro Leadership Conference on Africa—it has since disbanded—by black elites in the civil rights movement signaled the institutionalization of African-American pressure to protect and enhance African interests.

That trend has continued to develop, most notably in the creation of the lobby TransAfrica. In that body we find an interest in enhancing professionalism (as an organized lobby with its research staff and the recent addition of a research and educational affiliate called TransAfrica Forum); in developing specialized talents (as a full-time lobby with full-time concern with the outer black world); and in extending vision beyond a purely African one to include a Caribbean focus. Perhaps the fact that TransAfrica and similarly situated interests have not yet been able to affect the foreign policy process meaningfully is less important than the fact that the task of serious foreign policy political mobilization is under way in black America.

The extent to which black bureaucrats and diplomats have been able to exert significant influence on the foreign policy process, in the sense of being architects as opposed to being instruments, remains an open question. Certainly the kind of influence that Andrew Young was able to exert, at least for a while, was unique; and it is perhaps more significant that he was removed prematurely. It is of significance, however, that in February 1983 another institutional expression of this rising black American concern appeared in the form of an organization of black ambassadors, created for the long-run purpose of heightening an interest in foreign policy within the black community and encouraging young blacks to consider foreign service careers.

In a sense, these developing expressions of a linkage of interest with Africa through a foreign policy focus may be perceived as another stage in the fulfillment of a historic U.S. pattern of ethnic groups bringing their influence to bear on matters affecting their ancestral lands. Such developments are consistent with what may be formulated as a general rule: that the more heightened a sense of racial or ethnic identity, the greater the propensity for such expressions to transcend national boundaries.

But there is a particularly sharp edge to the rising African-American identification with African causes. There is, so to speak, a dual, racially significant attachment. Here we have a developing relationship not only conditioned by the facts of common racial origin but also impregnated with the realities of common racial traumas. One must pause here to question the impact of this dualism, what DuBois called "twoness," on the African-American role in U.S. foreign policy processes. It is equally important to note that black Americans do not have a monopoly on racial dualism. White Americans from Europe have a similar historical experience—the European soul and the American soul in one body. In this context the U.S. South prevails in the interest of national security. Black Americans are no exception.

CONSTRAINTS AND CHALLENGES

Professor Locksley Edmondson points out many constraints and opportunities for African-Americans in U.S. policy decision processes for Africa. Among some of the possible constraints on the effectiveness of blacks in influencing the foreign policy processes are the following:

1. The relative political powerlessness of blacks, despite significant gains, especially considering black underrepresentation in the critical administrative levels. Interestingly, there is an overrepresentation of blacks in the armed forces, though disproportionately concentrated in the lower ranks, with very uncertain implications with respect to the advancement of outer black world interests.

2. The historical and apparently continuing suspicion of the dominant decision makers regarding black inputs that tend to be less automatically supportive of the status quo

3. The limited maneuverability of the black bureaucratic/diplomatic ranks, constrained by wider institutional realities

4. With North-South relations being the critical component of U.S. relations with the outer black world, the extent to which black Americans are able to

identify with the demands for a new international economic order might be constrained by the gravity of the black economic predicament as a domestic priority; the possible perception that a restructuring of international economic relations may imply a diversion of difficulties of comprehending alternative development models, and thus being supportive of noncapitalist developmental paths

5. The pervasiveness of East-West strategic formulations in U.S. foreign policy, making it more difficult for those who may wish to highlight the North-South dilemma.[11]

Some constraints imposed by the external environment include the following:

1. The need for a multiple focus on Africa, a continent of over 50 nations, making perceptions more diffuse and complex

2. Item (1) is complicated by the "newness," and hence the relatively less settled state, of African nationhood, exhibiting more cleavages within and between nations than in the more established politics to which most other U.S. ethnic diasporas are linked

3. The need to relate to another "target area" besides the African homeland— the Caribbean, which in addition exhibits certain of the above-mentioned traumas of new nationhood

4. The more the clear-cut colonial and (as in the case of South Africa) racial issues in the outher black world become less salient, the greater the difficulties of discerning clear-cut issues of common concern.[12]

PROMISES AND CHALLENGES

Still, the promising trend is an increasing interest and involvement of black Americans in foreign policy, which

a. Is a demonstration of greater political maturity.

b. May serve to reduce the racist components in U.S. foreign policy.

c. May serve to sensitize U.S. foreign policy to the needs of a truly pluralistic world.

The current debate over U.S. policy toward the changing situation in South Africa resolves around questions of self-interest, of the economic/strategic importance of the country, the relevance of its system to U.S. domestic issues and human rights policy, and its relevance to broader African policy. Traditionally, Africa has been seen as of little or no significance to U.S. interests. Is this traditional view in the process of redefinition by U.S. policymakers? Will events, as they unfold in South Africa, come to be seen by Americans as of such significance that U.S. national interests will be perceived as involved in the outcome of the changes that will occur over the next decade? There is a need for black Americans in particular to examine the shifting significance of South Africa in U.S. policymaking, especially as the "threat of international Communism" continues to be the dominant factor in decision making.

Another important point I wish to make is the apparent self-imposed constraints and promises of black Americans and the U.S. foreign policy process. If black Americans are to be effectively involved in U.S. foreign policy precesses, especially in the Third World, we must revisit DuBois's concept of "twoness" as it may apply to black American interest in Africa. The question is whether black Americans can be effective in U.S. foreign policy toward Africa with two souls in one beautiful black body—the African soul and the American soul. One can only hope that black Americans can do for Africa what the Jews have done for Israel.

It is also important to note that black American effectiveness in U.S. foreign policy toward Africa will involve the preparation of black youth for a better understanding of Africa through education in homes, schools, churches, and black organizations. Black Americans must encourage their youth to seek employment in all branches of government, including the CIA and FBI. Above all, blacks must take advantage of the two-party system. No longer can black Americans put all their eggs in one basket. To put it bluntly, black Americans must be Democrats and Republicans.

Last, but not least, is the issue of race in U.S. foreign policy. To the extent that racism has become part of world civilization, especially in the United States and South Africa, it is difficult not to see the obvious. Surmise enough to argue that theoretically and operationally, U.S. policy is inextricably linked with national interest. These interests are usually determined by elected officials, who are products of a racist society. It therefore goes without saying that race has always been an important consideration in U.S. life. This trend will continue into the twenty-first century and beyond.

In conclusion, the following four points should be noted:

1. African-Americans have inextricably been involved in U.S. foreign policy issues, especially in Africa, since U.S. independence.
2. There are constraints, promises, and challenges for black Americans in U.S. foreign policy in Africa.
3. The more recent black American presence in U.S. foreign policy has had some impact in the direction of that policy in general, particularly regarding the Third World.
4. The future of this involvement is greater than ever before, and this future depends on black American initiative.

NOTES

1. Jake Miller, *The Black Presence in Foreign Affairs* (Washington, D.C.: University Press of America, 1978), pp. 1–58.

2. Herschell Challenor, "The Influence of Black Americans on U.S. Foreign Policy Toward Africa," in Abdul Said, ed., *Ethnicity and American Foreign Policy*, rev. ed. (New York: Praeger, 1981), pp. 143–182.

3. John A. Davis, "Black Americans and United States Policy Toward Black Africa," *Journal of International Affairs*, 23, no. 1, (1969), 236–249.

4. Milton Morris, "Black Americans and the Foreign Policy Process: The Case of Africa," *Western Political Quarterly*, 25 (September 1972), 451–463.

5. Brenda Plummer, "The Afro-American Response to the Occupation of Haiti, 1915–1934," *Phylon*, 43 (June 1982), 125–143.

6. Alfred O. Hero, "American Negroes and U.S. Foreign Policy, 1937–1967," *Journal of Conflict Resolution*, 8 (June 1969), 220–251.

7. Locksley Edmondson, "Race and Human Rights in International Organizations and International Law and Afro-American Interest," *Afro-American Studies*, 2 (December 1971), 205–224.

8. Donald McHenry, "Captive of No Group," *Foreign Policy*, 15 (Summer 1974), 142–149.

9. United States Department of State, *Realism, Strength, Negotiation: Key Foreign Policy Statements of the Reagan Administration* (Washington, D.C.: Bureau of Public Affairs, 1984), pp. 56–89.

10. Ibid., pp. 140–159.

11. Edmondson, "Race and Human Rights," 205–224.

12. Ibid.

Political and Economic Origins of African Hunger

Andrew Conteh

World food production has increased every year since 1945, with only two exceptions: 1972 and 1983, both years marked by drought in Africa. In 1986, records were again broken, with food production 2 percent higher than in 1985, and cereal production rising to an estimated 1.86 billion metric tons.

Although the 1986 gains were mostly smaller than in 1985, other features of the production pattern were encouraging. Food production increased substantially in the developing countries (2.9 percent), with significant gains in many countries in Africa, Asia, and the Near East. There were good cereal harvests in China and India, excellent ones in Pakistan and Turkey, and record crops in Nigeria, Morocco, the Sudan, and several Sahel countries. In the developed countries, by contrast, overall food production barely changed. Regions in which large food surpluses have accumulated for many years managed to reduce production significantly.

Cereal production in the United States fell by 10 percent and that of the European Economic Community (EEC) by about 5 percent, but these reductions were the result of poor weather as well as of effective reduction policies. Significant increases, however, occurred in Eastern Europe and the Soviet Union, where food production rose by 6.0 percent, overcoming decreases in North America and Australia.

Among the cereals, wheat production increased most (3.8 percent), with gains in both developed and developing countries. Surpluses rose by 7.5 percent, and meat and milk production both increased, particularly in the developing countries (meat by 3.3 percent and milk by 2.7 percent). Fish production in 1986 also increased, for the ninth year running, to more than 85 million metric tons. Aquaculture is providing an increasing share of total fish production, and is proving particularly important in augmenting food supplies in Asian countries such as China, Japan, the Republic of Korea, and the Philippines.

However, global surpluses, as always, disguise local shortages, and several countries—including Ethiopia, Mozambique, and Sudan—continue to face exceptional food shortages. In two decades, Africa has moved from a position of self-sufficiency in food production to one of rising deficits, despite a 2 percent annual growth rate in production since 1974.

As may be seen from Table 11.1, per capita food production decreased in most sub-Saharan countries over a decade, despite the considerable improvement in agricultural production in other Third World countries. The per capita daily calorie supply likewise declined, even though the area greatly increased its consumption of foreign cereals through importation and foreign aid. Children, rural inhabitants, and slum dwellers are especially vulnerable to hunger. Over time, hunger slows physical and mental development in children and leaves them more vulnerable to illness and disease. For example, respiratory and diarrheal infections are common in undernourished children, and even diseases like measles can be fatal. Other common dietary deficiency diseases are vitamin A deficiency (which can cause blindness), anemia (iron deficiency), and goiter (iodine deficiency). Undernourished adults lose weight, are progressively weakened, and become apathetic, less creative and imaginative, and more irritable.

Declining per capita food production in Africa is not only a cause of the crisis; it is an effect. Africa is the victim of a social and economic crisis that requires two kinds of remedial action: short-term emergency relief in the form of food, and long-term structural adjustment that will encourage both an agricultural recovery and rehabilitation of African economies.

CAUSES

The situation in most of Africa is the result of a combination of factors, both natural and man-made. Prolonged drought has served to trigger events that would probably have happened sooner or later, the most obvious being the decline in per capita food production.

Table 11.1
Food Indicators for Sub-Saharan African Countries

Country	Value added in agriculture (millions of 1980 $'s)		Cereal imports (thousands of metric tons)		Food aid in cereals (thousands of metric tons)		Average index of food production per capita
	1970	1985	1974	1985	1974/75	1984/85	1983/85
Angola	--	--	149	377	0	78	102
Benin	410	515	8	54	9	21	121
Burkino Faso	461	607	99	113	28	124	114
Burundi	468	598	7	20	6	17	106
Cameroon	1,233	2,245	81	139	4	12	107
Central Africa Rep.	256	333	7	17	1	12	105
Chad	416	--	37	134	20	163	106
Congo	147	184	34	90	2	1	104
Ethiopia	1,663	1,511	118	986	54	869	97
Ghana	2,320	2,398	177	292	33	94	118
Guinea	--	805	63	140	49	47	102
Ivory Coast	1,999	2,853	172	272	4	0	115
Kenya	1,198	2,263	15	365	2	340	99
Lesotho	88	--	49	118	14	72	93
Liberia	235	373	42	116	3	20	114
Madagascar	1,111	1,293	114	205	7	98	112
Malawi	258	426	17	23	(.)	5	105
Mali	717	816	281	281	107	266	114
Mauritania	200	222	115	240	48	135	94
Mozambique	--	477	62	426	34	366	98
Niger	1,466	1,070	155	247	73	218	96
Nigeria	17,943	18,858	389	2,199	7	0	109
Rwanda	295	614	3	24	19	36	106
Senegal	603	615	341	510	27	130	105
Sierra Leone	259	358	72	81	10	21	108
Sudan	1,754	1,511	125	1,082	46	812	103
Tanzania	1,834	2,088	431	231	148	127	108
Togo	238	325	6	79	11	23	103
Uganda	2,558	3,031	37	20	0	30	125
Zaire	2,518	3,362	343	331	1	138	113
Zambia	473	659	93	247	5	112	107
Zimbabwe	556	955	71	144	--	--	109

Source: World Bank, World Development Report (1987), Table 6.

The fact that African countries do not produce enough food stems from serious limitations of the natural environment, an imbalance in the global trade structure, and the government policies that have given low priority to food production.

Food Crisis and General Economic Malaise in Africa

The food crisis and the economic crises in Africa are linked, and both are associated with an underlying and fundamental crisis in agriculture. In most African countries agriculture is central to the resolution of economic problems.

Food production in the vast majority of African countries has been inadequate since the late 1950s, and probably earlier. Throughout the decade 1960–1970, the productivity of the food-producing sector of most African agricultural economies was virtually stagnant, in terms of output per worker and per unit of land. The agrarian paradox can be discerned not only in the Sahel drought area but also in East Africa, where the effects of climatic irregularity are not so severe.[1]

Mali is a country heavily affected by drought conditions and a principal recipient of emergency food shipments. The production of food crops for local consumption had fallen precipitously by the early 1970s. Corn production, for example, fell by more than one-third between 1969 and 1971, and millet, desperately needed to take up the slack, showed no increases whatsoever. During the same period, Mali's export crops attained bumper levels. During the crop year 1971–1972, cottonseed production reached a record high of 68,000 metric tons, a figure that reflected an increase of more than 400 percent during a six-year period. Peanut production totaled more than 150,000 metric tons that year, an increase of nearly 7 percent during a four-year period. Rice production, also largely for export, reached a record high. The agrarian paradox assumes a particularly cruel form when one or more of the crops being exported is a basic food item that could be consumed locally.

In Tanzania, food production for local consumption began to plummet disastrously during the early 1970s, a problem the government was inclined to attribute to climatic conditions but that was, it can be argued, to a far greater extent a consequence of peasant resistance to an unwanted program of socialist villages. By 1974, food production had fallen so low that the government had exhausted its entire reserve of foreign exchange to purchase food overseas. Additional shipments were being sent on an emergency relief basis, placing Tanzania in the same situation as Mali and other Sahel nations. At the same time, however, the export sector of the Tanzanian agricultural economy was flourishing, and the total level of production of export crops was approaching record highs. During the crop year 1972–1973, just before the massive importation of emergency food supplies, Tanzania exported over 120,000 metric tons of cotton, more than 100,000 metric tons of coffee, about 235,900 metric tons of sisal, and nearly 280,000 metric tons of cashews.[2] Thus it could be likened to Mali not only with respect to its dependence upon foreign supplies of food but also in the impressively successful accomplishments of its export-oriented agricultural economy.

Meanwhile, world food production managed to stay ahead of population increases in the 1970s, as it had done in the 1960s and most probably also in the 1950s. The general experience of developing countries taken as a group, including market and centrally planned countries, has been one of rising per capita food production: against an increase in population of about 2.5 percent a year in the 1970s, total food output increased at an annual rate of 3 percent in the 1960s and 1970s. After a slow start at the beginning of the 1970s, food output picked up in mid decade, when it reached a rate of increase of 4 percent a year. It fell off in the second half of the decade, especially toward the end, to below 3 percent; preliminary estimates show a relatively strong start for the 1980s.

The poor performance of cereals at the beginning of the 1970s and during 1972–1974, at a time of setbacks in output in some of the more developed countries, was largely responsible for the food (or, more strictly, cereals) crisis of the mid decade. Thereafter, cereal production increased steadily, although it faltered again toward the end of the decade, then rose in 1980 and 1981.

The long-run experience of many countries in Africa has been very different from the overall trend. In Africa as a whole, the food supply per inhabitant shrank, on average, by 10 percent during the 1970s. The effect on millions proved catastrophic.

Sharp fluctuations in production plagued many countries, even where the trend was upward. Of those countries that found it difficult to raise production to meet increases in population or in purchasing power, as long-term trends in cereal output illustrate (Table 11.2), many were able to offset a large part of the shortfall in domestic

Table 11.2

Annual Average Rate of Growth in Food Production by Region, 1971-1981 (percentage)

Developed market	2.5	1.9	1.6
Developing market	2.9	2.6	3.8
Africa	1.7	2.0	1.8
Latin America	2.9	3.7	3.6
Near East	3.9	2.5	0.7
Far East	2.9	2.4	5.3
Centrally planned	2.5	1.7	1.6
Asia	3.1	3.1	2.9
Europe and USSR	2.1	0.7	0.1

Source: Office for Research Development and Policy Analysis, Department of International Economic and Social Affairs, United Nations Secretariat; based on *FAO Monthly Bulletin of Statistics*, November 1981.

supply with imports. For many middle-income countries, rising food imports, even at rising prices, represented a relatively smaller claim on their foreign exchange resources as export revenues remained buoyant. The economic setbacks in the late 1970s and in the early 1980s curtailed the foreign exchange available to many developing countries for obtaining imports in case of temporary domestic food production setbacks. Reduced purchasing power among urban and other groups placed many of the poorer workers at the risk of hunger once again.

The reported incidence of food emergencies of a local or national nature increased as the 1980s began. The shipment of cereals under food aid schemes was not increased, remaining at between 9 million and 9.5 million metric tons of grain equivalent since 1976/1977. For low-income countries, such shipments accounted for 17 percent of their total cereal imports in 1980/1981, having fallen from about 25 percent of shipments in 1976/1977 and 50 percent in the early 1960s.

The overall world food supply position in the 1980s, as against the 1960s, can be said to be much improved, but with much more volatile food markets. Greater awareness of the need to limit the incidence of hunger following crop failure and a generally stronger agriculture in developing countries, capable of sustaining past production gains into the future, may be considered the most significant long-term advances of the 1980s.

Africa's problems of food production are not reducible to a matter of rainfall levels. They have to do fundamentally with a series of causes.

Dualistic Agricultural Economies

The scramble for Africa that resulted in the balkanization of the region into many small states, dictated the orientation of the African economy. Indeed, the African economy has been characterized by a system inhibiting the development by the region of its own resources for its own use and benefit. The total production structure and its supporting infrastructure were established to ensure the production for and transportation of raw materials to the colonizing countries. The consumption pattern was designed to ensure maximum dependence on imports. Thus, Africa was producing what it did not consume and consuming what it did not produce. The picture remains the same. African food production occurs within a context formed by the colonial experience. The structure of African agriculture has been heavily shaped by policies designed to integrate colonies into metropolitan trading networks and, sometimes, to protect settler populations.

Taxation policy was instrumental in stimulating the production of agricultural exports (West Africa) as well as in providing a labor force for mining or plantation production (Southern and Central Africa) or working on settler-operated farms (East and Southern Africa).

Concessions to European settlers and investors profoundly affected land tenure systems in East, Southern, and Central Africa. Trade patterns and the interests of European settlers shaped the development of infrastructure and commercial relations, agricultural technology, market access, and the direction of agricultural research.

While there were major regional differences, several common themes emerged:

1. African food production became a primarily subsistence activity, even in areas where substantial trade in foodstuffs existed before colonialism.[3]
2. Male participation in the off-farm work force or cash crop cultivation frequently made women more responsible for food production.
3. Lack of colonial interest in African food production meant little sustained research on food production and, hence, a relatively poor understanding of African production processes. Recommendations for change were frequently counterproductive. Research on export crops was more extensive, and generally more productive.

Throughout much of West Africa, the development of export-oriented agriculture was the mainstay of the colonial trade economy. The region had neither known deposits of minerals nor settlers. Colonization policies were therefore directed at developing tropical agricultural exports produced by African farmers themselves. Costs of production were kept low enough to prevent substitutes from being developed within European markets.

The coastal areas were linked directly with external markets, while the hinterland served as a pool of labor for the coast. In areas where land and labor were abundant, the initial cultivation of export crops did not come at the expense of food crop production. Food crops were grown for domestic consumption along with commercial export crops. Africans were frequently entrepreneurial cultivators, using traditional ties to increase export crop production. In other areas, however, introducing export crops dislocated subsistence food production. The marketing of export crops here, as in other regions, was generally handled by non-Africans, and the virtual equation of cash and export crops limited the commercialization of food marketing.

In Central Africa, the production of agricultural export crops was generally managed by European concessionary companies. Industrial plantations for producing export crops were established directly by European investors, and were worked by coerced or cheap labor. The African role in the commercial export crop was thus more limited. As elsewhere in Africa, food production remained largely a subsistence activity. Surplus production was sold on internal markets in Angola and the Belgian Congo, where large-scale production of staple crops never developed.

In Eastern and Southern Africa, colonial policy toward the agricultural sector was shaped by two forces: the labor requirements of mining and the presence of large settler populations. A major thrust of colonial policy was to create labor reserves, both for mining and for working settler-operated farms. The need to feed miners—often migrants from distant areas—created the potential for a commercial market in foodstuffs in some countries. Initially this market was served by African producers. However, restrictions on landownership and production reduced the role of African producers. Commercial procurement came primarily from larger white-owned farms, whose market position was supported by a wide range of government policies. The result was a dual land tenure system that had a major negative impact on African food production.

Agricultural dualism can also be held directly accountable for Africa's contemporary problem of inadequate food production, for the success of export production was achieved almost entirely at the expense of an economically impoverished, peasant, food-producing sector. Decades of overconcentration on export cultivation have left the continent's food-producing regions badly undersupplied with infrastructure, deprived of government services, desperately short of capital for development, and technologically prefeudal. As a result, any attempt to improve Africa's food-producing capability will need to concern itself with a fundamental structural transformation of the rural economy. Efforts to achieve this may well encounter considerable political difficulty. Policies that have the potential to undermine the established economic primacy of the export sector would run directly counter to the large and powerful array of social groups that have a stake in the profitability of the export economy. No small part of the difficulty will lie in the fact that some of those who profit from the present situation are in key positions of political power in their societies.

Strong political support for the export sector has been one of the major common denominators linking the policies of the colonial governments to those of independent African regimes. The political influence wielded by exporting interests is so strong that it helps to account for some of the enormous differences between the plantation and peasant sectors, as well as for the overemphasis on export production. It may, for example, explain why African governments have, with very few exceptions, been so consistently supportive of the institution of private ownership in the export sector, regardless of whether this has involved foreign corporations, foreign nationals, or local citizens, while the tradition of communal tenure in the food-producing areas has been left virtually intact. In addition, the strong political position of the exporting interests almost certainly accounts for the fact that their farms nearly always occupy the best arable areas, a matter of immeasurably greater importance than the proportion of a country's land in their possession.

The political influence of the exporting regions can also be held directly accountable for the fact that they benefit from the full array of government supports. The infrastructures of African nations—their road and railway systems in particular—are, time and time again, patterned in such a way as to facilitate the transportation of exportable agricultural commodities from the interior to the principal ports, rather than to improve the internal distribution of food. The agricultural extension services of most African governments are directed primarily toward the exporting areas; as a result, the farms that grow cash crops benefit from a wide range of scientific inputs, including fertilizers, pesticides, and new varieties of high-yield seeds.

Perhaps most important, government-sponsored irrigation schemes are almost always built to deliver an assured supply of water to export crop areas, with food-producing regions eligible only for the remainder after the needs of the large-scale cotton, rice, or peanut farms have been met. It is pertinent to note, for example, that Mali's record-high crop of rice in 1972–1973 was made possible by irrigation schemes in the Segou and Mopti areas. One of the reasons this rice had to be considered, to a large extent, as an export crop was that it was necessary to defray the cost of imported equipment and supplies used in construction. In a nutshell, then, African governments have provided an impressive variety of supports and services to the export sector, and in this way undoubtedly have furnished export agriculture with a substantial indirect subsidy.

The peasant food-producing sector has benefited from few, if any, of these supports or subsidies; as a result, it stands out as a model of agricultural backwardness. The technological stage of African peasant food growers, an assorted grouping that probably comprises about 90 percent of the population, can only be described as little advanced beyond the Iron Age. By far the most common implement is the hand-held hoe, a tool that disappeared centuries ago from most of European and North American agriculture. In contrast with the diesel tractors that perform much of the basic work in the plantation sector, the use even of animal-drawn plows is rare among African peasant farmers. The technological contrast between African export-crop production and food-crop cultivation could not be greater. The former involves the most advanced scientific inputs available; the latter uses techniques that are not much advanced over those employed when human societies first abandoned a hunting-gathering livelihood in favor of agricultural production. If any explanation of the utter stagnation of productivity among African peasant food producers were necessary, it lies here, in the almost complete absence of technological and scientific inputs of the modern age.

Africa's food producers are unsupported by the range of governmental services available to the export sector. The most conspicuous difference in this respect has to do with infrastructural services. Whereas the exporting regions normally benefit from the ready availability of road and railroad networks, Africa's food-producing regions continue to be badly deficient, even with respect to a minimal system of feeder roads. Even the most casual visitor to a food-producing area of the African countryside cannot fail to notice the extent to which the basic means of transportation usually consists of heavily loaded bicycles being pushed, not pedaled, sometimes for miles, along narrow, winding paths.

In many countries the difficulties of transporting basic food items from the countryside to the major cities are so great that large amounts of these crops often languish and spoil in rural markets, where they can be purchased for absurdly low prices, while urban demand, sufficiently strong to encourage greater production at a more reasonable price level, goes unsatisfied. Often there are not even the most elementary facilities for the storage of perishable food items, with the result that any given country's supply of basic staples tends to go through an extreme cycle that ranges from high availability during harvest season to severe scarcity or nonavailability during the agricultural off-season. Food items that could easily be stored and processed locally are, instead, imported from abroad at great cost in foreign exchange while local food producers lack sufficient capital to improve their land or purchase more up-to-date equipment.

This situation is also related to the absence of marketing agencies to assist in the transportation and sale of food items. Whereas farmers who grow such items as cocoa, coffee, tea, and other staples of the export trade can depend upon the assistance of governmental marketing boards with nationwide bureaucracies, the marketing of food crops normally proceeds on an almost anarchic, laissez-faire basis. The entire system of food distribution and sale has an extraordinarily haphazard quality. Demand prediction, price stabilization, and quality monitoring, all of which are now routine in the export sector, are virtually unheard of so far as locally produced food items are concerned. After 75 years of colonial rule and about 30 years of independent government, the establishment of a state-supervised marketing system for basic food items is not even a remote possibility in most nations. To the extent that institutional involvement is a barometer of concern, African governments exhibit more interest in the satisfaction of European coffee and tea drinkers than they do in the food consumption patterns of their own populations.

The same sort of situation often prevails with respect to agricultural extension services. Whereas export crops benefit from the full range of modern agroscientific inputs, food production is carried on without even the most elementary level of support. A 1970 survey by the U.N. Food and Agriculture Organization, for example, showed that the use of fertilizer per unit of arable land in Africa was lower than on any other continent and, in fact, only about one-third that in Asia, the second lowest continent in fertilizer utilization. While this can to some extent be accounted for by the greater availability of land per person in Africa, and by the greater unpredictability of other factors of production, including rainfall, the figure for Africa (7 kilos per hectare) is nevertheless indicative of the extent to which peasant producers are deprived of inputs that would enable them to boost their level of production. Indeed, when it is taken into account that export-crop-producing areas in Africa make extensive use of fertilizers along with other scientific inputs, the unavailability of modern supports for food production becomes all the more dramatic.

The impoverishment of the peasant food-producing sector in African agriculture is not the accidental by-product of benign neglect, but the unintended consequence of a misplaced overemphasis on export production. The reasoning behind this assertion borrows heavily from Rodolfo Stavenhagen's study of the impact of plantation production in both Africa and Latin America.[4] In addition to a high level of governmental support, and a continuous infusion of modern agroscientific inputs, the exporting plantations had one additional major requirement for their economic success: an abundant and readily available supply of low-wage agricultural workers. In order for the large-scale plantation to thrive, the African peasantry had to be forced to make itself available, at least during peak harvesting periods, as a pool of migratory workers. The only way to achieve this objective was to lower the living standards of nearby peasants to the point where their material survival was, at least partially, dependent upon rural wage income. Thus, Meillassoux is completely correct in viewing the modern fate of the African peasantry as a variant on the classic enclosure phenomenon.[5]

This pattern, shaped by colonialism, has not fundamentally changed in the postcolonial period. Few countries have been able significantly to diversify their exports, or to move away from primary exports to more highly processed goods. As a result, many government agricultural policies have supported the export activities that dominated their economies at independence, and that now provide much of their foreign exchange and tax revenue. Dualism in agriculture, as already pointed out, leads to the situation where women are the main subsistence farmers in most of Africa.

Land Conditions

Africa has a total land area of 2.886 billion hectares, of which 789 million hectares are potentially cultivable. The land area presently cultivated, however, is only 168 million hectares. Therefore, in many areas the limiting factor is not the availability of land but the distribution of population.

For example, Burundi and Rwanda have annual population growth rates of nearly 3 and 4 percent, respectively, and population densities of 165 and 390 persons per square kilometer. To maintain a secure supply of food, both countries have been forced to put marginal land under cultivation, reduce fallow periods, and increase crop density. But yields are very low because small amounts of selected seed and fertilizer are used and cropping practices are rudimentary. In contrast, Senegal, which has only 18 people per square kilometer, has a distribution of rural population that does not coincide with its potentially cultivable land. There is a high population density on land where it is no longer possible to increase the cultivable area, and low population density on land that has the highest potential for rain-fed agriculture.

The overworked soils are vulnerable to the powerful erosive forces common to Africa, such as prolonged drought, high winds, and violent rain. When the rains do come, there is little soil left to absorb the water. Flooding occurs and any topsoil remaining is washed away.

The cattle populations in some African countries have increased, often to levels that cannot be sustained from year to year, resulting in extensive overgrazing. This has contributed to a decline in available forage and also to degradation and desertification, particularly in the arid and semiarid areas.

The transformation of once fertile land to desert is not easily stopped. As the desert spreads, people and animals are driven before it, in search of fertile lands. The impact of this migration helps to accelerate the process of land degradation.

Use of fertilizers can minimize the effects of shorter fallow periods. From 1973 to 1983, fertilizer consumption in Africa increased 55 percent, but half of the countries on the continent use less than 3 kilos per hectare on arable land and permanent crops. Fifty to 60 kilos per hectare is estimated to be required for an intermediate level of production. In Kenya, for example, smallholders account for 75 percent of all agricultural holdings but for only 3 percent of total fertilizer consumption. Fertilizers, in many cases, are available only at major supply depots and trading centers that cater mostly to the relatively larger farmers. As a result, they often are not accessible to smallholders at planting time.

Constraints on the purchase of fertilizer in most countries are evident: increases in transportation and storage costs accounted for 44 percent of total marketing costs between 1978 and 1982. Even though the prognosis for a substantial increase in the use of fertilizer is not favorable, it is estimated that during 1985/1986, Africa's most seriously affected countries would require 642,000 metric tons, at a cost of $270 million.

While much of Africa is dry and could benefit from irrigation, little more is economically possible. As of 1982, only 8 million hectares out of a total cultivated area of 168 million hectares were irrigated, while in Asia 134 million out of 454 million cultivated hectares were irrigated. Of the 8 million hectares that were irrigated in Africa, only about 1.5 million were south of the Sahara (excluding South Africa).

Despite high costs of irrigation in Africa, substantial areas of land could benefit from it. There are some 12 million hectares available in the Sahel alone. In Chad, for example, river banks, the shores of lakes, and the large number of wadis offer good soil for irrigated crops.

A further economic barrier to expanding irrigation is the need to develop the area's infrastructure. Without roads, bridges, power supply, maintenance, and intensive farmer training, major irrigation projects are destined to fail.

The Environment

Acute food shortages in Africa have most commonly been triggered by droughts. The droughts that struck the Sahel during the late 1960s and early 1970s received worldwide attention, but the Sahel has suffered more than 20 other major droughts since the sixteenth century. Similar droughts, resulting in famine or near famine, have occurred in other parts of Africa. Eastern Africa, for example, is currently experiencing the latest in a series of serious droughts in just two decades. Countries in Southern Africa went through a major drought in 1978/1979. It is generally believed that droughts occur somewhere in Africa every year, that two or more droughts affecting large areas of the continent come about every decade, and that extremely protracted and widespread droughts occur about once every 30 years. There is thus every likelihood that, for a long time to come, various parts of Africa will continue to experience droughts of similar intensity, and farsighted action must be taken now.

In many parts of Africa rainfall is not only insufficient but also highly erratic. Effective rainfall is further decreased in some areas by high rates of evapotranspiration. In these conditions, droughts frequently start gradually, with below-normal rainfall for one or two years. This, followed by even a single year without rain in the right season, is usually enough for famine to set in, as food reserves are exhausted and no new crops are grown. Climatic factors are therefore important causes of drought, and thus contribute to the threat or occurrence of famine over a large part of Africa. In this connection, it should be noted that droughts affect the production of both food crops and cash crops. Therefore, just when communities and individual households cannot produce enough food for themselves, they can least afford to purchase food from elsewhere.

In two respects, however, climatic variations are not an adequate explanation of the recurrence of droughts, and even less of famine. First, it is necessary to emphasize that climatic problems by themselves would not have resulted in tragedies of the dimensions witnessed in Africa recently had they not been reinforced by man's damage to other aspects of the ecosystem. Second, account must be taken of the manner in which climate in Africa has been, and continues to be, affected by man and by an agriculture that remains predominantly subsistence-oriented. This, together with the nontraditional food consumption habits acquired by the emerging urban population, in large part explains the growing dependence of African countries on food imports. Moreover, in some cases, rapid urbanization has adversely affected food production owing to labor shortages that it creates in rural areas during peak seasons. The factors that have led to the high rate of migration to urban areas must, therefore, figure in an explanation of the food crisis in Africa.

The Failures of African Leadership

Since independence African peoples—both rulers and ruled—have generally been inclined to disregard both public morality and democratic rights. Many of Africa's leaders and their parties or clients have proved to be ineffectual, overly ethnic in orientation, and corrupt. The military rulers have seldom been an improvement. All too often, Africa's rulers have behaved as if public goods and concerns were private property. Friends, relatives, and clients have received appointments, favors, and high salaries, to the detriment of the common good.[6]

After achieving independence, Africa's new leaders sought economic growth and independence through Africanization, but they failed in their endeavors and often rendered their countries dependent on a kind of international dole. Africanization was promoted at the expense of efficiency and integrity. The public sector grew; the private sector declined. Development plans became fashionable, but they were seldom successful because the planners knew too little and often diverted resources to their own pockets, as in the various "Vouchergate" scandals of Sierra Leone during the presidency of Siaka Stevens.[7] Import-substitution schemes were instituted to protect local industries and encourage industrialization. These often failed to produce efficiently, and they brought higher taxes and high prices for the goods produced. Many leaders become politically intolerant and authoritarian; members of the opposition were imprisoned or exiled.

The poor performance of many African governments can be traced to regime factions. That is, the political elites did not possess effective legitimized authority, and this circumstance affected the capacity of the state to carry out its public policies. The required resources were not only material but also organizational, symbolic, and coercive. Because most African states lacked these resources, they were unable to build or to execute development schemes.[8]

African governments have given food production relatively low priority, a policy reflecting historical conceptions about subsistence production. Food is such an important matter in most African countries that governments frequently attempt to control supplies, regulate prices, and monopolize distribution of basic food commodities. Food policies followed by governments, either explicitly or implicitly, have sometimes derived from the immediate need to feed the urban population at noninflationary prices, not from the need to assist food producers in improving the productivity of their farms. The beneficiaries of such policies have been groups other than the food producers.

The dominant thrust of most food policies, at least until the early 1970s, was to keep domestic food prices low. In large part, these policies were designed to benefit urban consumers. Hence, farm prices were often set at low levels, which discouraged farmers from marketing more food through official channels and reduced the incentive to invest in making food production a commercial enterprise. Trade policies were oriented toward supplying urban consumers with cheap food, not with supporting farm income or attempting to build a strong internal marketing system for domestically produced food (as is the case in many industrial countries). While government-controlled marketing institutions were designed in some cases to eliminate the unsavory actions of middlemen, they also had a strong interest in controlling procurement while keeping costs down. Compulsory procurement requirements and attempts by some governments to operate state farms were shaped by the need to procure for the urban market.

In countries favored with mineral, oil, or export crop resources, government investment in these sectors has produced unbalanced growth detrimental to the development of a viable food-production sector by draining the countryside of young people. Practically nowhere in Africa has smallholder food production been seen as an engine of growth in national economic and social development. Consequently it has ranked low on governments' investment schedules. Thus, for a long time there has been a clear lack of priority attention to agricultural development and to national food policies.

The long-standing neglect of the food and agricultural sector, especially in respect to small farmers and food production, can be seen as a major factor in low production levels. This neglect has often been exacerbated by policies that favor low consumer food prices at the expense of price incentives to farmers.

At fault are pricing and investment policies that favor the production of agricultural exports rather than the production of food for local consumption.

Population

While Africa lags behind the rest of the world in its level and rate of economic development, there is one area in which the continent takes the lead: the rate of growth of its population. Africa's population could well double by the end of the twentieth century.[9] The population of Africa south of the Sahara is estimated at over 450 million, with an average density of 18 persons per square kilometer. Given the land area of the region, the size of the population cannot be considered too great. Having large families is a logical response to the conditions under which most Africans live. On the small family farms that produce most of Africa's food, the most important factor of production is family labor. The high birth rate is a response to this need for farm labor. People need to have many children in order to provide for augmenting meager family income. Many children are also needed to provide old-age security and to compensate for the high infant death rate. Moreover, high birth rates reflect the social powerlessness of women, which is exacerbated by poverty. In most cases, the greater the poverty, the greater the oppression of women. Furthermore, the high population growth rate becomes a problem when it surpasses a nation's aspirations and the capacity of that nation's resource base to meet the increasing demands. With an annual average population growth rate of 3.2 percent, the number of people in Africa will continue to exceed the support capacity of their economies unless serious efforts at the governmental level are undertaken to attain and maintain economic growth with a better distribution of national wealth.

A number of demographic considerations indicate a worsening of Africa's population problem in the years ahead. First, the African population is very young, with some 19 percent under 5 years of age and 45 percent under age 15. This indicates that even if the fertility rate were to be lowered considerably, the population would continue to grow through "demographic inertia."[10] The next generation of parents has already been born. Moreover, Africa's population exhibits the highest dependency ratio in the world. (The dependency ratio compares the number of very young and very old with those of labor force age who are capable of supporting them.)

The consequences of high population growth rates and the age structure of the population are felt most immediately in increased demand for food, education, and health services.[11] While in the rest of the world, the growth of food production has remained slightly ahead of population growth, this has not been the case in sub-Saharan Africa. Whereas food production and population in sub-Saharan Africa both grew at a rate of about 2.4 percent in the 1960s, by the 1970s the population growth rate of 2.8 percent was far ahead of a food production growth rate of only 1.4 percent. While Africa was basically self-sufficient in food in 1970, today more than one-third of its people are fed in some part by imports, thus reducing already scarce foreign exchange reserves.[12]

The high population growth[13] in Africa has been accompanied by worsening nutrition in recent years (food consumption per capita has actually declined since the late 1960s). The annual shortages of food have led to weight loss in both children and adults, causing such energy depreciation that adults cannot perform the full amount of work required to prepare for the next sowing season.

Protein calorie malnutrition, resulting in kwashiorkor and maramus, is one of the most serious nutritional problems in Africa, primarily affecting infants and children. Surveys have indicated that 2 to 10 percent of all children aged one to four suffer from overt protein calorie malnutrition, and 30 to 50 percent of those under five show a weight deficit that can be considered clinical malnutrition, often resulting in stunted growth.

Protein calorie malnutrition is associated with very high mortality. Without treatment, kwashiorkor may result in 20 to 50 percent mortality. When malnutrition begins in utero, it is known to affect the psychomotor and mental development of the infant, perhaps irreversibly. Kwashiorkor also causes mental retardation, and unless rehabilitative measures are undertaken to encourage mental development, the damage can be permanent.

Various degrees of protein calorie malnutrition have been observed in adult women as well, particularly pregnant and lactating women. Anemia, resulting from iron and/or folic acid deficiencies, occurs in 20 to 80 percent of all women and in some men as well. Deficiencies of riboflavin, a member of the vitamin B group, are also common,

Table 11.3
Sub-Saharan Africa: Population Estimates, Mid-1984

Country	Population Estimate mid-1984 (millions)	Persons per sq. km.	Birth rate (per 1000 population)	Death rate	Natural increase (percent annually)	Infant mortality rate[a]	Life expectancy at birth (years)
Sub-Saharan Africa, Total	433.5	18	48	17	3.1	112	49
Western Africa	162.3	26	49	18	3.1	120	47
Benin	3.9	35	51	22	2.9	145	43
Burkina Faso	6.8	25	48	22	2.6	145	43
Gambia	0.6	55	48	28	2.0	189	36
Ghana	13.0	54	47	14	3.3	96	53
Guinea	5.3	22	47	23	2.4	155	41
Guinea-Bissau	0.9	25	41	21	2.0	140	44
Ivory Coast	9.5	30	46	18	2.8	119	48
Liberia	2.1	19	48	17	3.1	109	50
Mali	7.8	6	48	22	2.8	145	43
Mauritania	1.8	2	50	20	3.0	134	45
Niger	5.9	5	51	22	2.9	137	43
Nigeria	92.0	100	50	17	3.3	111	49
Senegal	6.4	33	48	21	2.7	138	44
Sierra Leone	3.5	49	47	29	1.8	196	35
Togo	2.8	49	45	16	2.9	110	49
Eastern Africa	174.3	20	49	17	3.2	108	49
Burundi	4.5	161	47	20	2.7	134	45
Djibouti	0.4	18	47	21	2.6	---	--
Ethiopia	35.4	29	49	21	2.8	140	44
Kenya	19.8	34	55	14	4.1	79	54
Madagascar	9.7	17	44	16	2.8	65	50

Malawi	6.8	58	52	19	3.3	161	46
Mozambique	13.7	17	44	16	2.8	107	50
Rwanda	5.9	227	51	16	3.5	107	50
Somalia	5.4	8	46	21	2.5	140	44
Sudan	20.9	8	45	17	2.8	115	48
Tanzania	21.7	23	50	15	3.5	96	52
Uganda	15.2	64	50	14	3.6	91	53
Zambia	6.4	8	48	15	3.3	98	52
Zimbabwe	8.5	22	47	12	3.5	67	56
Middle Africa	60.7	9	45	17	2.8	117	48
Angola	8.5	7	47	22	2.5	145	43
Cameroon	9.5	20	43	17	2.6	114	49
Centr. Afr. Repub.	2.5	4	45	21	2.4	140	44
Chad	4.9	4	44	21	2.3	140	44
Congo	1.7	5	44	18	2.6	121	47
Equatorial Guinea	0.4	14	42	21	2.1	134	45
Gabon	1.1	4	35	18	1.7	109	50
Zaire	32.1	14	45	15	3.0	104	51
Southern Africa	36.2	13	40	14	2.6	91	54
Botswana	1.0	2	50	12	3.8	77	55
Lesotho	1.5	50	41	16	2.5	107	50
Namibia	1.5	2	45	17	2.8	112	49
South Africa	31.6	26	38	14	2.4	89	54
Swaziland	0.6	35	47	17	3.0	126	49

[a]Infant mortality rate = deaths under age one per 1,000 live births in the same year.

Sources: Population estimates: United Nations, Population Division, Estimates and Projections Section, "Demographic Indicators by Countries as Assessed in 1982," medium variant (New York: United Nations, December 14, 1983), computer printout; World Bank, World Development Report 1984 (New York: Oxford University Press, 1984), Table I and p. 276.

Table 11.4
Population Growth and Projections

Country	Average annual growth of population (percent)			Population (millions)			Population momentum
	1965-80	1980-85	1985-2000	1985	1990	2000	
Angola	2.8	2.5	2.9	9	10	13	1.9
Benin	2.7	3.1	3.2	4	5	6	2.0
Botswana	4.2	3.5	3.2	1	1	2	2.0
Burkino Faso	2.0	2.6	2.9	8	9	11	1.8
Burundi	1.9	2.7	3.1	5	5	7	1.9
Cameroon	2.7	3.2	3.4	10	12	17	1.8
Central African Rep.	1.8	2.5	2.9	3	3	4	1.8
Chad	2.0	2.3	2.5	5	6	7	1.9
Congo	2.7	3.1	3.6	2	2	3	1.9
Ethiopia	2.7	2.5	2.9	42	49	65	1.9
Ghana	2.2	3.3	3.0	13	15	20	1.9
Guinea	1.9	2.4	1.9	6	7	8	1.3
Ivory Coast	5.0	3.8	3.1	10	12	16	1.9
Kenya	3.9	4.1	4.0	20	25	36	2.0
Lesotho	2.3	2.7	2.7	2	2	2	1.8
Liberia	3.0	3.4	3.2	2	3	4	1.9
Madagascar	2.5	3.2	3.0	10	12	16	1.9
Malawi	2.9	3.1	3.3	7	8	11	1.8
Mali	2.6	2.3	2.7	8	9	11	1.8
Mauritania	2.2	2.1	2.8	2	2	3	1.8
Maurituis	1.7	1.3	1.2	1	1	1	1.7
Mozambique	2.5	2.6	3.1	14	16	21	1.8
Niger	2.7	3.0	3.2	6	7	10	1.9
Nigeria	2.5	3.3	3.4	100	118	163	1.9
Rwanda	3.3	3.2	3.7	6	7	10	1.8
Senegal	2.5	2.9	3.1	7	8	10	1.9
Sierra Leone	1.7	2.2	2.6	4	4	5	1.8
Somalia	3.3	2.9	3.1	5	6	8	1.9
Sudan	3.0	2.7	2.9	22	25	34	1.8
Tanzania	3.3	3.5	3.5	22	27	37	1.9
Togo	3.0	3.3	3.2	3	4	5	1.9
Uganda	2.9	3.0	3.2	15	17	23	2.0
Zaire	2.8	3.0	3.0	31	36	47	1.9
Zambia	3.1	3.5	3.5	7	8	11	2.0
Zimbabwe	3.1	3.7	3.1	8	10	13	2.0

Source: Derived from World Bank, World Development Report, 1987, Table 27.

leading to angular stomatisis, cheilosis, changes of the tongue, gum disease, and consequent tooth loss.

Vitamin A deficiency, affecting the eyes, is the most worrisome because it causes xerophthalmia, which, if untreated, can result in blindness. Its actual extent is not known, and a study of its prevalence is needed. In some parts of the continent, goiter, resulting from inadequate iodine supplies, is a major problem. Goiter can cause fetal deficiency; iodine deficiency in the mother can result in cretin births.

In economies like those of Africa that are dependent on agriculture, population growth threatens the balance between people and scarce natural resources. Furthermore, rapid population growth slows development by exacerbating the choice between higher consumption now and higher investment in future benefits for many. Rapid population growth makes it difficult to manage the adjustments necessary to promote economic and social change.

The rapid growth of population has also been associated, since the early 1970s, with much migration from the rural areas to the cities. The rapid urbanization has changed African eating habits. City dwellers have come to prefer imported wheat and rice to traditional foods like yams, cassava, and millet. This has placed an extra burden on the scarce financial resources of these countries and has worsened their balance-of-payments potential.

The Debt Burden

Dualism in their agricultural economies means that the African countries often depend on one or two export commodities for foreign exchange earnings. But the continuing economic recession has meant reduced demand for these commodities, lower prices, and hence lower foreign exchange earnings. The commodities affected are precisely those traditional commodities that Africa exports: cocoa, coffee, cotton, peanuts, and oilseeds. The low commodity prices and soaring interest rates, preceded by high oil prices, have severely restricted the ability to pay debts and purchase the food required for domestic consumption.

Part of the blame for the debt crisis lies with the aggressive lending policies of commercial banks toward Third World countries. Because foreign loans were perceived as highly profitable and risk free, banks overextended themselves in foreign lending.

The economic policies of certain developing countries also contributed to the debt problem. In the face of substantial and rising balance-of-payments deficits, they often chose to finance their deficits instead of implementing the difficult economic measures needed to adjust to the increasing debt. Increased capital outflows from developing nations to pay loans dwarf the funds available for longer-term development programs, contribute to economic destabilization, and exacerbate the hunger problem.

The most constructive long-term alleviation of the debt crisis would be improved trade with the developed countries in order to earn foreign exchange to service and repay debts. Yet a recent report of the International Monetary Fund indicates that industrial countries are increasing their trade barriers.

This is a two-sided coin. The developed world depends on Third World markets for exports, and the developed world's prospects for economic growth are tied to improved Third World economies. Weak markets in the Third World are partly responsible for the high unemployment in the developed countries.

The second step must be a major rescheduling of most of this debt from short- and medium-term to long-term debt. Without this there will be no end to the current crisis. When the debt was incurred, circumstances encouraged both lenders and borrowers to accept short-term agreements. The situation has changed dramatically, and the terms must be greatly extended.

It is simpleminded to say "The commercial banks got themselves into this mess—let them get themselves out of it." When a bank writes off a loan or sets up a loan-loss provision, taxpayers absorb up to 50 percent of the cost in the form of federal taxes. If a major crisis does develop over the debt issue, it will be governments (taxpayers) who foot most of the bill—not bank shareholders.

So, as a third step, the governments of the developed world and/or international financial institutions will have to assume some of the debt load now carried by the commercial banks. As recently as 1986 such an obvious action had little backing. But this attitude is changing. Increasingly, thoughtful observers are advocating such action as an essential part of the ultimate solution.

As a condition of having governments acquire some of the debt—thus reducing risk for the commercial banks—the banks should be required to write off some of the debt against which they have already made loan-loss provisions. (That a loan-loss provision has been set up means bank shareholders and taxpayers have already paid the penalty.) The problem is that the debtor has received no relief—the debt is still outstanding and interest is still accumulating. Bankers write off debts owed by commercial borrowers who cannot repay. It's time they faced up to this inevitable truth with some of their Third World debts.

Africa's debt, however, is considerably smaller than that of some middle-income countries in Latin America. But credit conditions are such that only about nine African countries are presently eligible for nonconcessional loans: Botswana, Cameroon, Congo, Ivory Coast, Mauritius, Nigeria, Seychelles, Swaziland, and Zimbabwe. Private foreign investment has virtually ceased, forcing many countries to confront the painful process of structural readjustments, which normally entail currency devaluations, limitations on imports, and modifications of price structure.

Research and Training

Colonial approaches to development facilitated the production and extraction of surpluses—copper, gold, cocoa, coffee—for external markets while paying little attention to investments in human capital, research on food crops, and strengthening of internal market linkages. For example, colonial governments gave little attention to the training of agricultural scientists and managers. By the time of independence in the early 1960s, there was only one college of agriculture in French-speaking tropical Africa. Between 1952 and 1963, only four university graduates in agriculture were trained in French-speaking Africa and 150 in English-speaking Africa. By 1964, there were three African scientists working in the research stations in the East African countries of Kenya, Uganda, and Tanzania.

The effects of colonial policies on present landownership patterns and agricultural research and training institutions are important contributors to the current food production and poverty problems. Many colonial regimes focused their research and development programs on export crops, and the needs of commercial farmers and managers of plantations. The modest investment in research on food crops could be defended during this period because the rate of population growth was low—1 to 2 percent per year—and surplus land could be "automatically" brought under cultivation by smallholders. But with annual rates of population growth now approaching 3 to 4 percent in some countries, research institutions must be restructured to devote more attention to food crops and the needs of smallholders and herders. Meanwhile, the continent continues to experience a worsening situation in vital agricultural research.

This situation was highlighted clearly by the 1985 Tokyo meeting of senior officials of the Consultative Group on International Agricultural Research (CGIAR). The increasing difficulty of funding essential research was a major concern of CGIAR. Persistent low priority status in the economic and development policies of national governments, together with inadequate assistance from international sources, combine to constrain agricultural research in Africa at a time when the need for expanded effort has never been so urgent. Africa's main hope of being able to feed itself in the future and to avoid famine disasters on an even larger scale than currently being experienced depends on the results of effective, sustained research.

The dilemma confronting CGIAR provides a disturbing example of the squeeze that is being inflicted even on internationally funded research. Research centers of particular importance to African agriculture that are supported by CGIAR include the International Institute of Tropical Agriculture, based in Nigeria; the International Livestock Center for Africa, based in Ethiopia; the International Laboratory for Research on Animal Diseases, based in Kenya; the West African Rice Development Association, based in Liberia; and the Indian-based International Crops Research Institute for the Semi-Arid Tropics, which is doing work of considerable value in West Africa.

All of them, and the 7,000 staff employed throughout the CGIAR system, are facing increasing economic pressures. In the 1985 financial year, donor countries provided funding of U.S. $173 million. In financial year 1986–1987 this funding was estimated at a mere $1 million—in real terms, this meant a reduction in activity for some centers, and overall there was no growth.

But the problem of research funding is not merely one of international aid. In February 1987 a World Food Council report pointed out that despite the public commitment of a number of African states to place increased emphasis on agricultural development investment, there is little evidence of this in either "budgetary ear-markings or actual expenditure," and investment in agriculture has stagnated. This neglect, ominously, includes investment in research.

While an increase in food production has been achieved in some parts of West Africa, this generally has not been the result of higher production per acre, but of an expansion of the land under cultivation. Even the occasional increase in volume of production is being outstripped by population growth by about 2 percent a year.

During the highly optimistic "green revolution" period, particularly between 1965 and 1980, it was believed by many that African agriculture would benefit about as much as the Asian countries. But while Malaysia, for instance, was investing 19 percent of its gross domestic product (GDP) in agriculture, Nigeria's total agricultural investment amounted to 12 percent, with some Nigerian states allocating only 3.5 percent. Tanzania's investment was reduced from over 20 percent in the mid-1960s to 10 percent for 1978-1979.

In succeeding years, the contrast between the rewards of investment policy in Asia and Africa has become obvious. While famine stalks Africa with an ever darkening shadow, in India—which not long ago was suffering severe shortages—in 1987 grain stocks reached a record level, with almost embarrassingly big harvests of rice and wheat causing severe problems of finding adequate storage facilities.

The inadequate attention given to research resources in most of Africa has been a significant factor in retarding production growth. A successful producer country like Zimbabwe, which in 1985 had a 20 percent increase in agricultural production, has not only improved price incentives but also has been investing approximately 2.5 percent of its agricultural GDP in research. Nigeria's investment has been only about 0.75 percent. It already has severe gaps in its research program in the major small livestock sector, for instance. In 1986 the Nigerian government ordered all 22 of its research centers to cut their staffs by one-third.

Ivory Coast's rate of investment has been only fractionally more than Nigeria's, and Sierra Leone's average contribution to its research sector has been a mere 0.21 percent.

In investment terms the rewards obtained by funding research are indisputable. World Bank studies show that agricultural research yields a rate of return more than two to three times greater than returns from most alternative investments.

The obvious neglect of national research institutions can be partly ascribed to the mistaken optimism of many African governments, based on the misguided belief that technology transfer and overseas research achievements could be cheaply and easily imported for home application without a major domestic research effort. This fallacy has been overwhelmingly demonstrated in recent years by the disappointing attempts to utilize new "super" varieties of crops developed in Asia and elsewhere. It has been assumed, for instance, that the high-yield rice cultivars developed by the International Rice Research Institute, based in the Philippines, could be utilized without substantial modification in Africa to provide large increases in production similar to those achieved in many areas of Asia.

But the director of the West African Rice Development Association (WARDA) has now said that after seven years of variety trials involving several thousand imported swamp rice varieties, only two have yielded as well as the best local varieties. This stimulated WARDA to disperse its own rice research program among several West African countries.

Similarly, the Indian-based International Crops Research Institute for the Semi-Arid Tropics (ICRISAT) was asked to organize a millet and sorghum improvement program for West Africa; it was launched in 1975 with importation of improved varieties. At the same time, ICRISAT research scientists were forecasting that within four to five years, new high-yield varieties would be available to local farmers. But, eight years later, the program leader was admitting that variations in rainfall, soils, and farming conditions probably explained why the importation of these high-yield varieties had been "relatively unsuccessful at the farmers' level." In fact, the varieties that proved more successful have been improved local varieties derived from indigenous West African genetic stock.

Plans for a new attempt to improve African crops have been announced by one of the founding fathers of the original "green revolution" in Asia. Geneticist Norman Borlaug, who was awarded a Nobel Peace Prize for his work, has told of plans for a privately organized international project for the creation of a technological package to achieve improvement in corn and sorghum production in an African version of the "green revolution." The long-term target will be to make Africa self-sufficient in food by the end of the 1980s though in many countries, Borlaug contends, it is possible to achieve this "green revolution" by 1988.

A cautionary comment on the scheme has already come from Thomas Odhiambo, director of the International Center of Insect Physiology in Kenya, who warned that techniques developed in India cannot be transferred directly to Africa. Much more research work has to be done on African staples, such as sorghum, cassava, and sweet potatoes. Odhiambo's caution is born of the harsh disappointments Africa has experienced in the wake of the first "green revolution" attempts.

It has to be recognized that progress in development of a narrow range of improved varieties of any food crop cannot in itself provide a panacea for Africa's basic agricultural problems. Even within the geographical boundaries of a single country there can be a wide variation in the performance of the same seed variety. This inevitably underlines the necessity of maintaining a pattern of research activity that is sufficiently dispersed and funded to be able to contribute to the needs of specific regions.

While every recruit in the quest for agricultural advancement in Africa is to be welcomed and every appropriate new project encouraged, there are already substantial research facilities in Africa that could contribute more significantly to the effort if adequately supported. The current position of many potentially vital research centers, however, is desperate. Among the bitter examples of the deterioration that is being suffered as a result of diminishing resources, Sierra Leone's Rokupr Rice Research Station provides a particularly sad spectacle. Established in the 1930s, Rokupr, under its original name of West African Rice Research Station, gained an illustrious reputation for its service to the whole of West Africa in rice development. New rice varieties bred at Rokupr were renowned for their pest- and disease-resistant qualities, and their yield capacities are still higher than the more recently imported "green revolution" varieties.

Rokupr's potential for even more significant achievements is considerable. Over 400 different indigenous rice varieties have been identified in Sierra Leone, offering an invaluable source of material for breeding and improvement programs. Yet, because of ludicrously inadequate funding, Rokupr's plant-breeding laboratories now lie mainly unused. Research scientists try to run vital programs without essential equipment, and extension staff are marooned at the station through lack of transport to visit farmers. Even the scarce and crucial foundation seed, which Rokupr is responsible for supplying to the country's multiplication program, is stored in buildings that are so inadequate that large amounts of seed are lost through environmental damage.

Paradoxically, this tragedy is occurring in a country that not only could produce enough rice to feed itself, but also could become a new exporter. Instead, Sierra Leone's dependence on food imports continues to grow.

It must be conceded that progress in and policies of agricultural research in Africa have been highly variable both in quality and in impact. There are obvious weaknesses in addition to that of financial resources—availability of sufficiently trained personnel and selection of program priorities are among them. These can, and must, be corrected.

The long-term nature of many important aspects of research in a time of economic recession is increasingly placing essential programs at risk. But Africa's deteriorating food situation demands more, not less, investment in this sector. Former director of the International Rice Research Institute and now head of research at the U.S. Agency for International Development (USAID), Dr. Nyle Brady, says: "The only way we are going to help Africa solve its food problems is to help Africans do their research programs themselves."

Up to now, however, there has been little indication that the international community, generous in its response to famine disaster, has become aware of the urgent needs of research, a basic component of agricultural development on which Africa's ability to defeat hunger ultimately depends.

An encouraging development on the research front is the formation of an informal working group of seven major bilateral donors to plan a long-term program for strengthening national agricultural research systems throughout Africa, with emphasis on food and livestock research. This shift to coordinate bilateral support for research is a welcome innovation, but it remains to be seen whether donors will have the courage to view research as a long-term investment and to provide guaranteed funding for a minimum of ten years. One refreshing change introduced by W. Peter McPherson, administrator of USAID, is the flexibility to authorize ten-year rather than five-year projects. For example, USAID has authorized funding for a ten-year, centrally funded, worldwide water research project and a nine-year tropical soils project.

The question is whether USAID's country priorities will remain stable enough to assure African countries of continuity in U.S. funding over a 10- to 20-year period. For example, the proposed allocation to the eight Sahel states was slightly reduced in real terms in fiscal year 1983 even though Congress had earlier endorsed a 20-year recovery program for the Sahel following the drought. On the other hand, U.S. economic assistance to the Sudan was dramatically increased in 1985 to over $100 million, exceeding total U.S. aid for the

Sahel. A rule of thumb is that an African country should never embark on a long-term program to upgrade its national agricultural research system with major support from only one bilateral donor.

An essential component of a long-range strategy is massive investment in human capital formation, including graduate training of several thousand agricultural scientists and managers. This is necessary to replace the foreign advisers, researchers, managers, and teachers in African universities, and to meet the needs of a science-based agriculture in the next century. Since it takes 10 to 15 years of training and experience beyond high school to develop a research scientist, the investments in human capital will not produce payoffs for Africa until the 1990s, at least.

Building graduate agricultural training programs within Africa necessitates a reexamination of the role of the African university in national development. The time is propitious for African universities to move from undergraduate to graduate training programs in science and agriculture. Before graduate education is expanded, however, some questions must be raised about priorities in undergraduate education. In many universities, undergraduate degree programs in agriculture are still embarrassingly undervalued and underfunded when compared with law, medicine, and history. For example, in Senegal the University of Dakar was formally established in 1957, and in 1960 the Senegalese assumed its administration. Today there are approximately 12,000 students at the University of Dakar, of whom several thousand specialize in law and economics. Not until 1979 was the National School of Agriculture established at Thies, north of Dakar. Students take their first-year science courses at the University of Dakar. The first group of undergraduates graduated from the Thies school in 1984–1985. That university-level teaching of agriculture was not initiated until 1979, 29 years after independence, reflects an enduring colonial legacy as well as the government's ambivalence about agriculture's role in national development. Although the structural reforms entailed in redesigning African universities to suit their countries' needs will require decades, it is time for donors to stop paying lip service to African universities. Whereas donors embraced African universities in the 1960s, they generally withdrew their support in the 1970s, instead promoting cash crop production, IBRD (International Bank for Reconstruction and Development) projects, and international agricultural research institutes. The money saved ($100 to $200 million) by phasing out the floundering crash projects cited above can be reallocated to selected universities with emphasis on faculties of agriculture. Donors should press for long-term structural reform of the universities in exchange for long-term aid commitments of 10 to 20 years.

Currently, graduate-level education for African students in the United States costs $1,850 per month, or $35,000–$45,000 for a master's degree over 24–30 months. USAID should gradually phase out master's-level training programs in agriculture and related fields in the United States. Instead, U.S. faculty members should be sent to Africa to help develop regional centers of excellence in graduate training in eight to ten African universities over the next 10 to 15 years. In order to achieve this goal, USAID will have to give greatly increased priority to aiding African universities, including ten-year authorizations to U.S. universities to facilitate this type of training program. In the final analysis, the initiative for this second phase—graduate training in agriculture in African universities—will have to come from within Africa.

The Huge Military Budget

Military budgets are used to equip forces of the state engaged in repressive campaigns against members of their populations. The death of about 2 million infants yearly may be attributed to increasingly high military budgets. John Clark notes in this regard:

The human race has within its power the ability to eliminate hunger, to eradicate the main killer diseases and to provide all basic needs of its members. This precious opportunity is being frittered away. It is not just the bombs that are dropped that cause destruction. The bombs that are bought, stored, displayed proudly in military displays but never dropped, cause destruction just as surely.[14]

While arms manufacturers and merchants abroad are the main financial beneficiaries of the Third World arms race, the overall profits for the arms-supplying country go well beyond the immediate calculation of a particular transaction. For instance, the French government reduced the cost of the 200 Mirage III jet fighters ordered by its air force a few years ago by selling 350 others, mostly to Third World states. These sales also helped to safeguard jobs in the French arms industry. In 1984, Britain's income from arms exports amounted to £2.4 billion, 75 percent of which came from the Third World.

Table 11.5

Arms Sales by Major Powers

Recipient	Total, all suppliers[a]	USSR	USA	France	UK	West Germany	Italy
Africa, Total[b]	17,200	9.900	725	1,800	150	925	700
Algeria	1,900	1,500	---	10	---	350	10
Angola	850	500	---	5	10	10	---
Ethiopia	1,800	1,500	90	10	---	5	30
Ivory Coast	160	---	---	100	---	---	---
Libya	6,900	5,000	---	310	10	160	450
Morocco	1,400	20	310	725	5	50	50
Mozambique	240	170	---	---	---	---	---
Nigeria	300	150	30	40	50	10	---
Somalia	440	210	---	20	5	10	30
South Africa	525	---	20	310	---	---	50
Sudan	400	10	120	---	---	230	---
Tanzania	440	300	---	---	5	---	10
Tunisia	170	---	50	10	5	10	30
Zaire	250	---	30	120	---	5	10
East Asia, Total[b]	9,500	2,000	5,400	120	440	140	90
China	625	210	---	50	350	---	---
Indonesia	440	---	120	20	---	10	---
Kampuchea	380	20	300	---	---	---	---
Korea, No.	575	280	---	---	---	10	---
Korea, So.	1,900	---	1,700	10	5	80	50
Malaysia	420	---	180	10	30	---	---
Philippines	250	---	190	5	20	10	5
Singapore	270	---	150	10	10	---	---
Taiwan	1,000	---	900	---	---	---	5
Thailand	430	---	320	---	5	---	30
Vietnam, No.	1,300	1,300	---	---	---	---	---
Vietnam, So.	850	---	850	---	---	---	---
Latin America, Total[b]	5,500	1,500	725	775	675	440	350
Argentina	975	---	90	270	60	110	80
Brazil	725	---	160	50	400	20	80
Chile	380	---	110	5	40	30	---
Cuba	875	875	---	---	---	---	---
Ecuador	575	---	40	280	70	110	5
Peru	1,100	650	100	110	10	40	80
Venezuela	410	---	110	10	60	80	110
Middle East, Total[b]	32,900	10,300	13,700	2,200	2,100	925	650
Egypt	1,500	250	250	490	110	180	60
Iran	8,700	650	6,600	200	310	430	340
Iraq	6,800	4,900	---	410	20	160	70
Israel	4,200	---	4,100	10	60	---	30
Jordan	600	---	500	---	20	5	---
Kuwait	800	50	350	150	210	20	---
Oman	370	---	10	---	330	---	---
Saudi Arabia	3,600	---	1,800	290	900	20	130
Syria	4,500	3,600	---	190	30	100	---
United Arab Emirates	410	---	10	350	30	---	20
Yemen, No.	625	210	110	80	---	5	5
Yemen, So.	600	575	---	---	---	---	---
South Asia, Total[b]	3,600	2,300	200	360	130	10	20
Afghanistan	470	450	---	---	---	---	---
India	2,200	1,800	40	40	100	10	20
Pakistan	875	20	180	320	20	---	---

[a]Includes transfers by six listed countries plus all other suppliers.

[b]Includes recipients listed plus all other recipients in region.

Source: U.S. Arms Control and Disarmament Agency, *World Military Expenditures and Arms Transfers, 1970-79* (Washington, D.C.: U.S. Government Printing Office, 1982), indicates deliveries of arms, ammunition, and related equipment, and excludes services and construction.

"This is not only a major source of foreign exchange, but also helps reduce the defence bill by charging overseas customers a good slice of the research and development costs involved in designing new weapon systems."[15]

Since 1981 the Third World has been a net exporter of capital to the West. According to Clark, debt payment has become the engine for this process of "decapitalization." Furthermore, Western aid to the Third World, if ever there was such a thing, is now eclipsed by this outward flow of Third World resources to the metropolis. "For every pound put in a charity tin," notes Clark, "the West's financial institutions take out 9."[16]

Western governmnets no longer feel the need to camouflage the very nature of what it calls aid. An apt example was the 1987 British sale of 21 Westland W.30 helicopters to India. For London, this sale, which was worth over £65 million, was the main chunk of the year's "aid" package to New Delhi. The Rajiv Gandhi administration did not want to accept this aid—but reluctantly agreed when told that it was unlikely to get the aid otherwise. It was the helicopters or nothing.

There are thus economic effects (and, by implication, social effects) in the widest sense: the effects of the arms race and military expenditures on trade, on aid, on technological and scientific cooperation, and on other kinds of exchange between countries. By diverting vast resources away from production and growth, and by contributing to inflation, military budgets impede full social-economic progress generally, and the people at large suffer greatly.

SOLUTIONS TO THE PROBLEM

At first glance, many people would say that assistance in the form of food donations (food aid) should be sent to the most severely affected countries by those who have plenty. Certainly this is a first and essential step in emergencies, and nearly 10 million metric tons of cereals are provided each year to poor countries as food aid. However, food aid is not a lasting solution to the problem. If poorly planned and delivered, it can have a harmful effect on the receiving country, upsetting local customs and eating habits. By depressing market prices, it can cut into the income of local farmers, and it can discourage the local production and use of traditional crops.

Therefore, an action plan against hunger must include the following measures:

1. Promoting greater self-reliance in countries suffering from hunger, thus gradually reducing the dependence on imports
2. Reexamining farm policies in developing countries to make sure that they encourage—rather than discourage—farmers to produce food on a dependable basis; government policies should aim at ensuring fair prices for farm produce, access to the means of production, and wise land and water use
3. Improving transportation, marketing, and storage systems to ensure that available food reaches areas where and when it is needed most
4. Reexamining food aid to make sure it reaches the hungry and does not disrupt national production
5. Greater cooperation among developed and developing nations to remove trade barriers and help stabilize international prices for agricultural commodities
6. Avoiding overconsumption and the waste of food in all countries
7. A realistic approach to the large debts owed by many Third World countries and their consequent need to devote inordinate proportions of export earnings to repaying loans; the debt burden hinders the ability of governments to make necessary investments in the food and agricultural sector.

For a permanent solution to the food problem in Africa, the fundamental requisite is a strong political will to channel a much greater volume of resources to agriculture, to execute essential reorientation of social systems, to apply policies that will include small farmers, to achieve higher productivity, and to set up effective systems and organizations for the formulation, implementation, and monitoring of relevant programs.

The chapter on agriculture in the Lagos Plan of Action and the United Nations Program of Action for African Economic Recovery and Development (1986–1990) provide further guidelines for action to resolve the problems in the development of agriculture in Africa.

NOTES

1. U.N. Economic Commission for Africa, *Survey of Economic Conditions in Africa, 1972* (New York: United Nations, 1973), ch. IV, esp. pp. 103–105.
2. *Daily News of Tanzania* (Dar-es-Salaam), June 30, 1974.

3. See E. S. Bretl, *Colonization and Underdevelopment in East Africa* (London: Heineman, 1973); Robert Rotberg and Ali Vlazriu, eds., *Power and Protest in Africa* (New York: University Press, 1970); Walter Rodney, *How Europe Underdeveloped Africa* (Washington, D.C.: Howard University Press, 1982).

4. See Rodolfo Stavenhagen, *Social Classes in Agrarian Societies* (Garden City, 1975), pp. 10–50.

5. Claude Meillassoux, "The Sahel Famine," *Review of African Political Economy* I (London, 1974), pp. 27–33.

6. See John R. Cartwright, *Political Leadership in New York* (New York: St. Martin's Press, 1983); Robert Jackson and Carol Rosberg, *Personal Rule in Black Africa: Prince, Autocrat, Prophet, Tyrant* (Berkeley: University of California Press, 1982); Richard E. Bissell and Michael S. Radu, *Africa in the Post-Decolonization Era* (New York: Transactions Books, 1984).

7. *West Africa*, August 28, 1987.

8. See R. Berins Collier, *Regimes in Tropical Africa: Changing Forms of Supremacy, 1945–1975* (Berkeley: University of California Press, 1982), p. 166.

9. *World Population Prospects* (New York: United Nations Fund for Population Activities, 1985), p. 146.

10. Margaret Wolfson, "Population and Poverty in Sub-Saharan Africa," in *Crisis and Recovery in Sub-Saharan Africa* (Paris: OECD Development Center, 1985), p. 96.

11. Ibid., p. 97.

12. World Bank, *World Tables* (Baltimore: Johns Hopkins University Press, 1980), p. 486.

13. See United Nations, Economic Commission for Africa "The Kilimanjaro Programme of Action of Population," ST/ECA/POP/1 UNFPA Proj. no. RAF/83/P02 (Addis Ababa, Ethiopia, 1984).

14. *West Africa*, March 1988.

15. Ibid.

16. Ibid.

Most of these government, private, and corporate efforts designed to raise agricultural production in Nigeria entail the massive importation of agricultural technology and other agricultural inputs. Will this importation accelerate the disintegration of the peasant mode of production, and in its place establish capitalist relations of production in the Nigerian agricultural sector? How realistic is the assertion that the importation of agricultural technology will lead to the revival of agricultural exports from Nigeria? How valid is the argument that the imported technology will act as an incubator for the indigenous development of agricultural technology in Nigeria? How will the entrenchment of capitalist relations of production in the agricultural sector affect class struggles in Nigeria? What class interests are behind the revival of agriculture in Nigeria? Can the new agricultural policies solve the food crisis in Nigeria, or will they only succeed in the greater consolidation of Nigeria's position as a dependent, neocolonial state within the international capitalist system?

This chapter seeks to answer these questions by qualitatively analyzing the policies, structures, and processes of the new agricultural programs, particularly as they relate to the importation of agricultural technology and other farm inputs. The chapter is divided into five sections. The first provides a brief overview of the dimensions of the food and agricultural crisis in Nigeria. The second examines state and corporate programs that have been devised to solve the crisis. The third analyzes in great detail the current policies and processes of the transfer of agricultural technology to Nigeria. It also identifies the class interests behind the various agricultural programs. The fourth section specifies and analyzes the contradictions in the Nigerian social formation and in the implementation of the new agricultural policies and programs in Nigeria. Such contradictions may tend to negate the supposed benefits of the importation of agricultural inputs. The final section addresses the claim that Nigeria will attain food self-sufficiency through a policy of using imported agricultural inputs to produce food and other agricultural commodities.

The scholarly analysis of state agricultural policies can be intellectually useful because it can help to clarify broader issues in the study of the political economy of a dependent neocolonial state. It is also useful because it can shed light on the nature of the relationship among the domestic ruling class, the state, and foreign economic actors. Finally, such a study may vividly illuminate how the structures and processes of the international capitalist system shape and condition policy responses to economic crises that are in large measure caused by the locational and functional role that Third World economies play within the international capitalist framework.

THE FOOD AND AGRICULTURAL
CRISIS IN NIGERIA

It used to be a cliché that agriculture was the mainstay of the Nigerian economy. Before the quadrupling of oil prices, agriculture was the main contributor to the gross domestic product (GDP). In 1964 the contribution of agriculture to the GDP was about 61 percent. Agricultural exports in the same year accounted for 71 percent of total foreign exchange earnings. However, by 1980 the share of agriculture in GDP had fallen to about 18 percent and foreign exchange earnings from agricultural exports were largely negligible.[1]

Although there has been a dramatic decline in the importance of agriculture and particularly of agricultural exports in the Nigerian economy, an overwhelming majority of Nigerians (over 70 percent) still earn their livelihood directly from agricultural production.

Another dimension of the agricultural crisis is the growing dependence on food imports to satisfy domestic food requirements. In 1971, Nigeria spent only about 88 million naira on food imports. Food imports rose to 703 million naira in 1977, and by 1981 had climbed to over 2 billion naira.[2]

Although there has been a dramatic rise in food import bills, it should be pointed out, as Yusufu Bala Usman observed, that fundamentally Nigeria's importation is "a process of the private transfer abroad of Nigerian wealth."[3]

Similarly, a Nigerian banker, Oladele Olashore, has estimated that Nigeria does not derive more than 25 percent value on its expenditures on imports; that is, of the total amount spent on imports, only 25 percent represents actual goods and services delivered. The rest represents fraud and transfer pricing.[4] Thus, a large bulk of the money said to have been spent on food imports may actually have gone to the private bank accounts of some Nigerian government officials, businessmen, and their foreign cohorts. Nevertheless, part of the huge food import bill does reflect genuine need for imported food to supplement (and supplant?) domestically produced food.

Earlier expectations within the ruling circles was that Nigeria need not be self-sufficient in food production because massive oil-based revenues would always pay for imported food. However, with the drastic fall in the price of crude oil, Nigeria can no longer afford to pay for the imported food, and since earlier massive food imports had depressed domestic production, this inability to continue to import food has aggravated the food crisis. The crisis of crude oil has thus become an economic crisis in general and a food crisis in particular.

A third dimension of the food crisis is that most food and agricultural experts in Nigeria believe that if domestic food output is not doubled soon, the food crisis will worsen.[5] The annual growth rate of food demand is estimated at 3–4 percent, while the rate of increase in domestic food supply is placed at only 2.2 percent per annum. The population growth rate is estimated at 2.5 to 3.0 percent per annum.[6]

There is an expected shortfall in the production of every food item in Nigeria, and it is even more acute for the major food crops, such as yams, corn, beans, rice, cassava, and millet. Anietie Usen and Soji Omotunde quoted food experts as estimating that by 1988, Nigeria would require 15.4 million metric tons of yams, 3.1 million metric tons of corn, 1.5 million metric tons of beans, and 2.1 million metric tons of wheat. This compares with the actual 1985 production of 4.9 million metric tons of yams, 1.02 million metric tons of corn, 475,000 metric tons of beans and 33,708 metric tons of wheat.[7]

A fourth dimension of the crisis is that even though production falls far short of expected demand, a sizable proportion of what is produced is lost through spillage, inadequate storage, and contamination and deterioration in storage. The director of the Nigerian Stored Product Research Institute, S. D. Agboola, has estimated that the above factors, in conjunction with losses from pests, deprive Nigeria of 15 to 20 percent of its total production annually. He added, "No amount of imports of fertilizer, pesticides and mechanisation can stop this kind of losses."[8] Also, the permanent secretary (political) in the office of the secretary to the Bornu state government estimated that in 1986 alone, the state lost about 800 million naira worth of crops due to pest invasion.[9] As a result of this invasion, the state government spent 6 million naira to import pesticides, herbicides, sprayers, and motorcycles to deal with the pests. (Agricultural workers ride motorcycles to the pest sites in order to kill pests.)

POLICIES AND PROGRAMS

Although retired generals, top businessmen, and other present and former state functionaries have become prominent farmers in Nigeria, the fundamental basis of agricultural production remains the small-scale peasant landholding.

Quite early in the colonial life of Nigeria, the British colonists chose to maintain the existing peasant mode of production as the basis for the exploitation of agricultural production. The efforts of the farmers were henceforth to be directed to the production of cash crops that would provide raw materials for industries in Europe. Thus, within the logic of the colonial economy, the peasant farmer was expected to perform numerous functions: to produce for European industries; to produce food crops to feed his family, urban industrial workers, and parasites of the colonial economy; to pay taxes for the upkeep of the colonial administration; and to purchase imported goods from Europe. The colonial trading companies were expected to make the bulk of their profits from the direct exploitation of the peasants.

This basic structure of the role of the peasant did not change with the attainment of political independence. As Yahaya Abdullahi found, "Between 1947 and 1970, the government removed as tax, 47% of the total value of cocoa, 30.6% of palm-oil, 47% of palm kernels, 27.6% of groundnuts, and 30.6% of cotton."[10]

Although both the colonial state and later the independent Nigerian state extracted much surplus from the peasants, neither state provided enough resources for an effective peasant-based economy. The colonial state did not bother to develop the peasant-based economy because exploitation, not development, was its objective. As for the relative neglect of the rural areas by the Nigerian government immediately after independence, the valid explanation is, as Falola and Ihonvbere pointed out, that the accumulative base of the Nigerian bourgeoisie is not agricultural investment.[11] At independence, therefore, there was no overriding concern on the part of the Nigerian bourgeoisie to transform the agricultural system.

However, it became apparent soon after independence that in order to extract greater surpluses from the peasants in order to fund national economic development, the peasant mode of production had to be transformed or more resources had to be allocated to the agricultural sector. Given the class interests of the domestic bourgeoisie (now in control of the state apparatus), the second option was chosen.

This second option entailed capital investments by the state in agriculture, particularly after 1975. Between 1962 and 1968 the federal and regional governments spent a total of 52.6 million naira on capital development in the agricultural sector. In 1975–1980 public capital expenditure on agriculture jumped to 2.3 billion naira, and in 1980–1985 it increased to 8.8 billion naira.[12] In association with the World Bank, large-scale agricultural development projects and river basin and rural development authorities were established in all regions of the country.[13]

In addition to the agricultural development projects, in the 1970s the federal government established companies to produce or process agricultural commodities. Many of these companies—for example, the Nigerian Livestock Production Company—were said to have sustained huge losses and were subsequently disbanded. A former minister of agriculture, Bukar Shuaib, said about these companies, "No doubt, most of the state-owned institutions involved in agricultural and livestock development are making heavy losses, adding little or no contribution to the economy."[14] The Nigerian Livestock Production Company, for instance, sustained losses of 21.7 million naira over four years.

Another dimension of the government's involvement in agriculture is the policy of heavy subsidization of farm inputs such as fertilizers, seeds, herbicides, and insecticides to farmers. This policy was most prominent during the second civilian regime of 1979–1983. For instance, in January 1980 the federal government imported 200 tractors, 900,000 naira worth of vaccines and veterinary drugs, 500,000 metric tons of fertilizers, 500 corn shellers, 500 rice threshers, 500 irrigation pumps, and 10,000 breeding cattle for distribution to farmers.[15] Before the year ended, an additional 200 tractors, 50 ten-metric-ton-trucks, 250 rice threshers, 44 publicity vans, 250 sorghum and millet threshers, and 1,800 corn shellers were imported by the federal government. Many of these subsidies provided avenues for private enrichment of the dominant class.

In some instances, the government's involvement in agriculture entailed haphazardly designed publicity campaigns aimed at urging farmers to redouble their efforts and encouraging city dwellers to take up farming. "Operation Feed the Nation" and other programs of sloganeering were taken seriously; the government imported helicopters, "publicity vans," and other gadgetry to put across its message about the values of farming. Although some people made money from these programs, the campaigns contributed nothing to agricultural production.

Another program designed to demonstrate the government's greater attention to the agricultural sector was the establishment of the Nigerian Agricultural and Cooperative Bank. By 1986 this bank had made agricultural loans totaling 400 million naira to various elements of the Nigerian bourgeoisie. The government also directed all commercial banks to reserve a portion of their loan portfolios to individuals for the purpose of agricultural investments. In addition, more money was allocated to the seven agricultural commodity boards, though by 1983 those boards were said to have incurred losses of 426.5 million naira.[16]

All these programs, particularly the increased financial allocations to the agricultural sector, did not result in any appreciable increase in agricultural productivity. If anything, the agricultural crisis seemed to get worse.

Although agricultural investment is not the principal basis for capital accumulation among the Nigerian bourgeoisie, the massive capital allocation to agriculture and the various agricultural programs became lucrative avenues for private appropriation of societal wealth. As Usen and Omotunde discovered, "So much money had been pumped into the River Basin Development Authorities (RBDAs) for importation of machines, construction of dams and houses that at a time the RBDAs were richer than some state governments."[17]

When the Ministry of Agriculture decided to sell off the commodity boards to private investors, on the grounds that they were incurring huge financial losses, the National Union of Public Corporations Employees pointed out that the boards were incurring losses because they were subsidizing food and agricultural processors in Nigeria. In 1982, the Ministry of Agriculture ordered the Nigerian Grains Board to buy 100,000 metric tons of corn at 290 naira per metric ton and resell to private feed millers at 250 naira per metric ton.[18]

CURRENT POLICIES ON AGRICULTURE AND ON AGRICULTURAL TECHNOLOGY TRANSFER

As crude oil began to supplant agriculture as the major foreign exchange earner, the cash crop sector of Nigerian agriculture was almost completely abandoned. Nigeria even began to import agricultural commodities, such as palm oil, of which it had once been a leading exporter. Ironically, much of the present emphasis on agricultural development can be explained by the collapse of the crude oil market. Revenues from crude oil played a crucial role in the current interest in agricultural development. As was pointed out above, from about 1975 the government began to make massive capital allocations to the agricultural sector. Virtually all these allocations were possible because of the huge revenues from crude oil. Since state expenditure on agriculture had become an important accumulative base for a section of the bourgeoisie, it was expected that the revenues from oil would continue to flow without interruption, so that more capital could be allocated to agriculture. Thus, the intention was not so much to make allocations to the agricultural sector in order to improve productivity as to create avenues, through state expenditure, for private capital appropriation.

Another important consequence of the influx of oil-based revenues was that they strengthened the material base of the Nigerian bourgeoisie. Top state functionaries, businessmen, and top military and police officers used their official positions or access to official positions to amass personal wealth. Although many of them used their accumulated capital for investments in the industrial and commercial sectors, because of the continued dominance of these two sectors of the Nigerian economy by multinational corporations, they also had to find alternative outlets for investment. Agriculture thus became increasingly attractive. Virtually all the retired brigadiers and generals, including Gen. Olusegun Obasanjo, the former head of state, have established large-scale mechanized farms.

To establish a proper framework for the analysis of the current policies and programs on agricultural technology transfer, it is important to restate briefly the major arguments that are advanced in support of the current policies and programs.

One of the most prominent justifications for the new policies and programs is the claim that they will transform the agricultural sector so as to enable Nigeria to diversify its sources of foreign exchange earnings. Thus, the expectation is that a revamped agricultural sector will increase agricultural exports and spare Nigeria the vagaries and volatilities associated with oil prices and the overdependence on a single export commodity.[19]

Agricultural commodities that are touted as viable for export include such traditional items as cocoa (and its derivatives cocovite, cocoa liquor, cocoa butter, and cocoa cake), palm oil, palm kernels, hides and skins, peanuts, and cotton. Other commodities being suggested include such food crops as yams, plantains, bananas, garri, cassava, cashews, and shea nuts.[20]

Another argument that has been advanced in favor of the new policies is that they will save Nigeria foreign exchange. The argument is advanced that since Nigeria can produce most of the food items and other agriculturally based industrial raw materials that it now inports, the foreign exchange that is spent on such items can be put to better use. Gamaliel Onosode expressed this sentiment eloquently when, in reference to the money Nigeria spends on fish imports, he said, "Under our current economic conditions, it is most unlikely that we can afford to devote so much of our scarce foreign exchange to import a product which, with moderate efforts, can be produced locally."[21]

Another justification for the current programs is that a revival of the agricultural sector will drastically reduce unemployment. Some of the new agricultural programs are designed to provide jobs for unemployed university graduates. Many of the 19 states have established agriculture self-employment schemes. Col. D. B. Laoye, the executive chairman of Oyo State Integrated Self-Employment Scheme, explaining why the government found it necessary to set up this scheme, said, "My own Scheme is a baby of need. It is one of the answers by the Oyo State Government to solve the unemployment riddle in the state."[22]

Olu Falae, secretary to the federal government, said in justification of the new economic programs, "If manufacturers and farmers increase their productions, there will be not only additional employment, but some growth in agriculture and manufacturing output."[23]

Finally, arguments have been advanced to the effect that the new programs not only will solve the "unemployment riddle," but also will help check rural-to-urban migration and end armed robbery and other vices.

The center of the current program is the Directorate of Food, Roads and Rural Infrastructure. Its location in the office of the president indicates the seriousness with which the president regards agriculture and rural development in the new scheme of things. The responsibilities of this agency include the construction of rural roads and of other rural infrastructure, such as markets. It is also charged with creating a favorable climate for the enhancement of food production.

Much money has been allocated to this agency since it was established in 1986. About 1.1 billion naira were allocated for various rural development projects in 1987. Some specific highlights of the new program include the allocation of 37.085 million naira for a project to cultivate 50 million trees and vegetables to "provide the minerals and vitamins required to balance the Nigerian diet."[24] A livestock program was established "to provide more protein to the Nigerian diet as well as attempt to bring the price of most [livestock] down."[25] A 23.64 million naira project was designed to provide improved seed production to "bridge the gap between supply and demand."[26]

With funds from the United Nations Development Program, the government has embarked upon a program "under which traditionally nomadic cattle rearers will be made to live sedentary lives."[27] The main objectives of the program are to discourage "impulsive sale of cattle" by the Fulani nomads and to "provide a known assured source for livestock." Under the program, the government provides, free of charge, 200–250 hectares of land for every 2,500 head of cattle. These plots of land are equipped with bore holes, and the cattle rearers are provided with grass seeds and fertilizers to cultivate fodder for the cattle. The drilling machines for digging the bore holes, the fertilizers, and the grass seed are imported by the government.

With the assistance of the U.N. Food and Agriculture Organization, fishing trawlers, boats, nets, and other fishing equipment are imported for distribution to fishermen.[28]

Using loans from the World Bank, the Nigerian government imports fertilizer for distribution to farmers. In 1986, 590,000 metric tons of fertilizer were imported; in 1987, 950,000 metric tons. Herbicides and pesticides are also imported by the government. In 1986, 100 flight hours were logged and over 15,000 liters of Fenitrothium pesticide were used to combat locusts and quelea birds.[29]

The federal government, in partnership with foreign investors, is setting up factories for the manufacture of such agricultural inputs as fertilizers and farm machinery. In partnership with M. W. Kellogg, Inc., a fertilizer company, the National Fertilizer Company of Nigeria (NAFCON) has been established. The government owns 70 percent and Kellogg owns 30 percent of the shares in the company. It is expected that NAFCON will produce 413,000 metric tons of urea, and 300,000 tons of nitrogen, phosphorus, and potassium fertilizers annually. The capital cost of establishing NAFCON is estimated at 797 million naira. Of this amount, export credit loans from the United States and Japan totaled 294 million naira. A consortium of Nigerian banks provided 70 million naira in loans, and the Nigerian government provided 328 million naira in equity funds. Kellogg's equity capital is 35 million naira.[30] Kellogg, responsible for the construction and management of NAFCON, has a free hand to bring into Nigeria the machines and other technological inputs for the construction and management of the company.

Other areas for joint ventures between the Nigerian government and foreign investors include irrigation, food processing, and establishment of factories for the local assembly of agricultural machinery.[31]

Although emphasis has shifted from the World Bank-designed huge agricultural development projects, the government has not given up on these gigantic projects. The private sector has been given generous incentives within the new agricultural program to encourage it to invest in agriculture. The new tax regulation exempts from taxation dividends declared by companies "engaged in agricultural production in Nigeria or processing of . . . agricultural products produced within Nigeria."[32] The new tax regulation also provides for generous depreciation allowances. It gives a 25 percent tax credit for research and development for the first year and 12.5 percent for subsequent years. An initial allowance of 25 percent is provided for motor vehicles, and after the first year such vehicles can be depreciated by 20 percent annually. It also allows exporters to keep the entire proceeds from their exports. In addition, the restrictions on foreign direct investments in the agricultural sector have been eased. Foreigners can now own as much as 60 percent of the equity in agricultural enterprises.

Other government programs to encourage large-scale private investments in agriculture include generous and liberalized credits and easy access to large tracts of land. Investors in agriculture also are exempted from paying the minimum wage to their employees.

These and other incentives have led to greater interest on the part of the private sector in agricultural investments. Numerous partnerships are being established between private Nigerian investors and foreign investors. The partnerships are set up to produce or process agricultural products. Food processing is most evident in the construction of flour mills and rice mills, and of plants for the canning of fruit and vegetable juices. The designs and machinery for these factories are supplied by the foreign partners. Partnerships also are formed to produce rice and wheat. Poultry and livestock breeding are other popular investments. Items imported for livestock breeding include breeding stocks, machinery, storage facilities, and feeds. Prominent companies that have invested in this and other sectors of agriculture include Rao Imex, Otto Wolf, DEG, Beatrice Foods, and Top Foods. Other foreign companies, such as Ford Motors, International Harvester, and Occidental Petroleum, are involved in exporting farm machinery, such as tractors and combine harvesters, to Nigeria.

A sizable proportion of the new private investment in agriculture has been made by such historically entrenched multinational firms as UAC, Lever Brothers, PZ, Guinness, and John Holt. Some of these firms have taken to farming to source their own raw materials; others, to take advantage of the new incentives on agricultural investments and to diversify their holdings. The brewery and textile industries have turned to farming to source their raw material needs locally. Afprint Limited, a major textile company, has set up a 2,000-hectare cotton farm through its wholly owned subsidiary, Afcott Limited. Afcott plants cotton seeds on a 1,600-hectare farm and runs it directly, while the remaining 400 hectares are cultivated by peasant farmers under the technical and financial guidance of Afcott. The farm employs 500 workers. The farm has its own airstrip . . . tractors and ploughs. Its managing director boasts that it is the largest mechanized cotton farm south of the Sahara.[33]

Nigerian firms such as Afprint are now interested in locally sourcing their raw materials because the dwindling foreign exchange earnings from oil have forced them to use local resources or be forced, for lack of imported inputs, to cease operation. Many of these firms were set up during the heady days of the oil boom, as part of the drive for import-substitution industrialization. They were all heavily import-dependent, but as long as Nigeria derived huge revenues from oil exports, there was sufficient foreign exchange to import the raw materials, machinery, and other items that make this type of industrialization possible.

Although some of these companies voluntarily decided to locally source their raw materials, others were literally coerced into doing so. For instance, the government has given notice of its intention to ban the importation of wheat, barley, and oats. The wheat millers and the bakeries are thus being forced to use Nigerian grain in order to continue to produce. At first the breweries objected to the ban on the importation of barley and oats, claiming that beer brewed with Nigerian grains would not be good enough for the Nigerian palate. Now, however, they have been able to make the switch, and some of them are touting the superior qualities of beer brewed with Nigerian grains.

The commercial banks are heavily involved in the new agricultural programs. All the banks have agricultural loan schemes. The Allied Bank, for instance, believes that small-scale farmers play a vital role in the nation's economy. Its loan package involves the provision of a "soft loan package to cover the expenses of farm inputs and operation such as tools, seeds, fertilizers, labour, transport, storage, marketing, etc."[34]

Many of the new loans to small-scale farmers are targeted to the new kind of farmers—unemployed university graduates, who would seem to be perfect candidates for loans for small-scale farming. With their education, they are not as "backward" as the illiterate peasant farmers, and can use modern agricultural methods to raise production. Their desperate position is unlikely to make them a threat to the status quo. It is hoped that using university graduates as small-scale farmers will raise agricultural production without the necessity to transform the peasant mode of production.

Both the federal and the state governments join the commercial banks in extending loans to unemployed university graduates. The Lagos state government gives a 5,000-naira loan to each participant in a program to raise corn production. The federal program gives a loan of 20,000 naira to each selected unemployed graduate to set up a firm to process peanut or palm oil or tomatoes, or for rice milling.

CONTRADICTIONS

The first major contradiction within the Nigerian social formation under which the new agricultural programs operate is the ambiguity of the role of the peasants. The new programs are constrained by two opposing perspectives within the ruling class about the usefulness of the peasant mode of production.

One view, which can be broadly characterized as the World Bank perspective, sees the peasant mode of production as nonviable and urges the replacement of the peasants by agribusinesses and progressive farmers. In Nigeria, progressive farmers are multinational firms farming on their own or in partnership with the state and local capital, and retired generals and other former top state functionaries. They will not necessarily produce food crops but will grow what Nigeria has a comparative advantage in producing. In fact, the emphasis will be on production for the external market.

The other perspective, articulated by the tobacco, textiles, and beverage industries, acknowledges that the farming methods of the peasants need to be modernized but argues that the small-scale farmers will be indispensable to the national economy for the foreseeable future. The greater faith in the peasants shown by this perspective could be accounted for by the fact that these industries have traditionally relied on the peasants to grow the cash crops on which they depend. Since the peasants, using their primitive methods, produced enough cash crops for them in the past, these industries feel that there is nothing intrinsically wrong with the peasant mode of production and that the peasants are no longer able to produce as much as they used to because of the general neglect of agriculture.

The Nigerian Tobacco Company, for instance, believes that with modern farming techniques, the small-scale farmers not only will produce sufficient cash crops but also can grow enough food to feed everyone. Acting on this belief, it has established farm training centers aimed at "equipping young farmers with modern knowledge . . . in the areas of mechanisation, livestock, crop science, soil science, economics and sociology."[35] Twenty thousand selected peasant farmers cultivate tobacco for the company, which provides assistance in the form of loans, advice, and chemicals. This relationship between the peasant farmers and the company is one of the primary reasons why it made a profit of 17.248 million naira in 1986.[36]

Another major contradiction is between the desire to produce for export in order to diversify Nigeria's export earnings and the desire to satisfy local needs. Christopher Kolade, the managing director of Cadbury Nigeria Limited, in a speech to the Association of Food, Beverage and Tobacco Employers, warned that the three Nigerian cocoa processing firms (Cocoa Industries, Cocoa Products Industry, and Ile Oluji Cocoa Products Company) would be forced to close down if the government did not take steps to control the export of cocoa beans.[37]

The cocoa processors are apprehensive that if cocoa exports are not tightly controlled, almost all the cocoa beans produced in Nigeria will be exported and Nigerian beverage manufacturers, such as Cadbury, Food Specialities, and Ovaltine, will be forced to reimport the processed cocoa beans in order to make cocoa-based beverages. The three cocoa processors used to get their cocoa beans directly from the Nigerian Cocoa Board. This board and six other commodity boards have been abolished, and cocoa exports have been decontrolled. Since an economy like Nigeria's, which depends on imports to satisfy domestic consumer goods, cherishes foreign exchange that can be earned through exports, a domestic manufacturer is placed at a disadvantage if it has to compete with foreign buyers for the same raw materials. With the current emphasis on exports, the three cocoa processors and the beverage manufacturers will be forced to close down or will raise their prices, thus negating the objective of satisfying domestic needs.

With the abolition of the Cocoa Board and with the generous incentives to exporters, cocoa exporters have been earning fabulous profits. In seven months, the price of cocoa jumped from 1,600 naira per metric ton to between 4,500 and 5,300 naira. Afro-Continental, Basic Finance, Ime Ebong and Associates, and M.K.O. have monopolized the cocoa export market.[38]

Since what is in the interest of these cocoa exporters seems to be detrimental to the interests of the cocoa processors and the beverage industry, Kolade, in his speech, urged the government to "reject any policy that seeks to promote the exportation of primary products for which the country has processing capacity either already in place or capable of being installed in the near future."[39]

Similarly, the Nigerian Tanners Council, through its spokesman, Shehu Kaikai, has argued that the export of hides and skins threatens the Nigerian shoe and leather industry.[40] He urged the government to ban the exportation of hides and skins, and to make it illegal for Nigerians to eat animal skins, in order to guarantee the supply of hides and skins for the shoe and leather industry.

A further contradiction of the new policies and programs is the high degree of external support on which the implementation of the programs depends. As we have seen, these new policies require a lot of foreign inputs in the form of finance, machinery, fertilizers, pesticides, and other goods. These are brought into Nigeria by the government, foreign partners or vendors, private Nigerians, or private corporate bodies. The new policies do not dramatically depart from the old ones. As Zuwaghu Bonat put it, the new policies are designed to reinforce the existing relationship whereby "the foreign bourgeoisie remained controllers of technology, while the local agents supplied cheap labor, operating capital, infrastructures, political stability, and guaranteed the repatriation of profits."[41]

It should also be noted that whereas the ideological interests of a section of the Nigerian bourgeoisie propel the state in the direction of privatization, the new agricultural programs cannot be executed without strong and active state support. Thus, the new policies are likely to intensify contradictions within the Nigerian dominant class.

Another contradiction is that the huge appropriations of land that the new agricultural programs demand will increasingly bring the peasants (whose lands are being appropriated) into direct conflict both with the state and with the rich Nigerians and large corporations that are appropriating the land.

Finally, although the need to earn additional foreign exchange is one of the primary motivations for the new policies, the government seems to have negated this objective by allowing exporters to keep all the proceeds from their exports.

CONCLUSION

This analysis has shown that the present quest for food self-sufficiency is largely a mirage. A self-reliant form of development cannot be attained by making the economy more dependent on external inputs.

It may be argued that dependence on imported machinery and other agricultural inputs may be better than external food dependence. Without going into the merits of this argument, we can point out that since the policy of importation of agricultural technology is implemented within an overall framework of a dependent neocolonial economy, its consequences for the mass of the Nigerian people will be largely negative.

The oil crisis has forced the frantic search for alternative and/or additional commodities for export, and this is what largely provides the current impetus for agricultural development. Although these new programs are being sold on the grounds that they will enable Nigeria to attain self-sufficiency in food supply, the external orientation of these programs is not hidden. Much of the agricultural commodities that will be produced through these programs will not be food items. Thus, the success of these programs will actually worsen the food crisis.

The current programs, particularly the subsidies, satisfy the interests of the dominant class in Nigeria. The multinational corporations that have been making huge profits as the mass of the Nigerian people sink deeper into poverty have discovered new outlets in which to reinvest part of the enormous profits that they have been making since the government embarked upon "austerity programs" in 1983.

As Yusufu Bala Usman correctly pointed out:

The agricultural problems are caused neither by lack of appropriate technology, nor by resources scarcity. The problems of agriculture are the nature and manner in which production is socially organised, and the relationship between people which this organisation entails and reproduces.[42]

The huge capital expenditure on agriculture in Nigeria during the second civilian regime, which did not result in a commensurate increase in productivity, should clearly indicate that massive capital allocations alone will not solve the food crisis. Given the parasitic dependence of the Nigerian bourgeoisie, such expenditures merely create opportunities for them to appropriate societal resources. As Heinrich Bergstresser concludes in his analysis of agribusiness in Nigeria:

Although agrobusiness strengthens the political and economic power of the Nigerian ruling class, it cannot be regarded as a solution to the general socioeconomic crisis in Nigeria, since it deepens Nigeria's dependence on and integration into the world market, and, at the same time, fails to promote the integration of the deprived into a social and economic system which is in transition.[43]

NOTES

1. See Alkasum Abba et al., *The Nigerian Economic Crisis: Causes and Solutions* (Lagos: Academic Staff Union of Universities of Nigeria, 1985), p. 18.

2. Ibid., p. 25; Toyin Falola and Julius Ihonvbere, *The Rise and Fall of Nigeria's Second Republic: 1979–1984* (London: Zed Books, 1985), p. 133.

3. Yusufu Bala Usman, *Nigeria Against the I.M.F.: The Home Market Strategy* (Kaduna, Nigeria: Vanguard Publishers, 1986), p. 39.

4. See *Business Concord* (Lagos, Nigeria), October 21, 1983.

5. Anietie Usen and Soji Omotunde, "Nigeria's Battle for Food," *Newswatch*, November 25, 1985, p. 20.

6. Ibid.

7. Ibid.

8. Ibid.

9. See *National Concord* (Lagos, Nigeria), December 29, 1986, p. 11.

10. Yahaya Abdullahi, "The Privatisation of Agricultural Sector," *The Analyst*, November 1986, p. 13.

11. Falola and Ihonvbere, *The Rise and Fall . . .* , p. 123.

12. T. A. Abdullalri, "Comments on Press Briefing by Minister of Agriculture," *New Nigerian*, February 18, 1985, p. 2.

13. Some examples are the Funtua, Gusau, Gombe, Ayangba, Lafia, Bida, and Ilorin agricultural development projects.

14. Quoted in *Newswatch*, November 25, 1985, p. 20.

15. Falola and Ihonvbere, *The Rise and Fall . . .* , p. 129.

16. See *Newswatch*, November 25, 1985, p. 20.

17. Usen and Omotunde, "Nigeria's Battle for Food," p. 21.

18. "NUPCE Blasts Privatisation," *New Horizon*, June 1986, p. 31.

19. This is the wisdom behind the 1987 fiscal year federal "budget of consolidation"; see text of the budget in *National Concord* (Lagos, Nigeria), January 3, 1987, pp. 7-10.

20. "Export Drive Now in High Gear," *Sunday Times* (Lagos, Nigeria), January, 4, 1987, pp. 1, 7.

21. Willie Nwokoye, "Nigeria's Fish Crisis," *African Concord* no. 73 (January 1986): 31.

22. See *New Nigerian*, January 3, 1987, p. 5.

23. *National Concord* (Lagos, Nigeria), December 20, 1986, p. 1.

24. "Briefing of Media Executives by Chief of General Staff," *The Standard* (Jos, Nigeria), January 3, 1987, p. 5.

25. Ibid.

26. Ibid.

27. "Government to Create New Homes for Fulani Nomads," *The Guardian* (Lagos), November 23, 1986, pp. 1, 2.

28. *The Standard* (Jos, Nigeria), January 3, 1987, p. 5.

29. Ibid.

30. Stephen Agwudagwu, "The 70 Million Naira Last Lap," *Newswatch*, August 11, 1986, p. 41.

31. For a review of some of these joint ventures, see Okello Oculi, "Multinationals in Nigerian Agriculture in the 1980's," *Review of African Political Economy* no. 31 (December 1984): 87-91.

32. See *Daily Times* (Lagos), January 5, 1987, p. 3.

33. "Afcott's Cotton Farm," *Thisweek* 2, no. 7 (November 24, 1986): 30.

34. Ibid., p. 43.

35. Fred Ohwahwa, "Beyond Cigarettes: NTC Trains Young Men for Small-Scale Farming," *African Guardian* 2, no. 25 (July 2, 1987): 26.

36. Ibid.

37. Economist Intelligence Unit, *Nigeria: Analysis of Economic and Political Trends Every Quarter*, no. 3, 1986 (London: Economist Publications, 1986), pp. 17-18.

38. *African Guardian*, January 29, 1987, p. 20.

39. Economist Intelligence Unit, *Nigeria*, p. 18.

40. *Sunday Standard* (Jos, Nigeria), December 7, 1986, p. 1.

41. Zuwaghu Bonat, "Who Decides Economic Policy in Nigeria?" *The Analyst*, November 1986, p. 11.

42. Usman, *Nigeria Against the I.M.F.*, p. 116.

43. Heinrich Bergstresser, "Nigeria: Agro-business—eine Lösung der Krise?" *Afrika Spectrum* 2 (1986): 50.

The Southern African Development Coordination Council

Robert E. Clute

On the eve of Zimbabwe's independence, the so-called Front Line States (Angola, Botswana, Mozambique, Tanzania, and Zambia) met at Arusha, Tanzania, on July 3–4, 1979, and discussed possible co-operation to develop the region of Southern Africa and to reduce its dependence on South Africa. On April 1, 1980, the heads of state of the Front Line States, joined by those of Lesotho, Malawi, and Swaziland, met in Zambia and adopted the Lusaka Declaration, which created the Southern African Development Coordination Council (SADCC). They were joined by Zimbabwe when it became independent. Because of Zimbabwe's relatively developed economy and its transportation system, which serves the area north of the Limpopo River, the latter's membership was crucial to SADCC. President Mobuto Sese Seko applied for Zaire's admission but was rejected, presumably because of Zaire's border incursions into Zambia in 1980 and the accusation that Angolan rebels were being provided a haven in Zaire.[1]

The SADCC area contains approximately 4.9 million square kilometers, about 42 percent of Africa, and in 1986 it contained 77.7 million inhabitants, about 13.3 percent of the continent's population. The area is extremely well endowed with minerals, including diamonds, copper, cobalt, nickel, iron, chromite, gold, magnesium, manganese, tin, phosphate, lead, silver, tungsten, lithium, coal, and petroleum products. Mineral exports make up a significant portion of the incomes of Angola, Botswana, Zambia, and Zimbabwe;[2] and if mineral resources were exploited, they could be an important source of income for a number of SADCC states. Certainly, if developed, the area could supply most of the Western world's needs for critical strategic minerals as an alternative source to South Africa.

The majority of the population is engaged in agriculture. With the exceptions of Zambia and Malawi, the per capita food production index is relatively low. Recent droughts, poor agricultural policies, and disruptions created by civil war have created famine conditions in Mozambique, and the area as a whole has faced food shortages. Except for Malawi and Zimbabwe, which are net exporters of grain, SADCC countries must import a fairly large percentage of their cereals, which puts a financial strain on already weakened economies. Gross national product (GNP) per capita is relatively low, and external public debt for the area is high and growing. Exports are principally agricultural or mineral commodities. With the exception of Angola and Tanzania, SADCC members are extremely dependent on the South African transportation system and economy. In 1982 about 17 percent of SADCC exports were to South Africa and 22 percent of its imports were from South Africa. The transportation advantage has been extremely profitable for South Africa, which in 1985 had a surplus of $2.2 billion on trade in goods and nonfactor services with SADCC states. Because of the low rate of industrialization and poor transportation networks, only 5 percent of total SADCC trade in 1985 was between member states.[3] Another important source of income for some SADCC members is contract labor sent to South Africa. In mid-1986, in addition to an estimated 700,000 to 1,000,000 "illegal" immigrants to South Africa, there were about 300,000 contract laborers from Botswana, Lesotho, Malawi, Mozambique, Swaziland, Zambia, and Zimbabwe. Remittances from such workers are an important source of foreign exchange. For example, remittances from contract workers account for 50 percent of Lesotho's GDP.[4]

SADCC OBJECTIVES AND
ORGANIZATIONAL STRUCTURE

The objectives of SADCC, as set forth in the Lusaka Declaration of 1980, were to reduce economic dependence on South Africa; to forge strong links in order to create a real and equitable integration of the region; to mobilize the area's resources for the implementation of national, interstate, and regional policies; and to create concerted international cooperation within the strategy of SADCC for the economic liberation of the member states.

All member states, with the exception of Angola and Mozambique, had been under British rule. With the exception of the latter states and Tanzania, the transportation, communication, and economic systems of the member states had been intertwined with South Africa, which made them very dependent on the latter. Botswana, Lesotho, and Swaziland were, and still are, part of the South African Customs Union. Thus, to many of the member states, decolonization is tantamount to removing the existing dependency on South Africa.

These objectives place great demands on member states that have not yet been fully realized. The diversity of the group is enormous; they vary in area from Angola, with about 1,247,000 square kilometers, to Swaziland, with 17,400 square kilometers. The per capita GNP varies from $210 in Malawi and Tanzania to $910 in Botswana. Ideologies vary as greatly as the economies. It would be relatively easy for a larger state with a more developed economy, such as Zimbabwe, to dominate the others. National development strategies must be harmonized, and greatly differing resources must be directed toward common goals. Above all, the search for foreign assistance must be coordinated to increase SADCC's bargaining power.

SADCC members have arrived at a peculiarly African administrative structure, which is highly decentralized and nonbureaucratic, and functions on the basis of consensus. Carol Thompson refers to it as ". . . more of a sequence of conferences than a tenth state in the region."[5] The SADCC states examined the structures of other regional groupings in Africa and concluded that they were hampered by a ponderous bureaucracy. They therefore consciously adopted a lean bureaucratic structure.[6] It has a very small secretariat, composed of a secretary general and four officers, with headquarters in Gaborone, Botswana. SADCC activities are divided into sectors. Each sector is coordinated by a member state that is responsible for the success of that sector's activities.

The supreme authority of SADCC is the summit, which meets annually and is composed of the heads of state of the nine members. It provides overall policy and direction. The Council of Ministers, composed of one minister from each member state, is the working body responsible for the strategy of policy implementation, the supervision of SADCC programs, and the covering of periodic meetings with donor states and organizations. The council may appoint special ministerial committees to deal with the functional areas, but thus far the only such committee created is the Southern African Transport and Communications Commission, under the leadership of Mozambique. The council is assisted by the Standing Committee of Officials, which meets annually and operates more or less as SADCC's committee on committees. The Standing Committee appoints subcommittees to assist the council in dealing with the sectoral areas and to meet frequently with the member government delegated the responsibility for that particular sector.[7] Usually the committee members are the member states' ministers responsible for that sectoral function. For example, a meeting on the transportation sector would usually be attended by the transportation ministers of the member states. At all levels decisions are reached by consensus.

The main work of SADCC is through the functional sectors. Each sector is assigned to a member state that is responsible for coordinating the sector's activity and the division of responsibilities. This loose structure respects state sovereignty and ensures that the larger states will not dominate or dictate overall SADCC programs. SADCC participants not only become acquainted with their counterparts in other member states but also learn to appreciate the particular problems of the other states. Although this loose structure seems to have worked fairly well, it does present problems in the overall development of the area, and sometimes national policies do not fit—or may even duplicate—the overall policies of the sectors. The duties of the sectors and the states responsible for coordinating their activities may be seen in Table 13.1.

SECTOR ACTIVITIES

The sectors are obviously designed to develop Southern Africa and to decrease dependence on South Africa. The scope of this work will not permit a detailed examination of all sector activities.

Energy Development

Over half of Africa's coal is located in SADCC member states, especially in Botswana, Mozambique, Swaziland, Tanzania, and Zimbabwe. Angola is the principal producer of petroleum, with most of its production going to the United States. Petroleum deposits are also lo-

Table 13.1
Sectoral Responsibilities for SADCC Programs

Member State Coordinator	Sectoral Function
Angola	Energy Development
Botswana	Animal Disease Control, Agricultural Research
Lesotho	Soil Conservation, Land Utilization
Malawi	Fisheries, Forestry, Wildlife
Mozambique	Transport and Communications
Swaziland	Manpower Training and Development, Health Training Facilities
Tanzania	Industrial Development, Industry and Trade
Zambia	Foreign Aid Through South African Development Fund, Mining
Zimbabwe	Food Production, Distribution and Security

cated in Tanzania, and Mozambique has deposits of natural gas.[8] In 1982, Angola offered to supply oil to SADCC members on special terms, but this offer has not yet materialized.[9] The SADCC area produces one-fifth of Africa's hydroelectric power, principally through the Cuneri, Cabora Bassa, and Karbia dams. Although the area has a large surplus generating capacity, some member states experience critical electric shortages. Ironically, Mozambique, which has the single largest generating capacity in the Cabora Bassa dam, has imported electric power from South Africa. The energy sector, coordinated by Angola, is in the process of constructing national security grids to permit electricity from the various dams to be sent to deficit areas as far away as Tanzania.[10] This sector has been most successful in attracting funding. The 1987 SADCC conference decided that future emphasis would be placed on new and renewable energy sources, fuel wood, and small-scale electricity projects.[11]

Animal Disease Control and Agricultural Research

These sectors are coordinated by Botswana, which was previously dependent on South Africa to perform these functions. A 25-year research program to develop drought-resistant strains of millet and sorghum has established a large research station at Matopos, Zimbabwe, and smaller satellite stations in the other member states. The Matopos station is growing over 6,000 varieties of sorghum and millet to meet the needs of the diverse ecological zones of the area. Future plans include research stations for cowpeas, legumes, and peanuts. Hoof-and-mouth disease, which formerly infected the cattle of Botswana, Swaziland, Zambia, and Zimbabwe, has been practically eliminated from the region.[12]

Food Production and Distribution

This sector, which is coordinated by the government of Zimbabwe, is extremely important to the area. With the exception of Zimbabwe and Malawi, the members of SADCC are not able to feed their populations from their own resources. Agricultural policy of many SADCC governments has left much to be desired.[13] Policy within this sector has been left to national government plans and does not address many of the rather dubious agricultural policies of member states. A nine-point plan to safeguard the region's food supplies was submitted to an SADCC donor conference held at Maseru, Lesotho, in January 1983. The plan concentrated on the building of a food reserve, an early warning system, programs to reduce losses of food after harvest, and the creation of standardized agricultural statistics.[14]

Between 1977 and 1982, food imports to SADCC members rose by 67 percent and were consuming massive amounts of foreign exchange. From 1981 to 1983, cereal production in the area dropped by 1 million metric tons per annum. The drought increased in intensity during 1984, and peasant farming was hampered by a shortage of draft animals due to the loss of cattle and the weakened condition of many of the remaining animals. The fourth annual consultative conference of SADCC, held at Lusaka, Zambia, in 1984, gave emphasis to agriculture. Executive Secretary Arthur Blumeris warned of dwindling food resources and the threat of famine. At this meeting stress was placed on the creation of irrigation systems throughout the area, the creation of storage facilities to handle food reserves, early drought warning systems, disease control, and the rehabilitation of agricultural infrastructures.[15]

At the sixth annual meeting of SADCC at Mbabane, Swaziland, in 1985, Zimbabwe's minister of agriculture, Denis Norman, who is responsible for coordinating this sector, noted that it was time to go beyond mere studies and to ". . . get some concrete projects off the ground."[16] At the Mbabane conference the United States agreed to assist in financing irrigation projects for Zimbabwe.[17] At the 1987 SADCC conference in Gaborone, emphasis was placed on household and national self-sufficiency in food, and on improving rural incomes through agriculture and agro-industries, but this likewise seems to be in the early planning stages.[18] Obviously the sector has had more success in attracting food aid than in developing plans and attracting donor funds to improve overall agricultural production and development.

Mining

Minerals represent one of the greatest assets of the SADCC region. The mineral potential of SADCC is at least equal to that of South Africa. However, large areas, such as Angola and Mozambique, have not been prospected and many known deposits in SADCC countries have not yet been exploited.[19] Under Zambia's coordination the mining sector has developed a strategy. A five-year plan was drafted at the meeting of SADCC ministers of mines on August 30, 1985. The cost was estimated at $2.2 billion and donor commitments of $600,000 have already been received. The plan covers a manpower survey, small-scale mining, an inventory of mineral resources, foundries, fabrication, iron and steel industries, and the mining of chemicals.[20]

Since independence there has been an increasing mistrust of the foreign ownership of natural resources that in many cases has resulted in the nationalization of foreign mining interests. The threat of nationalization, the rising capital expenditures required before a mine becomes operational, and the falling prices of mineral commodities combined to discourage direct foreign investment in mining activities during the 1970s. However, the lending institutions of a number of developed countries are now encouraging firms to take an increased role in mining projects in the Third World. There has also been a noticeable trend for oil companies to diversify their holdings by moving into the mining sector, as Standard Oil has done in Zaire and Zambia.[21]

Samuel Asante notes that there has been a tendency to restructure transnational mineral agreements into forms that may be more attractive to both host governments and foreign investors. Joint ventures are being contracted whereby the host country acquires a majority interest in the assets of local subsidiaries of transnational corporations. Host countries may negotiate service contracts with foreign corporations whereby a transnational company agrees to carry out the actual mining operations, to provide the necessary technical services, and to market the output. Production-sharing contracts may also be negotiated, as has been done in Indonesia, whereby the transnational corporation provides the necessary financial and technical assistance, bears the operating costs, and shares in the profits of the exported commodity.[22]

Perhaps these new approaches to mining ventures, which have already had some application in Botswana, Malawi, Swaziland, Zambia, and Zimbabwe,[23] will prove to be more attractive to foreign investors in the SADCC region than has been the case in the past. However, these innovations are dependent on the national policies of member states, and thus far SADCC has not developed an overall policy to attract foreign investments in the mining sector. With the unstable conditions in South Africa and the Reagan administration's claim that the Western world's supply of strategic minerals is endangered, it might be wise for both donor countries and private investors to build up alternative sources for such minerals within the SADCC area.

Communications

The communications sector, under the coordination of Mozambique, is establishing earth satellite stations to provide telecommunication links among all SADCC members. Prior to the establishment of SADCC, six of the states were dependent on South Africa for telephone, telex, and telecommunications.[24] In 1985 Italy agreed to provide $12.7 million for equipment for switching centers, training, and technical assistance;[25] and Malawi, Zambia, and Mozambique signed a contract valued at 30 million rand with a Norwegian firm for the construction of SADCC's telecommunications and microwave projects.[26] Completion of these projects will greatly decrease the region's dependence on South African communications.

Industrial Development

The industrial development sector is directed by Tanzania. Although there is some overlap between SADCC and the Preferential Trade Area (PTA), their goals are quite different. Lesotho, Malawi, Swaziland, and Zimbabwe belong to both organizations; Tanzania is not a member of PTA. The aim of PTA has been to increase trade among members by the reduction of tariffs, removal of trade barriers, and the creation of integrated markets aimed at a free trade area.[27] SADCC has been somewhat skeptical of the success of other attempted free trade areas in Africa, and has concluded that initial priority should be given to an increase in the production of goods and services. The executive secretary of SADCC stated, ". . . it doesn't help to reduce or eliminate trade barriers when you have nothing to trade."[28] SADCC relies on production to increase trade. Intra-SADCC trade is still minimal, and in 1982 comprised only 5 percent of the $14 billion total SADCC trade.[29] With a population equal to that of West Germany and a wealth of essential resources, the SADCC area could produce many of the finished products it now imports. However, since the area is now principally an exporter of mineral and agricultural commodities at relatively low world prices, and an importer of manufactured products that are steadily rising in price, it will not be able to finance industrialization without considerable foreign assistance.

The SADCC structure stresses the coordination of national development plans rather than a balanced overall SADCC plan for the development of the region. This is an attempt to bridge the diversity of interests of the member states. Small countries such as Botswana would prefer more stress on regional development in order to avoid domination by larger members. Douglas Anglin notes, "Anxious as Gaborone was to escape the South African frying pan, it was determined not to land in the Zimbabwean fire."[30] On the other hand, diversity discourages regional planning. Political styles of members states vary from monarchies in Lesotho and Swaziland, to authoritarian regimes such as Malawi, to a relatively liberal democracy such as Botswana. Economies range from open market economies, such as Botswana, Lesotho, Malawi, and Swaziland, to varied socialist systems based on state capitalism, such as Angola, Mozambique, and Tanzania, to mixed economies with varying degrees of private sector enterprise, such as Zambia and Zimbabwe.

The situation is further complicated by the varying degrees of development of the member states. The national development plans coordinated by this sector have placed little emphasis on avoiding duplication of industries and have not been successful in reducing the growing gap between the economically stronger states and the weaker states. SADCC has not been conspicuously successful in attracting donor funds to this sector. There has been some criticism that SADCC has been developing "shopping lists" rather than coordinated plans. Some progress has been made in promoting complementary production. For example, although most SADCC members produce textiles, only Botswana and Tanzania produce textile chemicals. Production of phosphate and ammonia fertilizers in member states is planned to avoid duplication. Botswana, Malawi, and Zimbabwe have achieved a healthy growth in the export of goods to other SADCC states.[31]

On the whole this is probably one of the weakest sectors in SADCC planning. The investments for industrial development have been woefully inadequate. At its 1987 conference in Gaborone, SADCC stressed "investment in production," and 120 representatives of the business community attended a seminar on February 4. The discussions emphasized the need for better incentives, less government control, more realistic exchange rates, and a less suspicious attitude toward the private sector.[32] If foreign private investment is to be attracted, there must be considerable changes in the policies of some SADCC member states, which now discourage foreign private investment. Success in this sector will require massive foreign assistance, the attraction of foreign private investment, and improved regional coordination and planning before the situation will improve to any great extent.

Transportation

Obviously the transportation sector, coordinated by Mozambique, is the most important factor in the SADCC program to reduce dependence on South Africa. With the exception of Tanzania and Angola, SADCC member states are greatly dependent on the South African transportation system. For Botswana, Lesotho, and Swaziland, the dependence is nearly complete. This dependence gives South Africa a strong economic weapon to use against the SADCC area. If strong sanctions were imposed against South Africa by the international community, South Africa would retaliate by denying

SADCC members the use of its transportation facilities. Thus the development of alternative trade routes directed toward SADCC coastal ports is a prime target.

The Beira-Maputo, Beira-Malawi, and Zimbabwe-Maputo railways have become unusable due to the control of vast areas of Mozambique by the anti-government forces of the Resistencia Nacional Mozambique (MNR), backed by South Africa. The MNR has sabotaged the railroad from Malawi to Nacala, Mozambique, which deprives Malawi of its major link to the Indian Ocean. Due to the anti-government guerilla activity of the National Union for the Total Independence of Angola (UNITA), which is backed by South Africa, the Benguela Railroad between Zaire and Angola has been cut off for several years.[33] Thus four of SADCC's seven major railways with access to the sea have been rendered unusable.

SADCC has helped alleviate Zambia's problem by improving its links with Tanzania. During the imposition of sanctions against Rhodesia, a pipeline was constructed between Zambia and Tanzania. The Tazara Railway connecting the two countries was completed in 1973. In 1985 SADCC raised nearly half of the $150 million needed to rehabilitate the pipeline and the Tazara Railway. Great Britain and the World Bank pledged funds to build a railroad from Malawi to Mbeya, Tanzania, which is now completed, and will give Malawi access to the Tazara Railway.[34]

SADCC also has a $90 million project to rehabilitate the railway from Nacala, Mozambique, to Malawi.[35] The distance from Blantyre, Malawi, to Nacala is 840 kilometers, but much of Malawi's goods must now be shipped 3,342 kilometers to Durban, South Africa. Unfortunately, the Malawi-Nacala road is still not very secure from MNR sabotage, which jeopardizes the success of the project.[36]

One of SADCC's most promising transportation ventures is the rehabilitation of the 200-mile road-railroad-pipeline network connecting Zimbabwe to the port of Beira, Mozambique. Disruptions by MNR sabotage had reduced the portion of Zimbabwean trade passing through Beira from 56 percent in 1982 to less than 20 percent in 1985. At an international donors' meeting in Brussels, during October 1986, new pledges were obtained that brought total funding to $185 million, 90 percent of the amount needed to cover rehabilitation work for the first three years of the project. Funds were provided principally by the African Development Bank, the Nordic countries, and the European Economic Community, with smaller amounts from the United States and East Germany. The first phase of the project was to reconstruct the railway lines, to provide new rolling stock, and to raise the capacity of the railroad. This phase has been completed, and the capacity of the railway has been increased from 3,000 to 8,000 metric tons per day.[37] The second phase, now in progress aims to improve the infrastructure and the capacity of the port. The final phase, to begin in 1990, is concerned with ancillary projects.

The port of Beira has been dredged to handle its 1975 level of 3 million metric tons per annum. During the second phase it will be dredged to attain a capacity of 5 million metric tons. Zimbabwe has stationed 12,000 troops to protect the railway and pipeline from further sabotage.[38] Minor sabotage still occurs, but the system is operative. However, in 1986 trade through Beira was only 900,000 metric tons, although SADCC had estimated that it would be 1.5 million tons. Zimbabwean businessmen have been somewhat reluctant to ship to Beira, and have continued to use the port of Durban because of fear of sabotage and sporadic pilferage in Beira. Another problem is caused by the fact that only 20 shipping lines call at Beira, and cargo sometimes must sit for long periods awaiting shipment.[39] Success of the port will require SADCC to convince a larger number of shipping lines to call at Beira.

Despite SADCC's enormous efforts to supply alternative transportation lines, 50–60 percent of the trade of Malawi, Zambia, and Zimbabwe, and 80–100 percent of the trade of Botswana, Lesotho, and Swaziland was still using the South African transportation system in 1986.[40] As a matter of fact, South African-based guerrilla activity and sabotage carried out by UNITA and MNR have undoubtedly been increased in an attempt to close down the SADCC lines to Angola and Mozambique. However, if the South African borders were closed to SADCC countries due to increased sanctions, there is little doubt that the upgraded transport sector of SADCC would be able to handle much of the traffic except for that of Lesotho and Swaziland.

FOREIGN AID TO SADCC

SADCC has been relatively successful in attracting foreign aid to support its programs. In mid-1986 Simbarshe Makoni, executive secretary of SADCC, noted that the program had outlined 400 projects, the completion of which would cost $5 billion in 1985 U.S. dollars.

Of this, SADCC had secured $1.1 billion and another $1.16 billion was in various stages of negotiations.[41] The European Economic Community, the Nordic countries, and Canada have been firm supporters of SADCC. Although the Middle Eastern OPEC countries have given strong verbal support, they have been reluctant to commit funds. The Soviet Union and the COMECON states likewise have not been contributors to SADCC aid, although East Germany has given some support.[42] However, the Soviet Union was represented for the first time at the 1987 SADCC conference and expressed interest, along with representatives from the Eastern bloc, in the transport and heavy industry sectors of the SADCC program.[43] The United States gave $103.375 million in direct aid to SADCC from 1980 to 1987, which was 4.36 percent of total SADCC funding. In addition, U.S. bilateral aid to SADCC member states was $1.3 billion during the same period.[44] This is a relatively low contribution in view of the large U.S. gross domestic product (GDP).

Despite this rather massive amount of foreign aid, the SADCC region is extremely weak economically. SADCC's foreign debt in 1986 was U.S. $16.5 billion, 60 percent of the region's GDP.[45] Military expenditures, caused to a great extent by South Africa's destabilization measures, have been a heavy economic drain. In 1983 Angola was spending 25 percent of its central government expenditures on the military. The latest figure on Mozambique was 27.8 percent in 1980. In 1984 military expenditures as a percent of total central government expenditures for selected SADCC states were Lesotho, 28.5 percent; Tanzania, 12.8 percent; Zambia, 20.9 percent; and Zimbabwe, 15 percent.[46] Aid assistance must be offset by losses experienced through South Africa's destabilization program.

SOUTH AFRICAN DESTABILIZATION IN SADCC

Many SADCC activities have been somewhat negated by South African policy designed to maintain hegemony over the area. South Africa has carried out a comprehensive program to weaken the economies of the SADCC states by backing insurgency movements such as MNR in Mozambique and UNITA in Angola. South Africa signed the Nkomati Accord with Mozambique in 1984 whereby the latter agreed to expel the African National Congress and not permit Mozambique to be used as a base for operations. South Africa in turn was to halt support of the MNR. In the Lusaka Agreement of the same year, South Africa agreed to withdraw military forces that had occupied parts of Angola for several years, and Angola was not to permit the South-West African People's Organization to use Angolan territory as a base for attacks on Namibia.[47]

Despite these commitments South Africa has with impunity continued to back both the MNR and UNITA. The latter groups control large portions of territory in Angola and Mozambique, thereby depriving SADCC of four major railways needed to transport goods to the ports of these two countries. Both UNITA and MNR have engaged in widespread sabotage of railroads, pipelines, electric pylons, and power stations, activity that has greatly disrupted the SADCC economies. SADCC member states have been further weakened by 250,000 deaths due to civil strife and the economic costs of a large refugee population created by the prolonged insurgency.[48]

South Africa has constantly harassed transport from SADCC members passing through its territory. In 1980–1981 it withdrew locomotives on loan to Zimbabwe. In 1986 it carried out an economic blockade of Lesotho that resulted in a coup in that country. The Commonwealth nations voted to impose sanctions against South Africa, which retaliated by imposing a tax on transit goods from Zambia and Zimbabwe.[49] Zambia and Zimbabwe have experienced "technical" problems in moving steel and beef through South Africa. Since Mozambique's independence in 1975, South Africa has reduced its traffic through the port of Maputo by 85 percent and has expelled 69,000 Mozambican contract laborers, thus depriving Mozambique of two major sources of foreign exchange.[50] In 1987, the puppet bantustan of Bophutatswana, under South African control, stopped train engineers from Botswana and Zambia from entering its territory unless they obtained visas. Both countries refused to comply, as they feared such visas would imply recognition of Bophutatswana.[51] South African military forces have made repeated armed attacks into the territories of all SADCC member states except Malawi and Tanzania.[52]

As a result of South African destabilization efforts, the SADCC programs have been harmed greatly. At the fifth SADCC conference in Harare, Zimbabwe, during January 1986, the organization estimated that South Africa's destabilization acts of the previous five years had cost $10 billion, in contrast with the $1.2 billion aid that SADCC had received for the support of its projects.[53] By the end of 1985, SADCC losses were running at $4 billion per annum.[54] At the

Harare conference, Botswana's vice-president, Peter Mmusi, said "We do not know how much it costs South Africa to inflict this damage on us, but we know that its abilities to carry the cost are underpinned by its economic relations with the rest of the world."[55]

Some SADCC members perceived that the South African economy must be weakened by international sanctions in order to put an end to that country's disruptive and damaging activities in Southern Africa.

THE SADCC POSITION ON SANCTIONS

In the past, SADCC members have been somewhat divided on the question of the imposition of sanctions against South Africa. Tanzania has been the most vociferous advocate of sanctions; Botswana, Lesotho, and Swaziland, the most dependent on South Africa, have been reluctant to advocate sanctions. However, in recent years the cost of South African destabilization has been so great that many formerly lukewarn states have moved to advocate sanctions.

Despite British opposition, an August 1985 meeting of the Commonwealth states in London advocated a list of voluntary sanctions. A summit meeting of nonaligned nations was held at Harare, Zimbabwe, in August 1986. The Commonwealth states (35 of the nonaligned states are Commonwealth members) were offered guest status. The meeting decided to demand full sanctions against South Africa within the United Nations. It was realized that sanctions would be ineffective without the support of Western Europe, the United States, and Japan. A team of foreign ministers from nonaligned states was selected to visit the United Kingdom, the United States, and Japan. Shridath Ramphal, secretary general for the Commonwealth, wrote letters to South Africa's leading trade partners advocating full sanctions.[56]

At the SADCC meeting in Harare of January 30, 1986, Peter Mmusi, vice-president of Botswana, eloquently expressed the thoughts of many SADCC member states: "Like a woman in labor, Southern Africa is prepared to suffer the pain resulting from economic sanctions provided they give birth to the peace and stability vital to the achievement of SADCC aims."[57]

The costs of destabilization are now so high that sanctions are a viable alternative. However, the question remains of whether the international community will back effective sanctions.

U.S.-SADCC RELATIONS

The Reagan administration's policy of constructive engagement with South Africa not only has been extremely unpopular but also has resulted in low levels of aid to SADCC states. The administration's overriding concern over the Soviet threat has caused it to withhold support from Angola and Mozambique, although both countries are necessary routes for SADCC goods to reach ports outside of South Africa. In the sub-Sahara, U.S. policy has concentrated on Kenya, Somalia, and Sudan because of the perceived Soviet threat in the Horn of Africa. For example, from 1980 to 1984, U.S. aid to Somalia exceeded bilateral aid to the nine SADCC states. The United States has refused to supply military aid to Angola and Mozambique to resist the South African-backed rebels, who have raised havoc with SADCC transport facilities. Indeed, the United States has aided the UNITA forces against the government of Angola. U.S. military aid to SADCC states from 1980 to 1984 was $24.3 million, whereas military aid to Kenya during the same period was $152.3 million.[58] Although the Soviet Union has not given appreciable economic aid to SADCC members, from 1980 to 1985 the value of its arms transfers to SADCC states was $3.475 million, of which $3.375 million went to Angola and Mozambique.[59]

In fact, the unwillingness of the United States to supply military aid needed to stop the sabotage and acts of terrorism by guerrilla movements, particularly in Mozambique, may be a greater source of discontent than the relatively low level of economic aid to SADCC. Zimbabwe also is unhappy with the lack of U.S. military aid. Military operations to protect the Beira corridor have been costly, and military expenditures in Zimbabwe's 1986–1987 budget comprise 16 percent of the total government expenditures.[60] In the case of Angola, U.S. policy has been somewhat schizophrenic, in that the income from U.S. oil companies provides 60 percent of the costs of the Angolan government at the same time that the United States backs the Angolan insurgents. Angola has been much more of a Soviet client state than Mozambique, and the presence of Cuban troops and Soviet naval forces may indeed be viewed as a threat to Western interests. However, the Mozambican government has steadfastly refused to permit Soviet bases, has abandoned many of the Marxist-Leninist economic policies it had adopted, and has made numerous overtures for a closer relationship with the United States.

Better U.S. relations with Mozambique, along with increased economic and military aid, would not only benefit the United States but also would greatly improve SADCC's possibilities of developing transport routes in that country.

The myopic concern of the Reagan administration over perceived socialist influences has resulted in picayune policies that have been damaging to relationships with SADCC states. For example, in 1984 the United States cut Zimbabwe's aid from $70 million to $40 million to punish that country for its voting record in the United Nations. Later the United States offered to fund a project to develop drought-resistant strains of millet for SADCC, but tried to exclude Tanzania, Angola, and Mozambique from the project because of their leftist leanings.[61] Zimbabwe's aid was reduced to $30 million in 1985 and to $25 million in 1986, presumably because of its pro-Soviet policies.[62]

It appears that Mozambique could, like Egypt and Somalia, break its ties to the Soviet Union. A supportive U.S. policy could well aid in that process. Certainly the United States needs to improve its relations with SADCC, for if apartheid is indeed crushed, South Africa would probably be a member of SADCC. If apartheid continues and South Africa is able to withstand the present disruptions, SADCC would offer a viable alternative source of strategic minerals, a major concern of the Reagan administration. Thus the time is now ripe for a major change in U.S. policy toward SADCC. If one uses U.S. aid as a measure, obviously SADCC does not rank very high in the present administration's priorities in Africa.

Many had hoped that the passage of the Comprehensive Anti-Apartheid Act of 1986, which imposed sanctions on South Africa, heralded such a change in U.S. policy toward Southern Africa. The act states: "The United States policy toward other countries of the Southern African region shall be designed to encourage . . . an end to cross-border terrorism and economic development." Under Section 104(B) of the act, the United States is to work toward such ends in southern Africa by

. . . (4) promoting economic development through bilateral and multilateral economic assistance targeted at increasing opportunities in the productive sectors of national economies . . . (6) encouraging, and when necessary strongly demanding that all countries of the region take effective action to end cross-border terrorism . . . (7) providing appropriate assistance, within the limitations of American responsibilities at home and in other regions, to assist regional economic cooperation and the development of interregional transportation and other facilities for economic growth.[63]

Subsequent U.S. policy provides little evidence of attempts to implement these lofty aims.

CONCLUSIONS

SADCC has developed a relatively successful program to decrease dependence on South Africa and has been extremely successful in attracting foreign aid. However, due to the shortage of bilateral and multilateral foreign aid, the SADCC states need to make strenuous efforts to attract foreign private investments. SADCC has been more successful in areas like transportation, energy, and communications than in industrial development. The SADCC structure is overly concerned with national sovereignty, which has interfered with the creation of an even and comprehensive industrial development plan for the area. SADCC successes have to a great extent been offset by drought, South African destabilization measures, and heavy military burdens. Undoubtedly the area would not have been able to survive these problems without the SADCC program. However, despite its successes SADCC has worked very hard in order to stand still.

Strong sanctions against South Africa are necessary to inhibit its policy of destabilization and to end apartheid. The international community will need to supply massive amounts of economic and military assistance to enable SADCC countries to develop and to defend themselves against both South African incursions and the South African-backed insurgents. Without such support SADCC will merely go down in history as a noble experiment.

NOTES

1. Douglas Anglin, "Economic Liberation and Regional Cooperation in Southern Africa: SADCC and PTA," *International Organization* 37 (1983): 687.

2. U.S. Department of the Interior, Bureau of Mines, *Mineral Industries of Africa* (Washington, D.C.: U.S. Government Printing Office, 1984).

3. U.S. Department of State, *A U.S. Policy Toward Africa*, Department of State Publication 9537 (Washington, D.C.: U.S. Department of State, 1987), p. 4.

4. Ibid., p. 34; *Africa Research Bulletin*, Economic Series, 22 (August 31, 1985): 7832.

5. Carol B. Thompson, "SADCC's Struggle for Economic Liberation," *Africa Report* 31 (July–August 1986): 59.

6. Margaret Novicki, "Simbrashe Makoni, Executive Secretary, Southern African Development Coordination Conference," *Africa Report* 31 (July–August 1986): 37.

7. J. Barron Boyd, Jr., "A Subsystemic Analysis of the Southern African Development Coordination Conference," *African Studies Review* 28 (1985): 50–51; Thompson, "SADCC's Struggle," p. 59–60.

8. U.S. Department of the Interior, *Mineral Industries of Africa*, pp. 18, 90, 124.

9. Wolfgang Zehender, *Cooperation Versus Integration: The Prospects of the Southern African Development Coordination Conference* (Berlin: German Development Institute, 1983), p. 25.

10. Thompson, "SADCC's Struggle," p. 61.

11. *Africa Research Bulletin*, Economic Series, 24 (February 28, 1987): 8540.

12. Thompson, "SADCC's Struggle," p. 60; Novicki, "Simbrashe Makoni," p. 36.

13. Robert E. Clute, "The Role of Agriculture in African Development," *African Studies Review* 25 (1982): 1–20.

14. Zehender, *Cooperation . . .* , p. 14.

15. "SADCC Moves to Tackle Drought," *Africa* (London) no. 135 (May 1984: 75.

16. *Africa Research Bulletin*, Economic Series, 22 (February 28, 1985): 7869.

17. Ibid.

18. *Africa Research Bulletin* 24 (February 28, 1987): 8540.

19. Zehender, *Cooperation . . .* , p. 14.

20. *Africa Research Bulletin*, Economic Series, 22 (February 28, 1985): 7589.

21. Werner Olle, "New Forms of Foreign Investment in Developing Countries," *Intereconomics*, May–June 1983, p. 196.

22. Samuel K. B. Asante, "Restructuring Transnational Mineral Agreements," *American Journal of International Law* 73 (1979): 335–371.

23. Ibid., pp. 344–45, 349; U.S. Department of the Interior, *Mineral Industries of Africa*, pp. 19, 81.

24. Novicki, "Simbrashe Makoni," p. 36.

25. *Africa Research Bulletin*, Economic Series, 22 (February 28, 1985): 8482.

26. Ibid., December 31, 1985, p. 8482.

27. Novicki, "Simbrashe Makoni," p. 37.

28. U.S. Department of State, *A U.S. Policy Toward Africa*, p. 34.

29. Anglin, "Economic Liberation," p. 706.

30. Carol B. Thompson, *Challenge to Imperialism: The Front-Line States in the Liberation of Zimbabwe* (Boulder, Colo.: Westview Press, 1985), pp. 283–289; Zehender, *Cooperation . . .* , pp. 28–35.

31. Thompson, *Challenge to Imperialism*, p. 61.

32. *Africa Research Bulletin*, Economic Series, 22 (February 28, 1987): 8539.

33. Ronald Walters, "Beyond Sanctions: A Comprehensive U.S. Policy for Southern Africa," *World Policy Journal* 4 (1986–1987): 97.

34. "SADCC Back-Slapping," *Africa Confidential* 27 (January 2, 1986): 6.

35. Novicki, "Simbrashe Makoni," p. 36.

36. Thompson, *Challenge to Imperialism*, p. 60.

37. *Africa Research Bulletin*, Economic Series, 23 (November 30, 1986): 8422.

38. Walters, "Beyond Sanctions," pp. 97–98.

39. Colleen Lowe Morna, "Doing Business in Beira," *Africa Report*, July–August 1987, pp. 61–69.

40. U.S. Department of State, *A U.S. Policy Toward South Africa*, p. 34.

41. Novicki, "Simbrashe Makoni," p. 36.

42. Anglin, "Economic Liberation," pp. 697–698.

43. *Africa Research Bulletin*, Economic Series, 24 (February 28, 1987): 8539.

44. U.S. Department of State, Bureau of Public Affairs, *Southern African Development Coordination Conference: Gist* (Washington, D.C.: The Department of State, November 1987).

45. *Africa Research Bulletin*, Economic Series, 23 (September 20, 1986): 8348.

46. U.S. Arms Control and Disarmament Agency, *World Military Expenditures and Arms Transfers 1986* (Washington, D.C.: U.S. Government Printing Office, 1987), Table 1. By the 1986–1987 budget year, Zimbabwe's military expenditures comprised 16 percent of that country's total expenditures. See Coleen L. Morna, "Preparing for War," *Africa Report*, January–February 1987, p. 56.

47. Walters, "Beyond Sanctions," p. 91; Robert M. Price, "Southern African Regional Security: Pax or Pox Pretoria?" *World Policy Journal* 2 (1985): 534–535.

48. Thompson, *Challenge to Imperialism*, p. 61.

49. Walters, "Beyond Sanctions," p. 95.

50. Ibid., pp. 95–96.

51. "Botswana: The Transport Weapon," *Africa Confidential* 28 (February 18, 1987): 7.

52. Walters, "Beyond Sanctions," p. 93.

53. *Africa Research Bulletin*, Economic Series, 23 (February 28, 1986): 8086.

54. Thompson, *Challenge to Imperialism*, p. 62.

55. *Africa Research Bulletin*, Economic Series, 23 (February 28, 1986): 8068.

56. Ibid., September 30, 1986, pp. 8348–8349.

57. Ibid., February 28, 1986, p. 8068.

58. U.S. House of Representatives, "Hearings and Markup Before the Subcommittee on Africa of the Committee on Foreign Affairs, *Foreign Assistance Legislation for Fiscal Year 1982 (Part 8)*, 97th Cong., 1st Sess. (Washington, D.C.: U.S. Government Printing Office, 1981), pp. 156–157; U.S. House of Representatives, "Hearings and Markup Before the Subcommittee on Africa of the Committee on Foreign Affairs, *Foreign Assistance Legislation for Fiscal Years 1984-85 (Part 8)*, 98th Cong., 1st Sess. (Washington, D.C.: U.S. Government Printing Office, 1984), pp. 95–96; U.S. House of Representatives, "Hearings Before the Subcommittee on Appropriations," *Foreign Assistance and Related Appropriations for 1983 (Part 4)*, 97th Cong., 1st Sess. (Washington, D.C.: U.S. Government Printing Office, 1982), pp. 187–188.

59. U.S. Arms Control and Disarmament Agency, *World Military Expenditures and Arms Transfers 1986*, Table III.

60. Coleen L. Morna, "Preparing for War," *Africa Report*, (January–February 1987): p. 56.

61. Boyd, "Subsystemic Analysis," p. 55.

62. Walters, "Beyond Sanctions,' p. 100.

63. *United States Code Congressional and Administrative News 1986*, 99th Cong., 2nd Sess., Vol. 1 (St. Paul, Minn.: West Publishing, 1987), p. 1091.

Nicaraguan Death Trip

Thomas D. Lobe

Revolutions, after the successful seizure of state power, pursue the radical transformation of society. Immediately after the revolutionary victory, each twentieth-century Marxist revolution has exuded exhilaration, idealism, boundless energy, and optimism. It is not that these people are quixotic, or have never confronted future difficulties. Take the memorable scene from the movie *The Battle of Algiers*, as Ben M'Hidi speaks to Ali: "Starting a revolution is hard, and it's even harder to continue it. Winning is hardest of all. But only afterward, when we have won, will the real hardships begin." So true. Both these brave Algerian revolutionaries were dead before the film had ended. Though the exuberant revolutionary forces gained power at the end of the film, off camera the Algerian revolution was soon compromised, if not solidly francophone.

So, too, the Soviet Union, China, Vietnam, Cuba, Angola, Mozambique, and Nicaragua: The obstacles and pitfalls that bedevil these socialist governments in their efforts to consolidate revolutionary gains and transform their societies are always more painful, more obstinate, than was ever imagined. Socialist goals are frustrated, revolutionaries' energies sapped, and radical social changes compromised and distorted. At worst, the fear develops that counterrevolutionary reactions from inside and outside the society may combine to thwart, if not destroy, the revolutionary process.

Nicaragua's experiences since the late 1970s is the latest example of this ruthless dynamic. A popular national uprising against the

Somoza dynasty and its hated security forces, the National Guard, catapulted the Sandinista National Liberation Front (FSLN) to state power. Most scholars of the Nicaraguan revolution agree that there was a hopeful expectation, an optimism, that the Sandinistas would bring Nicaragua a better, more just society. The purpose of this chapter is to describe the dynamic that so quickly leads from national exhilaration to bitterness and despair. For one tragic result of the Nicaraguan Revolution is the death and destruction of the best and brightest of this poor country. The death is physical, spiritual, and metaphorical. The war, the terror, the assassinations, the battles have been as vicious as any other revolution–counterrevolution conflicts; and the destruction of the economy, the social reforms, the promises have led to a loss of morale, a spiritual morass, and thus to cynicism, corruption, and expatriation.

Three factors combine to frustrate revolutionary goals: poverty, cultural imperialism, and U.S. intervention. Each interacts with the others and compounds their difficulties. This leads to deepening dilemmas for the Sandinista party and Nicaraguan state, and evolves toward the Nicaraguan death trip.

Nicaragua is a predominantly poor, peasant country. The nature of a socialist revolution in the midst of poverty creates enormous problems. The economic and technical infrastructure lacks strength and coherence; the social and economic tasks are insurmountable in the face of illiteracy, poor public health, and a tradition of minimal political participation. In short, the basic requisites for national growth, as well as for fulfilling some of the egalitarian, social justice goals of the revolution, are lacking in this weak and vulnerable society. The Somoza dynasty had never shown concern for these issues and was generally hostile to spreading the wealth much further than family members' pockets. The 1972 Managua earthquake and the 1978–1979 uprising had further weakened and bloodied the economy and the national infrastructure.

The FSLN, a vanguard party, had not, by 1978, developed into a mass-based party. The Sandinista cadre was committed and talented, but few in numbers. Most Sandinistas were rugged revolutionaries, having fought in distant jungles or languished in dank prisons. They did not have the technical resources (human or physical) to keep Nicaragua running efficiently, much less transform it into a socialist society. Yet this is the issue, for the Sandinistas were intent on delivering social programs to the vast majority of Nicaraguans who had previously been disenfranchised, ignored, and exploited: medical care to peasants who had never been examined by a physician; literacy to those who had never been inside a school; all-weather roads and titled lands to rural people who had previously been cut off from the national economy; and decent housing and support services to poor urban dwellers who had known only shacks, or worse. In order to fulfill its ambitious socioeconomic goals, the revolutionary government required many more doctors, nurses, teachers, engineers, construction workers, accountants, and other technical personnel. Also urgently required were all kinds of material aid: more buses, medical supplies and equipment, construction materials, seeds, and spare parts for everything. These needs were more serious and vulnerable because of past dependence on U.S. goods; the Somoza government had linked its economy to the United States. Simply to maintain equipment acquired during the Somoza era, to keep trucks and buses on the roads, and to keep the X-ray machines operating in the hospitals, the revolutionary government had to obtain U.S.-made spare parts.

Several strategies were developed by the Nicaraguan government to cope with these difficulties. Human resources and expertise were gained both through mass popular mobilization measures and through the importation of friendly foreign experts. Literacy and health-care mobilization programs were organized and had an immediate positive impact on many Nicaraguans. Many technical position needs, from physicians to economic planners, were staffed by Spanish-speaking experts from countries all over the world: Cuba sent the largest contingent of doctors, military technicians, bureaucrats, teachers, and construction workers. Thousands of professionals from the United States, Europe, and Latin America traveled to resource-poor Nicaragua to work in essential social sectors, devoting months, if not years, to their tasks.

Nicaragua's vulnerable economy was battered by three factors emanating from the world capitalist system. First, the socialist program frightened away capitalist investment. As in all postrevolutionary situations, suspicious foreign investors and nervous multinational corporations and banks took flight to economies more friendly to capitalist, profitable investment. Second, U.S. hostility toward the Nicaraguan government was translated into economic terms from early 1981 on. The U.S. goal has been the isolation and economic strangulation of the Nicaraguan government. U.S. bilateral economic assistance was cut off, and the U.S. government successfully vetoed most World Bank and International Monetary Fund grants and loans to the Nicaraguans. Since 1985 the U.S. trade embargo against Nicaragua has made it difficult, if not impossible, for potential investors, for normal U.S. trade relations with Nicaragua, and, most damaging for the Nicaraguans, for importation of essential spare parts. In addition, the U.S. government pressured other countries to cease all bilateral and multilateral aid, loans, and trade with the Nicaraguans. Third, two of Nicaragua's most profitable export crops, cotton and sugar, plummeted in value. Nicaragua's dependent economy was dramatized by the collapse of these two commodity markets and the consequent losses in export earnings.

If poverty structures the objective conditions under which the Nicaraguan revolution must operate, cultural imperialism creates a sociopsychological framework. Even before the U.S. Marines occupied Nicaragua in 1912–1925 and 1926–1933, and helped shape its values and expectations, much of Nicaragua had looked north for leadership, economic support, and cultural sustenance. Decades of U.S. cultural penetration, whether education, entertainment, advertising, architecture, or religion, is part of the texture of Nicaraguan life. The road between the United States and Nicaragua is well traveled: almost everyone in Nicaragua has a relative in the United States. The rich and the middle class send their children to U.S. universities; every boy, irrespective of class, dreams of playing major league baseball; and every household with a television watches endless hours of "Dallas," "Wide World of Sports," and "Knight Rider." The good life, whether influenced by the values of "Miami Vice," "Bonanza," or "Davy Crockett," includes the desire for private property and material wealth, as well as a prideful, rugged individualism.

None of this makes it impossible for the revolutionary vanguard to transform Nicaraguan society. But propagating self-confidence and self-sacrificing notions to the masses, educating children in the history of the Nicaraguan revolution, and developing a national and socialist consciousness conflicts with past generations of ideological conditioning. Attitudinal dependence runs deeper than economic dependence.

The most immediate impact after the revolution was the flight north of the rich and the skilled. As the Sandinistas began restructuring Nicaraguan society, many wealthy landowners and professionals with skills that were easily converted into jobs trekked to the land of infinite promise. Doctors, engineers, accountants, dentists, and professors emigrated in search of societies that allowed them their immodest wealth. Essential human and technical personnel were lost. Poor Nicaragua was suddenly depleted of a vital resource, and was poorer for it. Over 90 percent of all Nicaraguan doctors have left the country, making the government's promise of delivering medical care to all citizens difficult. High-status professors left in droves, leaving the universities with junior faculty, instructors, and visiting foreign teachers. The same situation developed in other professions. As mentioned above, foreign advisers and professionals filled some of the gaps left by the fleeing upper class. But this highlights the immediate shortages Nicaragua faced in accomplishing its fundamental social tasks.

Just as ominous, if not worse, was the attitude of those professionals who stayed behind. Their motives for remaining in Nicaragua were all too often that they did not have skills that would be of value abroad, or that they were afraid or too lazy to leave. They represented midlevel bureaucrats, small business people, and landowners who neither were able to sell out nor had liquid assets. Such Nicaraguans felt trapped, were uncommitted to the new government, and harkened back to better times. As severe shortages of U.S.-made games, foods, cars, and hard currency developed, the very guts and meaning to their lives emptied.

A dreadful pact was signed between the government and the professionals who stayed behind: The Sandinistas needed what technical skills they had, and placed them in the burgeoning social service bureaucracies. But their work habits and attitudes were lackluster. Petty corruption and short work hours permeated the social hierarchies. "Serving the people" was a notion foreign to their past experience, and they were not about to begin in the 1980s. Though they lived in a revolutionary society, their hearts and brains, as well as their stomachs, remained in the more comfortable past. These people were indispensable, at least in the short term, but they were untrustworthy, were uninvolved in their work, and communicated counterrevolutionary attitudes to colleagues and subordinates.

Moreover, both these older professionals and more recently educated skilled Nicaraguans shared an aversion to working in the hinterland. Modern professionals find greater material rewards and a more pleasant social life in the cities. Yet the poor reside in isolated rural outposts and crowded urban shantytowns. The Sandinista platform was committed to delivering social services, land reform programs, and infrastructural development to that lower-class sector. But few were willing to accomplish these tasks. Only the most idealistic and self-sacrificing were willing to serve the poor and the peasants.

This is not the first time a revolutionary regime has faced this dilemma: China, the Soviet Union, the East European governments, and Cuba each had relatively few individuals who were both committed revolutionaries and talented professionals able to accomplish complex state-building tasks. But in Nicaragua the poverty is more entrenched, the needs greater, and the lack of professional competence more absolute. Other revolutionary governments have educated, trained, and propagandized the mass line. This transformation process may take generations, but the long-term goal is to broaden the cadre base so that larger numbers of committed and trustworthy citizens contribute to the process. At the same time, more schools and universities are opened and competent young people from all classes are encouraged to develop their talents. In other words, future generations should be prepared to serve the people by being both "red and expert."

That is the long-term strategy of the Sandinista government. State schools and the state-owned media attempt to propagate Sandinista values; mobilizations are organized with the goal of integrating the youth into the revolutionary process. Medical school enrollment has multiplied; business schools and schools of public administration and education have opened and expanded; and students are sent all over the world on government scholarships to gain professional competence. On their return, the government hopes these newly educated people will enthusiastically work with the poor. But early evidence suggests a mixed record.

Many young people, both in the university and in recently gained professional positions, are ambitious, self-serving, and materialistic. Too many are cynical about revolutionary values and goals. Making money and gaining status are more important reasons for professional training than serving the revolution. Similarly, joining the FSLN, the militia, or a mass organization may be a career move rather than an ideological commitment. Often their attitudes toward subordinates and the lower classes are authoritarian and paternalistic. Accusations of corruption and nepotism are increasingly heard. For many a major activity is to figure out how to make money out of the revolution.

Many young people are making modest fortunes. Speculation, private trading, and black marketeering have become dominant forms of economic intercourse. Many talented people see an opportunity to exploit Nicaragua's vast needs by developing a network of middle-man contacts and technicians for sale. If the government exerts excessive pressure against such pecuniary activity, the expatriation option can be taken.

Lurking in the background is the United States and the possible pleasures of living in Miami or Los Angeles. The lure is primarily negative: a dislike of the Sandinistas' politics, of the military draft, or the lack of economic and social opportunities previously available to upper- and middle-class Nicaraguans. Perhaps they have grown tired of the dimmed lights of Managua, of long lines, and of scarcities of consumer goods. The model, the standard, is the United States. As long as Nicaraguans can have U.S. culture inside Nicaragua, whether it be fast-food restaurants or fashionable clothes, all is well. But the scarcer U.S. consumables are, the greater the longing for the tastes and the textures that are made in the United States.

Nothing makes this clearer than the number of people studying English. University night courses, high schools, and private classes are offering programs in the English language. When asked why they are taking English, middle-class students and adults usually answer that it is to keep open the option of expatriation to the United States. A fascination with, if not a love for, the United States continues among this element of the population. Unless the Sandinistas reverse their revolutionary program and give the middle and upper classes more usable wealth, the exodus from Nicaragua will continue.

Since 1985, as the economy has worsened, the lower classes have taken on some of these attitudes. This is, perhaps, most disheartening to the Sandinista leadership: to see rural peasants leave the countryside in pursuit of a better life in the cities; to see poor urban dwellers sell goods at exploitively high prices at the Eastern Market; to see co-operative and state farm dwellers sell their goods to middle-man traders at high prices, rather than to the state at set prices. These are painful blows to a government intent on developing a new consciousness. Yet profit-making attitudes pervade the society. Cynicism has led to profiteering and selfishness.

Further, these "popular classes" have fewer options than those with money. Without salable skills or convertible wealth, they cannot easily leave the country. For many, the United States is their model, but there is no clearly marked road to Miami. Yet bitterness, exhaustion, and economic deprivation can lead to disenchantment and opposition. The road to Tegucigalpa is short, and the payoff is immediate.

U.S. intervention and sponsorship of the Contra attacks against Nicaragua form the third dramatic factor that further impoverishes Nicaraguan society and exacerbates the human resource dilemma. As the conflict has escalated, so have Nicaragua's defense budget and manpower needs. By 1985 over 50 percent of the overall budget went to defense, compared with 16 percent in 1982. Also in 1985, the government was forced to reassess its priorities: survival issues were to take precedence over economic development and consolidation of the revolution. If the Contras were not defeated, if the Nicaraguan people were not secure from Contra attack, then the government would not have the opportunity to implement its socioeconomic program. Hence, a portion of the budgetary and manpower resources that were formerly planned for health, education, housing, and infrastructural development were diverted to defense and survival. This, in turn, lowered social service delivery and economic performance.

It also drew the most qualified and most talented young people into the military campaign. The needs of any military force are insatiable, but in Nicaragua these imperatives target the very people who perform well in schools and universities. Techniques of mass organization, personnel management, handling complex weaponry, and map reading are some of the skills essential to modern warfare. Students with intelligence and skill are drafted or recruited into the Nicaraguan military. A small core of idealistic, committed, and self-sacrificing youth volunteer for the armed forces and the militia. Military training and indoctrination increase this propensity. This has resulted in a talented and disciplined Nicaraguan armed force. But recruiting idealistic Nicaraguans into the military has drained some of the most energetic and loyal Nicaraguans from other social sectors.

Other Nicaraguans serve in defense-related fields. Many spend time in the militia, while some work during the coffee and cotton harvests, either standing guard or picking the crop. Whether they are part of the militia or part of the mobilization to harvest an export crop, their danger is a surprise Contra attack. Though these tasks necessitate fewer technical skills, only committed youth volunteer for this work. Often they must spend months in the rural danger zones, sacrificing their time and ambitions, away from their families and their work, for the defense of their country and the revolution.

But it is not just that priorities have been forced to shift tragically toward survival and defense; nor is it that the most talented and motivated youth are funneled into military functions. It is that they are the first victims of the war. As a result of their loyalty, they are dying for their country. They die in firefights with the Contras, or explode into pieces when their truck trips a land mine, or are mortally wounded by shrapnel while defending a cooperative or coffee harvest. The Nicaraguan revolution is being bled; and, as in other things, the best, the most praiseworthy, die first.

Many Nicaraguans have volunteered for, or have been recruited by, the Contras. Reasons for joining the Contra guerrilla force vary, but most scholars agree that the Contras depend on U.S. support for their existence. Without U.S. intervention there would be neither salaries for the Contras nor logistical and technical training and equipment. The Contras also gain some pride in working for and with U.S. government advisers. The cultural links between the imperial United States and dependent Nicaragua are vividly drawn along the Honduras-Nicaragua border. Nicaraguans whose motive for joining the Contras stem from a religious anti-Communism interact with U.S.-based religious right-wing relief organizations. Former members of the National Guard, their relatives, and their friends congregate around U.S. military advisers, swapping stories and arguing about weapons. There are also those drawn to the border for the money: their links with small-time U.S. traders, hustlers, and speculators is the stuff of dreams.

The Contras also have suffered a deadly casualty rate. Many brave and idealistic young people have sacrificed their lives in this civil conflict. They were persuaded that the Sandinista government was illegitimate.

Nicaragua's poverty was one pole of Contra consciousness. The perceived record of economic failures, mismanagement, and broken promises was a backdrop for personal disappointment and bitterness. Cultural imperialism and penetration was the positive pole. The Sandinistas' version of history conflicted with the historical memory of many Nicaraguans; revolutionary values and undertakings contradicted those of the capitalist, materialist, and wealthy United States. The Sandinista government, in attempting to transmit new attitudes and social forms to Nicaraguan society, was forced to the defensive. Nicaraguans who perceive that their government is antagonistic to their church, to political pluralism, and to private property look to the United States for sustenance and support. The third ingredient, U.S. active intervention, has been the yeast for the other poles of consciousness. For without the cutoff of U.S. aid, the trade embargo, and the determined sponsorship of the Contras, the economy would not have crumbled so totally. Without the long history of institutional, attitudinal, and personal connections between the two countries firmly established, the opportunity to oppose the Sandinista government would not have arisen. Without the emphatic, undisguised hostility of the U.S. government, disgruntled Nicaraguans who looked to the United States for guidance would have had less choice about the nature of their opposition.

This is not to suggest that there are no committed and talented revolutionary Nicaraguans. Many students, poor peasants, and workers, and especially women from the barrios, have risen to the vast challenges. Leadership and expertise have been drawn from new sectors of the population that are loyal to the Sandinista party and the legitimacy of the Nicaraguan government. But the sense of national exhaustion and disillusionment runs deep. The gaps in talent and commitment in the party, state, and professional bureaucracy are serious. Whether the Nicaraguans can disentangle themselves from this downward spiral remains to be seen.

15

The Third World Debt Crisis and U.S. Policy

Sheikh R. Ali

Third World nations are of great importance to the United States. Developing countries occupy more than half of the world's surface and embrace 75 percent of its population. They contain vast material and human resources, and are of great consequence to the U.S. economy as suppliers and markets.

One-third of U.S. manufactured exports go to the Third World, which also takes about 40 percent of U.S. agricultural exports. A high percentage of U.S. oil imports comes from the Third World, as does the bulk of certain industrial raw materials. For example, about two-thirds of U.S. bauxite imports comes from Jamaica and Guinea. Nearly two-thirds of the U.S. requirement of tin is imported from Thailand, Malaysia, Indonesia, and Bolivia.

The strategic locations of many developing countries invest them with special military and geopolitical significance to the United States. Some, like South Korea, Pakistan, Thailand, and the Philippines, are close allies; others provide access to important military facilities; still others deny the Soviets such facilities.

Beyond this, the countries of the Third World collectively represent an important political force. Over time, they have given various organizational expressions to their shared perspectives and aims. The Nonaligned Movement (NAM) was formally organized at the Belgrade summit convoked by Marshal Tito in 1961. But the roots of Third World efforts to define foreign policies independent of the superpowers can be traced back even further—to the Bandung Conference of 1955. The leaders of the movement at that point were primarily Asians—among them Nehru, U Nu, Sukarno, and Chou En-lai.

In the 1960s the newly independent countries of Africa sought strength in numbers and found common cause in efforts to protect their independence and promote development. Their influence was registered in the brief appearance of the Afro-Asian Peoples Solidarity Organization and, more permanently, in the expansion and growing voice of the NAM.

As attention shifted from the protection of sovereignty to economic development, the Latin American countries—most of which had attained independence in the nineteenth century—found they shared many common aims and common afflictions with the Asians and Africans. Indeed, the Latin Americans asserted a strong lead in the first United Nations Conference on Trade and Development at Geneva in 1964. The Group of 77 (G-77)—which increased its numbers but kept the acronym—became the principal lobbying organization through which developing countries pressed for radical adjustments of the international economic system.

In the 1970s certain Arab states—particularly those with oil—found their place in the forefront of the NAM and G-77. The success of the Organization of Petroleum Exporting Countries as a supplier-cartel, able to manipulate supplies and administer prices, fueled a growing sense of power among all developing countries. A number of them—Algeria, in particular, comes to mind—took the lead in pressing for a new international economic order. They sought an order based on the premise that the structural economic problems of developing countries were the responsibility of the developed world and that the latter countries had an obligation to redistribute global wealth and economic power as compensation for past transgressions.

By the mid-1980s, a changing international economy and the success of some developing countries with market-oriented economic development had taken much of the steam out of efforts to legislate a new international economic order. The NAM maintained ritual support for far-reaching structural economic reforms, but attention returned strongly to political issues.

Economically, the differentiation of Third World nations is well advanced. Nor do they speak with a single voice politically, Yet, to enhance their collective influence in the international forum, they have coordinated closely, through the NAM, on many politico-economic issues.

PRINCIPLES OF U.S. POLICY

Let us turn to some of the principles that inform U.S. policy toward the Third World, peoples and nations so heterogeneous and so diverse in their claims on U.S. interest that there can be no simple U.S. policy. However, the United States approaches the Third World with a number of general policy guidelines in mind.

The United States attaches high importance to the economic development of the Third World. This is a matter of self-interest but also reflects the U.S. sense of responsibility for helping to create a stable global environment in which all share a stake.

Before World War II, investment in developing countries accounted for about two-thirds of total foreign investment. If we could return to that ratio, there would have been $18 billion of new money flowing into developing countries in 1985 from the United States alone. What a tremendous difference that would have made! The money is there, but it must be attracted.

There is no doubt that the funds for capital investment are there. The value of U.S. assets overseas is now over $1.1 trillion, compared with some $350 billion in the late 1970s.[1] In 1986, U.S. individuals and corporations invested $28 billion overseas. Unfortunately, only about 5 percent of that ($1.4 billion) went to developing countries.

The United States has been the leading source of financial and technical assistance to developing nations since the introduction of the Marshall Plan after World War II. The United States sponsored most of the interational financial institutions that have assumed a growing share of the burden for financing development.

The U.S. capital market has been fully open to borrowers from developing countries. By 1984, U.S. commercial lending institutions had lent some $140 billion to Third World countries.[2] Equity investment in the Third World exceeded $50 billion, roughly a quarter of U.S. total overseas investment.[3] U.S. transnational corporations have taken the lead in fostering the global diffusion of industrial know-how, technology transfer, and capital movement.

The sustained growth of the U.S. economy and the open access it affords others to U.S. markets are perhaps the major contributions of the United States to the growth of developing countries. Policy lines in so vast a field are difficult to summarize, but we proceed on the basic premise that, for Third World countries as well as for others, the path to sustained growth lies in the efficiency of free and open markets, encouragement of entrepreneurial activity in the private sector, and the full use of opportunities available for mutually beneficial economic transactions in international trading and financial systems.

Despite severe budgetary constraints arising out of the national deficit, the United States continues to lead the world in bilateral economic assistance and in its support for multilateral development banks and other financial institutions. The Reagan administration increased U.S. development assistance from $6.5 billion to $8.8 billion a year—a level well above that of other industrial nations and about four times that provided by the Soviet Union.[4] Contrary to popular misconception, the bulk of U.S. bilateral aid is not military assistance but economic aid. The United States has been the principal source of financial relief to those struggling with debt problems. The Americans have repeatedly taken the lead in organizing relief efforts in response to natural calamities such as the African drought, the El Salvador earthquake, and the Bangladesh flood.

The developing countries understandably want trade more than aid—an opportunity rather than a handout. Such an attitude serves U.S. interests as well and explains why the Americans have kept their markets more open to Third World exports than has any other industrial nation. The objective must be further to reduce the impediments to free and fair trade—particularly by removing nontariff barriers to trade.

THIRD WORLD DEBT CRISIS

Foreign debt levels in the developing countries have grown enormously in the past. More than two dozen nations have faced problems in servicing their foreign debt since the debt crisis erupted in 1982 in Mexico.[5] Mexico owes some $108 billion; Brazil has $110 billion of outstanding debt. They are not alone, however. Argentina owes $52 billion; Egypt, $44 billion; Venezuela, $34 billion; the Philippines, $34 billion; and Nigeria, $23 billion. About 34 percent of the more than $1 trillion total is owed by Latin American countries and 22 percent by African countries.[6]

By its very nature, the debt crisis underscores the interdependent character of the global financial system. When debtors cannot pay, creditors also suffer. The United States is by far the largest single creditor to the Third World. U.S. commercial banks have some $123 billion in outstanding debt of developing countries. The U.S. government is also a sizable lender to developing countries, with the Export-Import Bank holding about \$12 billion of this debt.[7]

European and Japanese banks also have stake in this complex network. They now account for about 70 percent of total commercial bank loans to the Third World. The World Bank and other development banks, in contrast, have loaned less than 5 percent of the \$1 trillion total.

These high foreign debt levels would not be a problem were it not for the fact that the economies of many Third World countries are simply not growing fast enough for them to meet the interest payments, much less to reduce the principal. The interest payments alone amount to something over \$90 billion a year. Unsound economic policies, inefficiency, and corruption have constrained growth, and rising interest rates and falling commodity prices have compounded the problem.

THE BAKER PLAN

In 1985, U.S. Secretary of the Treasury James Baker presented his program for sustained growth. It recognized that the only way the borrowers would ever work their way out of the problem was to re-establish growth in their economies; to do that, they must establish sound economic policies, including balanced government budgets and a larger role for market forces and private enterprise.[8]

There were other features of Baker's plan that were helpful then and remain valid today. The World Bank commented on the Baker plan: "The analysis underlying the Baker initiative of September 1985 remains valid."[9] However, as yet there is no such consensus for action with regard to the problems faced by the debtors. The Baker plan recognized that developing countries are different from one another. Some nations already have good policies and mainly need financing to get through a rough patch. Chile falls into that category. Others are moving in the right direction but may need a little push and some understanding. Turkey might be an example. Countries like Argentina need extensive policy reform and the financing for it, and will be serious problems for a long time. Mexico and Brazil have large debts, as well as great growth potential over the longer term and with the right policies. Finally, there are the very poorest countries that need special attention from their foreign creditors. Recognizing these differences, the Baker plan proposed a case-by-case approach, understanding that any kind of generalized plan would not be wise.

The Baker initiative also recognized that any plan for compulsory cancellation or forgiveness of debt would be disastrous. It would discourage the bankers from ever lending again, and it would show the borrowers that there was no penalty for continued unsound and ineffective economic policies. The Baker plan also insisted that there be no government bailouts. This is essentially not a government problem. It is a private sector problem. To bail out the borrowers or the lenders would not be economically desirable or politically feasible.

Finally, the Baker initiative called for a substantial infusion of new money to help facilitate growth-oriented economic reforms. It called for continued lending by the International Monetary Fund (IMF), and this has taken place. Just as important, it gave the IMF a key coordinating role. The Baker plan also proposed an increased lending role for the World Bank. This has also begun to take place. Last, it urged increased lending by the commercial bankers.

Although commercial banks have been cooperative and responsive, new bank lending cannot really be expected to go very much higher. This is understandable and not surprising. The banks were badly burned by the near defaults. They had overloaned to a group of poor creditors, and their eyes were on how to get their money back, not on how to lend more. We do not see that attitude changing very much, at least not until real economic prosperity comes to the developing world.

CAPITAL INVESTMENT

Growth is necessary if debtor countries are to overcome their debt crisis, and in order to grow, these countries need money. Loans from governments and private sector banks provide much of this money now. But another element is needed to supplement these loans and really stimulate growth.

That element is capital investment. The Third World debtors need to begin to look at capital investment—whether from external or internal sources. To be successful, they will have to find ways to make it easier for those with capital to invest in their countries. They also must give investors a fair chance of realizing gains and, in the case of foreign investors, repatriating their profits. And they must develop economic policies that will free markets to grow and make profits more likely.

To restore growth, the developing countries must attract capital, not just seek more loans, because loan capital is not going to be enough. They must seek capital investment from individuals and from corporations, and they must seek it from within their own countries and from outside.

Capital investment has a very important advantage to the recipients: they do not have to pay interest on it, and they do not have to pay it back. It earns a return if the project is successful. Capital investment is attractive to the recipient for another reason; it keeps debt from growing ever higher. We must remember that it was too much borrowing, coupled with too little productive investment, that caused the debt problem in the first place. An overreliance on borrowing, for a country as well as for a business, is risky and could merely worsen the problem. Capital investment serves the dual purpose of reducing the need for loans and, under the right conditions, channeling funds into productive uses.

A particular advantage of foreign investment is that it brings not only money but other important inputs as well. Foreign investment often involves the transfer of new technology not available locally. The investing company may bring management and marketing skills, technical expertise, and trained manpower, all of which improve the efficiency of domestic enterprises and enable them to compete more aggressively in the world market. These benefits can sometimes be more important to a developing country's economy than the money itself.

FLIGHT CAPITAL

Unfortunately, in recent years many of the developing countries have been the victims of capital disinvestment, more commonly known as flight capital. Investors in these countries became panicky and began to pull their capital out. Indeed, as fast as funds came in the front door from new borrowings, capital flew out the back door, and the debt burden grew as the capital base shrank. This flight capital may represent the largest pool of money available to debtor countries, totaling between $80 and $100 billion.[10] If the capital were to return in the form of new productive investment, developing economies would boom and the debt problem in many countries could disappear.

Mexico provides an instructive example of this reflow of capital. From 1983 to 1985, nearly $14 billion more flowed out of Mexico than flowed in. But starting in 1986, as a result of a creative refinancing package, the beginnings of sound economic policies, and the easing of rules on foreign ownership limits and dividend remittances, flight capital has flooded back into Mexico, fueling a stock market boom and a foreign reserve surplus in a country considered a major problem just a year or two ago.

The debtor countries should take a hard look at the economic history of some of the Pacific Basin countries. In 1955, South Korea was one of the poorest countries in Asia, with a per capita income of $110. In 1986, 31 years later, its per capita income, in nominal terms, had grown more than 20 times, to over $2,300. Its Communist neighbor, North Korea, saw its per capita income only double during the same period.

How did Korea do it? It generated a high level of internal saving and investment, and through market-oriented policies put these funds to productive use. These are the kinds of policies that would attract foreign investment. The Korean people were encouraged—indeed, required—to save and to invest their savings in their economy. Koreans now save and invest about 30 percent of their gross domestic product (GDP).

Singapore is another example of a country that has sustained a rapid pace of economic growth through high levels of capital investment. It benefited not only from an extraordinarily high rate of domestic savings—over 40 percent of GDP—but also from large foreign investment flows. By 1986, foreign investors had poured more than $11 billion into Singapore's economy. As a result, foreign borrowing accounts for only 20 percent of Singapore's external liabilities, compared with as much as 90 percent in such developing countries as Brazil, Mexico, and Argentina. Had these countries been able to obtain the same levels of foreign investment, they would not be experiencing the financial difficulties they face today. The lesson is that favorable debt-equity ratios are just as important for countries as they are for business enterprises.

Other Asian nations have benefited from large foreign investment flows. Malaysia, which has a foreign debt of $27 billion, has received

$8 billion in investment flows. Hong Kong has $5 billion in foreign investment and only $8 billion in foreign debt. Also noteworthy is the fact that Singapore and Hong Kong, as well as Taiwan, are now receiving large inflows of foreign portfolio investment through their stock markets because of attractive returns on equity. The potential for increased financial flows is there, but developing countries must seek out these funds aggressively.

Most of the external investment flow from the United States is now going to Europe and Japan. It is an unfortunate fact that in most parts of the developing world, foreign direct investment has declined in recent years and, in many countries, foreign portfolio investment is nonexistent.

HOW TO ATTRACT INVESTMENT

What should governments in developing countries do to stimulate saving and investment? The prescriptions are widely known. Countries with high levels of saving and investment generally maintain sound market-oriented economic policies. Market forces, not government regulation or planning, have the greatest influence over production, prices, and wages. Successful countries do not let government spending get out of hand. Successful countries control inflation. They avoid controls on interest rates and lending, and encourage private commercial banking. They have supported the development of securities markets and the diversification of investment instruments. As a general rule, they try to ensure that government intervention in the economy does not present unreasonable barriers to productive investment. Countries with high levels of foreign investment have been careful to address the particular concerns of foreign investors. They have clear policies of welcoming foreign investors and protecting their rights. These are the kinds of issues to which debtor countries need to pay more attention if they are to stimulate domestic and foreign equity in a developing-country enterprise. The debtor country benefits by a reduction in its foreign debt. The foreign investor gains by receiving a premium when the loan is exchanged for local currency. And the bank receives at least partial compensation for a loan whose full repayment was questionable.

Chile has already authorized conversion of $2 billion, about 14 percent of its foreign bank debt, into domestic equity. Argentina,

Mexico, and Brazil are starting to use swaps to reduce their foreign debt. Debt-equity swaps are likely to lead not only to increased foreign investment but to domestic saving as well. Establishing a debt-equity swap program forces the government to examine carefully the overall regulatory framework for investment that all investors find attractive.

U.S. COMMITMENT

U.S. commitment to market forces as the key to economic development has found increasing resonance in the Third World. Nothing invigorates the global economic system today more than the economic recovery that has been under way in the United States since the early 1980s. Success invites emulation. Many Third World countries are abandoning the economic dogmas of the immediate postcolonial period. There is a growing recognition of the connection between individual initiative and economic progress—a growing realization that the talents of individual human beings are the greatest resource a society can bring to the task of national development.

At the U.N. Special Session on the Critical Economic Situation in Africa, held in May 1986, the African nations—including those hardest hit by collectivist planning—issued an extraordinary document calling for more open markets and less intervention by the state. This was a concerted position that they brought with them to the United Nations after deliberations in their regional body, the Organization of African Unity. It seems that U.S. ideas are taking hold. Thus, there are very important opportunities.

It is ironic that at a time when global trends favor the United States and it has opportunities to pursue more constructive relations with Third World countries, pressures are mounting within the United States to turn its back on the world. U.S. national budget cuts severely impair the ability to protect important U.S. interests in Africa, Asia, Central and South America, and the Caribbean. The budget cuts also have affected U.S. funding for the multilateral development banks, which are crucial to Third World economic recovery and growth. They also have reduced U.S. leverage for real reform in the budget and administration of the United Nations. They would result in the closing of some diplomatic posts and the reduction of U.S. official personnel abroad.

CONCLUSIONS

The debt crisis affects many developing countries. The two hardest-hit areas are sub-Saharan Africa and Latin America, but some Middle Eastern, North African, Caribbean, and Far Eastern countries also suffer: "In Africa, bad policies and inadequate institutional structures have compounded the extraordinarily difficult natural and historical circumstances of many countries."[11] By contrast, most Asian countries have avoided serious debt problems by not overborrowing and by promoting export-led growth so that they can afford to service their debts.

Looking back over the period since 1981, both borrowers and lenders can point with some pride to substantial progress on the debt problem. At a time of crisis in 1982, Western governments, commercial banks, international financial institutions, and debtors pulled together to prevent major disorder in the international financial system. Since then, all interested parties have come to recognize that the core of the problem is the need to return to the fundamentals of sound, market-based economic policies. As the Baker plan stressed, growth must continue to be the central thrust of our approach to the debt problem. Sustainable, rapid economic growth cannot be adequately financed without increased levels of private-sector capital flows. Investment funds must supplement loan capital in developing countries to a far greater extent than has occurred so far.

If the United States cannot work out a viable solution to the debt difficulties, the situation may grow worse and multiply conflicts between the debtor nations and the United States in the future. Debtor country default may cause great damage to the framework of international finance and the global economy, potentially as serious in its consequences as the banking failures of the 1930s.

NOTES

1. U.S. Department of State, *Third World Dilemma: More Debt or More Equity* (Washington, D.C.: Bureau of Public Affairs, U.S. Department of State, 1987).

2. Ibid.

3. Ibid.

4. Ibid.

5. Richard S. Weinert, "Swapping Third World Debt," *Foreign Policy* 65 (1986–1987): 85–97; Wayne Curtis, "Here Comes the Repo Man," *The Nation*, May 2, 1987.

6. U.S. Department of State, *Third World Dilemma*.

7. Ibid.

8. Ibid.

9. World Bank, *World Debt Tables: External Debt of Developing Countries* (Washington, D.C.: World Bank, 1988), p. ix.

10. U.S. Department of State, *Third World Dilemma*.

11. World Bank, *World Debt Tables*.

Selected Bibliography

Abba, Alkasum, et al. *The Nigerian Economic Crisis: Causes and Solutions.* Lagos: Academic Staff Union of Universities of Nigeria, 1985.

Abbas, Alnasrawi. "OPEC: The Cartel That Is Not." *OPEC Bulletin* (Vienna) 12 (1981).

Abbott, Freeland. *Islam and Pakistan.* Ithaca, N.Y.: Cornell University Press, 1966.

Abdulghani, Jasim M. *Iraq and Iran: The Years of Crisis.* London: Croom Helm, 1984.

Abdullalri, T. A. "Comments on Press Briefing by Minister of Agriculture." *New Nigerian*, February 18, 1985, p. 2.

Abir, Mordechai. *Oil, Power and Politics: Conflict in Arabia, the Red Sea and the Gulf.* London: Frank Cass, 1974.

Adnan, Al-Janabi. "Why OPEC Is Not to Blame." *OPEC Bulletin* (Vienna) 11, no. 14 (1980).

Africa Research Bulletin, economic series, 1985–1987.

African Guardian, January 29, 1987.

Alexander, Yonah, and Allan Nanes, eds. *The United States and Iran: A Documentary History*. Frederick, Md.: University Publications of America, 1980.

Anglin, Douglas. "Economic Liberation and Regional Cooperation in Southern Africa: SADCC and PTA." *International Organization* 37 (1983).

Anti-Communist Act. Law no. 643 (July 3, 1961). Superseded by Law no. 3318 (1980). For an English translation, see *Laws of the Republic of Korea.* 3rd ed. Seoul: Korean Legal Center, 1975.

Ariyo, Joseph A. "National Development Planning and Regional Policy: The Nigerian Case." Ph.D. dissertation. School of Urban and Regional Planning, University of Waterloo (Ontario), 1983.

Asante, Samuel K. B. "Restructuring Transnational Mineral Agreements." *American Journal of International Law* 73 (1979): 335-371.

Ayoub, Mahmoud M. *The Great Tidings.* Tripoli, Libya: Islamic Call Society, 1983.

Banks, Arthur S. *Cross-Polity Time Series Data.* Cambridge, Mass: MIT Press, 1971.

Banpasirichote, C. "Indigenous Knowledge and Development Theory." *New Asian Vision* 3, no. 2 (1986): 38-59.

Batscha, Robert M. *Foreign Affairs News and Broadcast Journalist.* New York: Praeger, 1975.

Bergstresser, Heinrich. "Nigeria: Agro-business—Eine Lösung der Krise?" *Afrika Spectrum* 2 (1986).

Binder, Leonard. *Religion and Politics in Pakistan.* Berkeley: University of California Press, 1963.

A Biography of Martyr Ayatollah Behesthi. Tehran: Council for the Celebration of the 3rd Anniversary of the Islamic Revolution, 1982.

Bitzes, John G. "Education and *Verstehen*—Prerequisites for the West in Its Treatment of the Third World." Paper presented at the Sixth Third World Studies Conference, Omaha, Nebraska, October 27, 1983.

Bloom, Allan. *The Closing of the American Mind.* New York: Simon and Schuster, 1987.

Bonat, Zuwaghu. "Who Decides Economic Policy in Nigeria?" *The Analyst,* November 1986.

Boyd, Barron J., Jr. "A Subsystemic Analysis of the Southern African Development Coordination Conference." *African Studies Review* 28 (1987).

Bretl, E. S. *Colonization and Underdevelopment in East Africa.* London: Heineman, 1973.

Bulletin of the Islamic Center (Washington, D.C.), June 24, 1983.

Business Concord. October 21, 1983.

Caporaso, James A. "Dependence, Dependency, and Power in the Global System: A Structural and Behavioral Analysis." *International Organization* 32 (Winter 1978).

Cartwright, John R. *Political Leadership in New York.* New York: St. Martin's Press, 1983.

Chowdhury, Anwar H. "Soviets Fear Islamic Contamination of Central Asia." *Tehran Times,* May 17, 1983.

CIA-America Supports the Usurpers of Palestine. Tehran: Ministry of Islamic Guidance, 1982.

Clute, Robert E. "The Role of Agriculture in African Development." *African Studies Review* 25 (1982): 1-20.

Collier, R. Beris. *Regimes in Tropical Africa: Changing Forms of Supremacy, 1945-1975* (Berkeley: University of California Press, 1982).

Cooley, John K. "Shah Plans to Restore Arms Cuts." *Christian Science Monitor*, February 28, 1977.

———. "How the Failure of Three Helicopters Changed History." *Christian Science Monitor*, April 28, 1980.

Curzon, George N. *Persia and the Persian Question*. Vols. 1 and 2. New York: Barnes and Noble, 1966.

Daily News of Tanzania (Dar es Salaam). June 30, 1974.

Daily Times (Lagos). January 5, 1987.

Darby, Michael R. "The Price of Oil and World Inflation and Recession." *American Economic Review*, 1982, pp. 738-751.

Dixit, Avinash. "Recent Development in Oligopoly Theory." *American Economic Review*, 1982.

Earle, E. M. *Makers of Modern Strategy*. Princeton: Princeton University Press, 1948.

The Economist Intelligence Unit. *Nigeria: Analysis of Economic and Political Trends Every Quarter*. No. 3. London: Economist Publishers, 1986.

El-Azhary, M. S., ed. *The Impact of Oil Revenues on Arab Gulf Development*. Boulder, Colo.: Westview Press, 1984.

———. *The Iraq-Iran War*. London: Croom Helm, 1984.

Ellis, Harry B. "Race to Modernize Before Oil Runs out." *Christian Science Monitor*, January 2, 1976.

Emmanuel, Arghiri. *Unequal Exchange: A Study of the Imperialism of Trade*. New York: Monthly Review Press, 1972.

England, Claude Van. "Iran Threatens Wider War in Response to Iraqi Threat." *Christian Science Monitor*, September 20, 1983.

Esman, M. J. "Some Issues in Institution Building Theory." In D. W. Thomas, H. R. Potter, W. L. Miller, and A. F. Aveni, eds., *Institution Building: A Model for Applied Social Change*. Cambridge, Mass.: Schenkman, 1972.

Falola, Toyin, and Julius Ihonvbere. *The Rise and Fall of Nigeria's Second Republic: 1979-1984*. London: Zed Books, 1985.

Far Eastern Economic Review, August 20, 1987.

Farid, Abdel Majid, and Sirriyeh Hussein, eds. *The Decline of Arab Oil Revenues*. London: Croom Helm, 1986.

Graham, Robert. *Iran: The Illusion of Power*. London: Croom Helm, 1978.

Graves, William. "Iran Desert Miracle." *National Geographic*, January 1975.

Guardian (Lagos), November 23, 1986.

Halberstram, David. *The Powers That Be*. New York: Alfred A. Knopf, 1979.

Hartley, William D., et al. "Persian Gulf Tension." *U.S. News & World Report*, November 5, 1979.

Hedley, Don. *World Energy: The Facts and the Future*. New York: Facts on File, 1981.

Heikel, Mohamed. *The Return of the Ayatollah: The Iranian Revolution from Mossadeq to Khomeini.* London: Andre Deutsch, 1981.

Huntington, Samuel P. *Political Order in Changing Societies.* New Haven: Yale University Press, 1968.

Jackson, Robert, and Carol G. Rosberg. *Personal Rule in Black Africa: Prince, Autocrat, Prophet, Tyrant.* Berkeley: University of California Press, 1982.

Kayhan International (Tehran), June 23, 1983.

Jaulin, Robert. *El ethnocidio a través de las Américas.* Mexico City: Siglo xxi, 1976.

Jazainy, Idriss. "The Facts About Oil Price Adjustments." *OPEC Bulletin* (Vienna) 13 (1982).

Keyes, Beach. "A Mideast Superpower Growing in Iran." *Omaha World Herald,* November 2, 1977.

Khomeini, Imam. *Islam and the Revolution.* Berkeley, California: Mizan, 1981.

────── . *Selected Messages and Speeches of Imam Khomeini.* Tehran: Ministry of National Guidance, 1981.

Khundmiri, Alam S. "A Critical Examination of Islamic Traditionalism." *Islam and the Modern Age* 2, no. 2 (May 1971).

Kifner, John. "Ethnic Arabs of Iranian Oil Region in South Worry Regime." *New York Times,* April 22, 1979.

────── . "Exile Back from America Helping Create a New Iran." *New York Times.* April 1, 1979.

Kolo, Jerry. "Institutional Design for Community Planning in Nigeria: A Conceptual Model." Ph.D. dissertation. School of Urban and Regional Planning, University of Waterloo (Ontario), 1986.

Krauthammer, Charles. "How to Deal with Countries Gone Mad." *Time,* September 21, 1987.

Kulshrestha, Samuel K. "A Proposed Concept of Polarized Activity Centers for Spatio-Economic Development." Ph.D. dissertation. Department of Urban and Regional Planning, Ahmadu Bello University, Zaria, Nigeria, 1980.

Lacouture, Jean. *Vietnam Between Two Truces.* New York: Random House, 1966.

Lieterman, Eloise. "Hope for Uniting U.S. Society Rests with Schools, Says Carnegie Educator." *Christian Science Monitor,* September 19, 1983.

Lipsey, Richard G. "Government and Inflation." *American Economic Review,* 1982.

Martial Law. Law no. 3442 (1981). For an English translation, see *Laws of the Republic of Korea.* Vol. 1, II–154 to II–156. Seoul: Korean Legal Center, 1983.

Mayer, William E. "Why Did Many G. I. Captives Cave in?" *U.S. News & World Report* 40 (February 24, 1956): 56–66, 67, 72.

McBeth, J. "'Guidelines' for the Press." *Far Eastern Economic Review,* March 19, 1987.

McKinnon, Ronald I. "Currency Substitution and Instability in the World Dollar Standard." *American Economic Review*, 1982.

McWhirter, William A. "The Shah's Princely Party." *Life*, October 29, 1971.

Morna, Colleen L. "Doing Business in Beira." *Africa Report*, July–August 1987, pp. 61-69.

Morris, Glenn T. "In Support of the Right of Self-Determination for Indigenous Peoples Under International Law." *German Yearbook of International Law* 29 (1986): 277-316.

Muller, Henry, et al. "A Government Beheaded." *Time*, September 14, 1981.

Muslim World 50, no. 2 (April 1960).

National Concord, December 20, 29, 1986; January 3, 1987.

Nawaz, M. K. "Some Aspects of Modernization of Islamic Law." In Carl Leiden, ed., *The Conflict of Traditionalism and Modernism in the Muslim Middle East*. Austin: University of Texas Press, 1966.

New Nigerian, January 3, 1987.

Newswatch, November 25, 1985; August 11, 1986.

Newsweek, September 14, 1981.

Nickel, Herman. "The U.S. Failure in Iran." *Fortune*, March 12, 1979.

Nietschmann, Bernard. "The Third World War." *Cultural Survival Quarterly* 2, no. 3 (1987): 1-15.

"NUPCE Blasts Privatisation." *New Horizon*, June 1986.

Nwokoye, Willie. "Nigeria's Fish Crisis." *African Concord*, no. 73 (January 1986).

Oculi, Okello. "Multinationals in Nigerian Agriculture in the 1980's." *Review of African Political Economy* no. 31 (December 1984): 87-91.

O'Donnell, Guillermo A. *Modernization and Bureaucratic Authoritarianism*. Berkeley: University of California Press, 1979.

Ohwahwa, Fred. "Beyond Cigarettes: NTC Trains Young Men for Small-Scale Farming." *African Guardian* 2, no. 25 (July 2, 1987).

Olle, Werner. "New Forms of Foreign Investment in Developing Countries." *Intereconomics*, May–June, 1983.

OPEC Secretariat, Statistics Unit. "OPEC and the World Crude Oil Trade." *OPEC Bulletin* (Vienna) 12 (1981): 10-31.

Organski, A. F. K. *The Stages of Political Development*. New York: Alfred A. Knopf, 1965.

Paletz, David L. *Media Power Politics*. New York: Free Press, 1981.

Population Reference Bureau. *World Population Data Sheet*. Washington, D.C.: Population Reference Bureau, 1986.

Potter, H. R. "Criteria of Institutional Change as Guidelines for Assessing Project Maturation." In D. W. Thomas et al., eds., *Institution Building: A Model for Applied Social Change*. Cambridge, Mass: Schenkman, 1972.

Price, Robert M. "Southern African Regional Security: Pax or Pox Pretoria?" *World Policy Journal* 2 (1985).

Psacharopoulos, George. *Education for Development: An Analysis of Investment Choices.* New York: Oxford University Press for the World Bank, 1985.

Quran. Sura 8, v. 53; Sura 22, v. 10; Sura 29, v. 69.

Report of Women's Vocational Training Project. New Delhi: International Labor Office, 1983.

Reuber, Grant L. *Private Foreign Investment in Development.* Oxford: Clarendon Press, 1973.

Riddick, W. W. "The Nature of the Petroleum Industry." *Academy of Political Science Proceedings,* 1973.

Rodney, Walter. *How Europe Underdeveloped Africa.* Washington, D.C.: Howard University Press, 1982.

Rotberg, Robert, and Ali Vlazriu, eds. *Power and Protest in Africa.* New York: Oxford University Press, 1970.

Roosevelt, Kermit. *Countercoup: The Struggle for the Control of Iran.* New York: McGraw-Hill, 1979.

Rostow, Walt W. *The Stages of Economic Development: A Non-Communist Manifesto.* Cambridge: Cambridge University Press, 1960.

Sachs, Jeffrey. "Stabilization Policies in the World Economy: Scope and Skepticism." *American Economic Review,* 1982, 56–61.

Sadat, Anwar. "In Search of Identity." *Time,* March 20, 1978.

Said, Edward W. *Orientalism.* New York: Pantheon. 1979.

Sayegh, Fayez. *Camp David and Palestine: A Preliminary Analysis.* New York: Arab Information Center, 1978.

Schmidt, Dana Adams. "Iran—Self-Appointed Guardian of the Gulf." *Christian Science Monitor,* January 29, 1975.

Seyyed-Javadi, Kamal, et al. *Echo of Islam: The Dawn of the Islamic Revolution.* Tehran: Ministry of Islamic Guidance, 1981.

Shaw, Donald L., Maxwell E. McCombs, et al. *The Emergence of American Political Issues: The Agenda-Setting Function of the Press.* St. Paul: West, 1977.

Siffin, William J. "The Institution Building Perspective: Properties, Problems and Promise." In D. W. Thomas et al., eds., *Institution Building: A Model for Applied Social Change.* Cambridge, Mass: Schenkman. 1972.

Simpson, John. "Along the Streets of Tehran." *Harper's,* January 1988.

Sirageldin, A. Ismail. *Saudis in Transition: The Challenge of a Changing Labor Market.* New York: Oxford University Press for the World Bank, 1984.

Smith, Anthony D. *The Ethnic Origins of Nations.* Oxford: Basil Blackwell, 1986.

Smith, Donald E., ed., "Emerging Patterns of Religion and Politics." In *South Asian Politics and Religion.* Princeton: Princeton University Press, 1966.

The Standard (Jos, Nigeria), January 3, 1987.

Stavenhagen, Rodolfo. "Ethnocide or Ethnodevelopment." *Development* 1 (1987): 74–78.

Stempel, John D. *Inside the Iranian Revolution.* Bloomington: Indiana University Press, 1981.

Sullivan, William H. *Mission to Iran.* New York: W. W. Norton, 1981.

Sulzberger, A. O. "New Fears Emerging for Iranian Students." *New York Times,* April 15, 1979.

Sunday Standard (Jos, Nigeria), December 7, 1986.

Sunday Times (Lagos), January 4, 1987.

Taher-Kheli, Shirin, and Shaheen Ayubi. *The Iran-Iraq War: New Weapons, Old Conflicts.* New York: Praeger, 1983.

Talbott, Strobe, et al. "Hope for the Hostages." *Time,* November 10, 1980.

Taylor, Charles Lewis, and David A. Jodice. *World Handbook of Political and Social Indicators.* 3rd ed. 2 vols. New Haven: Yale University Press, 1983.

Tehran Times, May 25; June 4, 1983.

Thisweek, November 7, 1986.

Thompson, Carol B. "SADCC's Struggle for Economic Liberation." *Africa Report* 31 (July–August 1986).

Triffin, R. "The Dollar, the ECU, Gold and Oil." *Forbes,* 1980.

U.S. News & World Report, December 3, 1979; March 3, 1980.

United Nations. *Charter of the United Nations and Statute of the International Court of Justice.* New York: United Nations, 1945.

United Nations Economic Commission for Africa. *Survey of Economic Conditions in Africa, 1972.* New York: United Nations, 1973.

United States Arms Control and Disarmament Agency. *World Military Expenditures and Arms Transfers, 1986.* Washington, D.C.: U.S. Government Printing Office, 1987.

United States Department of State, Bureau of Public Affairs. *Southern African Development Coordination Conference: Gist.* Washington, D.C.: U.S. Department of State, 1987.

United States Department of State, Secretary of State's Advisory Committee on Africa. *A U.S. Policy Toward Africa.* Department of State Publication 9537. Washington, D.C.: U.S. Department of State, 1987.

United States Department of the Interior, Bureau of Mines. *Mineral Industries of Africa.* Washington, D.C.: U.S. Government Printing Office, 1984.

United States House of Representatives. "Hearings and Markup Before the Subcommittee on Africa of the Committee on Foreign Affairs," 97th Cong., 1st Sess. *Foreign Assistance Legislation for Fiscal Year 1982 (Part 8).* Washington, D.C.: U.S. Government Printing Office, 1981.

––––––. "Hearings Before the Subcommittee on Appropriations." 97th Cong., 2nd Sess. *Foreign Assistance and Related Appropriations for 1983 (Part 4).* Washington, D.C.: U.S. Government Printing Office, 1982.

––––––. "Hearings and Markup Before the Subcommittee on Africa of the Committee on Foreign Affairs." 98th Cong., 1st Sess. *Foreign Assistance*

Legislation for Fiscal Years 1984-85 (Part 8). Washington, D.C.: U.S. Government Printing Office, 1984.

Usman, Yusufu Bala. *Nigeria Against the I.M.F.: The Home Market Strategy.* Kaduna, Nigeria: Vanguard Publishers, 1986.

Viola, J. W. *Human Resources Development in Saudi Arabia: Multinational and Saudization.* Boston: International Human Resource Development Corporation, 1986.

Wallerstein, Immanuel. *The Capitalist World-Economy.* Cambridge: Cambridge University Press, 1979.

Walters, Ronald. "Beyond Sanctions: A Comprehensive U.S. Policy for Southern Africa." *World Policy Journal* 4 (1986-1987).

Wells, H. G. "On History." *New York Times,* December 5, 1940.

West Africa, August 28, 1987.

Wiarda, H. J. "Ethnocentrism and Third World Development." *Society* 24, no. 6 (1987): 55-64.

Wilcox, D. L. "Black African States." In J. L. Curry and J. R. Dassin, eds., *Press Control Around the World.* New York: Praeger, 1982.

Winrock International Institute for Agricultural Development. *Agricultural Development Indicators.* Morrilton, Ark.: Winrock International Institute for Agricultural Development, 1987.

Wolfson, Margaret, ed., "Population and Poverty in Sub-Saharan Africa." In *Crisis and Recovery in Sub-Saharan Africa.* Paris: OECD Development Centre, 1985.

World Bank. *World Tables.* Baltimore: Johns Hopkins University Press, 1980.

World Population Prospects. New York: United Nations, 1985.

Yahaya, Abdullahi. "The Privatisation of the Agricultural Sector." *The Analyst,* November 1986.

Zehender, Wolfgang. *Cooperation Versus Integration: The Prospects of the Southern African Development Coordination Conference.* Berlin: German Development Institute, 1983.

Index

Abdullahi, Y., 145

acculturation: cultural diversity and, 38-40; differentiated from ethnocide, 39

Afprint, 152

Africa, 105-139, 161-178; communications technology in SADCC nations, 168; Consultative Group on International Agricultural Research (CGIAR), 130; debt burden, 127-129; dualistic agricultural economies, 111-117; environment, 119; food crisis, 105-139; food production and distribution network by SADCC, 166-167; foreign aid and debt, 16-17, 127-129, 196-197; foreign aid to, 176-178; "green revolution," 131; hunger in, 105-139; ICRISAT (International Crops Research Institute for the Semi-Arid Tropics), 132; industrial development in, 169-170; land conditions, 117-118; leadership failures, 120-122; Lusaka Declaration, 161-162; Mbabane conference, 167; military budgets in, 136-138; mineral exports, 161-162; mining in, 167-168; NAM and, 194; National Fertilizer Company of Nigeria (NAFCON), 150-151; Nigeria, 141-156; Nigerian agricultural crisis, 141-157; peanut production, 108; population growth, 15-16, 117, 122-127; Preferential Trade Area (PTA), 169; railroad transportation, 171; research and training in, 129-136; SADCC (Southern African Development Coordination Council), 161-178; South Africa's destabilization efforts against SADCC, 173-175; transportation in SADCC nations, 170-172; USAID (U.S. Agency for International Development), 134-136; U.S. foreign policy in, 95-103; U.S. relief efforts following catastrophes, 196; U.S.-SADCC relations, 176-178. See also SADCC

African-Americans, 95-103

Agboola, S. D., 144

agriculture: in Africa, 106–138; cocoa processing, 154–155; Consultative Group on International Agricultural Research (CGIAR), 130; dualistic economies, 111–117; environment in Africa, 119; fertilizers and, 118–119; food production and distribution network in Africa, 166–167; food production problems in Africa, 106–114; "green revolution," 131; ICRISAT (International Crops Research Institute for the Semi-Arid Tropics), 132; land conditions in Africa, 117–118; in Nigeria, 141–157; peanut production, 108; peasant farmers, 153–155; pest invasions, 144; small-scale farming, 153; in Third World, 17
Alfonzo, P., 69
Allah. *See* Islam; Muslim fundamentalism; religion
Anglin, D., 169
Angola, 161–178; energy development, 165; Lusaka Declaration, 161; military expenditures, 173; National Union for the Total Independence of Angola (UNITA), 171; size of, 163; U.S. aid and relations, 176–178; *See also* SADCC
animal diseases control, 166
apartheid, 178
aquaculture, in Africa, 106
Arab Gulf states (AGS), 70–71; human effects of oil economy on, 79–85; spillover effect, 74–76. *See also* OPEC
Arab league, 69–70
Argentina, foreign debt crisis, 196–197
Ariyo, 21
arms sale: British helicopter sale to India, 138; military budgets in Africa and, 136–138
Asante, S., 168

Baker, J., 17, 197–198
Baker plan, 197–198
Bandung Conference, 193–194
Bangladesh Flood, U.S. relief efforts following, 196
Beira-Malawi railway, 171
Beira-Maputo railway, 171
Belgrade summit, 193–194
blacks: Africa and, 95–103; in America, 95–97
Blumeris, A., 166
Bonat, Z., 155
Bophutatswana, 174
Borlaug, N., 132
Bornu, 144
Botswana, 161–178; energy development, 164–165; Lusaka Declaration, 161; per capita GNP, 163; stress on regional development, 169; transportation dependence on South Africa, 170. *See also* SADCC
Brady, N., 134
Brazil: Baker Plan for sustained growth and, 197–198; foreign debt crisis, 196–197
Buddhism, *See* religion
Burdick, E., 54
Burundi, population growth rates, 117
Bush, G., 98

Canada, SADCC support, 173
capital disinvestment. *See* flight capital
capital investment: in Africa, 130–133; government stimulation of, 201–202; in Third World, 198–202; U.S. commitment to market forces, 202–203
Caporaso, J., 28
Catholicism, in Vietnam, 50
cereals, 105–113; decline of, 109; production of, 105–106
Chad, land conditions, 118
Challenor, H., 96

Chile, Baker Plan for sustained growth and, 197-198

China: population growth, 15-16; production increases, 105

Christianity. *See* religion

Clark, J., 136, 138

climate, food production and, 117-121

cocoa, in Nigeria, 154-155

COMECON, SADCC support, 173

communications, in SADCC nations, 168

Consultative Group on International Agricultural Research (CGIAR), 130

critical perspective, of development, 28-29

cultural genocide. *See* ethnocide

Darby, M. R., 74

Davis, J., 96

debt: capital investment and, 198-202; crisis of Third World nations, 193-203; of Third World nations, 16-18, 127-129. *See also* Africa; foreign debt

"Decade for Women," 87-88

development: critical perspective, 28-29; goals of in Arab states, 82-84; mainstream perspective, 26-27; perspectives of, 26-29

Diggs, C. C., Jr., 97

disease: control, in Africa, 166; nutritional deficiences and, 127

dualistic agricultural economies, in Africa, 111-117

DuBois, W. E. B., 100

Eastern Africa: agriculture in, 111-115. *See also* Africa

Ebong, I., 155

economics: Baker Plan for sustained growth, 197-198; capital investment in Third World, 198-202; of debt crisis of Third World nations, 127-129, 193-203; dualistic agricultural economies, 111-117; of flight capital, 199-201; of food production in SADCC countries, 166-167; foreign aid and debt, 16-18, 127-129; growth strategy of Third World, 13-14; human effects of oil economy on Arab Gulf States (AGS), 79-85; index of repression (1960-67), 29-30; of industrial development, 169-170; international and Third World implications, 194; marginal propensity to save (MPS), 75-76; military expenditures and, 173; mineral exports, 161-162; of mining, 167-168; of oil business, 71-78; open, in Third World, 25-35; partnership agreements, 151-152; production-sharing contracts, 168; of SADCC nations, 162-163; of sanctions against South Africa, 175

Edmondson, L., 97, 100

education, in Africa, 129-136

EEC, cereal production, 105

Egypt, foreign debt crisis, 196-197

energy development: oil crisis and, 71; in SADCC countries, 164-165. *See also* OPEC

equity, as Third World objective, 83

ethnocide, 37-45; definition of, 37-40; mechanisms of and actors in the phenomenon, 40-45

European Economic Community (EEC), 173

Falae, O., 149

family unit, in Third World, 15-16

farming. *See* agriculture

fertilizers, uses of, 118-119

flight capital, and developing countries, 199-201

food. *See* agriculture

food production: in Africa, 105–111;
climate and, 117–121; and land
conditions, 117–118; leadership
failures in Africa and, 120–122;
population growth rates in Africa
and, 117, 122–127; in SADCC
countries, 166–167; shortages and
famines examined, 105–139. *See
also* agriculture

foreign aid: to SADCC, 172–173, 176–
178; to Third World nations, 16–18

foreign debt: Baker plan, 197–198;
capital investment and, 198–202;
crisis of Third World nations, 193–
203; economics of, 16–18, 127–129

foreign investment: production-sharing
contracts, 168; in Third World by
U.S., 195–196

foreign policy, U.S.–Africa, 95–103

foreign trade: fertilizers and, 118–119;
of SADCC nations, 162

FSLN (Sandinista National Liberation
Front), 184–190

fundamentalism. *See* Islam; Muslim
fundamentalism; religion

Gaborone, 169–170

government: centralization of, 16;
repression in Third World, 26–34

Group of 77 (G-77), 194

growth, as Third World objective, 83

Halberstram, D., 49

Hero, Al, 96

higher education, in Africa, 129–136

human capital, in Arab Gulf States
(AGS), 79–85

hunger, in Africa, 105–139

hyperinflation, 28

IB model, 19–20

IFIs (international financial institutions), 27

IMF (International Monetary Fund),
74

index of economic openness, 30–31

index of repression (1960–1967), 29–
30

India: British helicopter sale to, 138;
population growth, 15–16; production increases, 105; women's role
in, 87–94

Indonesia, production-sharing contracts, 168

industrial development, in SADCC
nations, 169–170

inflation, 28

institution-building (IB) strategy, 19–
20

International Crops Research Institute
for the Semi-Arid Tropics
(ICRISAT), 132

international financial institutions
(IFIs), 27

International Monetary Fund (IMF),
74

Iran, 69; religion in, 49–52

Islam: beliefs of, 58–59; Islamic revivals, 57–67; Muslim modernists,
62–64; Muslim pragmatists, 64–67;
Sunni traditionalists, 60–62; traditional Muslims, 60–62. *See also*
religion

Ivory Coast, investment in, 131

Japan, trade with Arab Gulf states
(AGS), 76

Judaism. *See* religion

Kaikai, S., 155

Kellogg, M. W., 150–151

Kenya: agriculture in, 118; U.S. aid
and relations, 176–178

Khilafat movement, 60

Khomeini (Ayatollah), 52–53

Kolade, C., 154
Kolo, 21
Korea, 200
Korean War, U.S. prisoners, 48–49
Kulshrestha, 21
Kuwait, gross domestic product of, 75–76

labor, 28; role of women in India, 87–94
Lacouture, J., 50
Laoye, D. B., 149
Latin America: foreign debt crisis, 196–197; Nicaraguan revolution, 183–192; United Nations Conference on Trade and Development (1964), 194
LDCs, 13; African hunger, 105–139; economic analysis of, 28–34; index of repression (1960–1967), 29–30; political instability (1958–1967), 30
least-developed countries (LDCs), U.N. classification of, 13. *See also* Third World
Lederer, W. J., 54
Lesotho, 161–178; Lusaka Declaration, 161; military expenditures, 173; transportation dependence on South Africa, 170. *See also* SADCC
Liberia, founding of, 95
Lusaka Agreement, 173–174
Lusaka Declaration, 161

McHenry, D., 97
McPherson, W. P., 134
mainstream perspective, of development, 26–27
Makoni, S., 172
Malawi, 161–178; Lusaka Declaration, 161; per capita GNP, 163. *See also* SADCC
Malaysia, investment strategies, 131

Mali: food crop production, 108; record crop, 114
marginal propensity to save (MPS), 75–76
Mayer, W. E., 48–49
Mbabane conference, 167
MDCs, 25, 27
Mexico: Baker Plan for sustained growth and, 197–198; flight capital, 199–201; foreign debt crisis, 196–197
Middle East: Arab league, 69–70; OPEC and, 69–77. *See also* Arab Gulf States (AGS); OPEC
Miller, J., 96
mineral exports, 161–162
Mmusi, P., 175
MNCs, 27
modernization, strategy of Third World, 14
more-developed countries (MDCs), 25, 27
Morocco, crop production, 105
Morris, M., 96
Mozambique, 161–178; Lusaka Declaration, 161; military expenditures, 173; transportation sector coordination, 170–172; U.S. aid and relations, 176–178. *See also* SADCC
Muslim fundamentalism, 57–67; basis of, 58–59; versus traditional Muslims, 60–62. *See also* religion

National Fertilizer Company of Nigeria (NAFCON), 150–151
neo-institutionalists, 15
Ngo Dinh Diem, 50
Nicaragua, 183–192; Contra attacks, 190–191; economic problems, 185–187; English language learning in, 189; FSLN (Sandinista National Liberation Front) in, 184–190;

Sandinista government, 187–191; Somoza dynasty, 184–186; U.S. and, 185–192; wealthy citizens flee from, 186–187

Nigeria: agricultural crisis in, 141–157; agricultural revival, 148–151; cocoa processing, 154–155; colonial period, 145; contradictory economic development policies, 151–156; crop production, 105; export economics, 147–151; farm loans, 152–153; foreign debt crisis, 196–197; foreign investment in, 146; import expenditures, 143; investment in, 131; NAFCON, 150–151; nutrition in, 150; oil income, 147–148; peasant farmers in, 153–155; United Nations Development Program assistance, 150; World Bank loans, 150–151

Nkomatic Accord, 173–174

Nonaligned Movement (NAM), 193–194

Norman, D., 167

nutrition, in Nigeria, 150

OAU (Organization of African Unity), 17

Obasanjo, O., 148

Odhiambo, T., 132

OECD (Organization for Economic and Cooperative Development), 17

oil: human effects of on Arab Gulf States (AGS), 79–85; Nigerian export of, 147–148; OPEC control, 69–73; in SADCC countries, 164–165; supply, demand, and prices, 73–75. *See also* energy development; OPEC

Olashore, O., 143

Onosode, G., 149

OPEC, 69–77; background of, 69–70; member states, 70; myths of in

West, 70–73; NAM and G-77 relations, 194; pricing policies, 74; SADCC support, 173; spillover effect, 74–76; supply factors, 73–75

open economics, in Third World, 26–34

Organization for Economic and Cooperative Development (OECD). *See* OECD

Organization of African Unity (OAU). *See* OAU

Organization of Petroleum Exporting Countries. *See* OPEC

Pahlevi, N., 50

partnership agreements, with Nigeria, 151–152

peanuts, production, 108–109

peasants, in Nigeria, 153–155

Philippines, foreign debt crisis, 196–197

Plummer, B., 96

political repression, in Third World, 26–34

population: growth of in Third World, 15–16; growth rates in Africa, 117, 122–127

Preferential Trade Area (PTA), 169

Qatar, 75–76

Quran. *See* Islam; Muslim fundamentalism; religion

railways, in Africa, 171

Ramphal, S., 175

religion, 47–54; in Iran, 52–53; Islamic revivals, 57–67; Muslim modernists, 62–64; Muslim pragmatists, 64–67; Sunni fundamentalism, 58–59; traditional Muslims, 60–62; in Vietnam, 49–51

rice, production, 108–109

River Basin Development Authorities (RBDA), 147
Rokupr Rice Research Station, 133
Rwanda, population growth rates, 117

Sachs, J., 74
SADCC (Southern African Development Coordination Council), 161–178; communications technology, 168; destabilization by South Africa, 173–175; energy development in, 164–165; food production and distribution network, 166–167; foreign aid to, 172–173; formation of, 161–162; industrial development, 169–170; Mbabane conference, 167; military expenditures, 173; mining economics, 167–168; objectives of, 162–163; oil and, 164–165; organization of, 163–164; Preferential Trade Area (PTA), 169; railway rehabilitation efforts, 171; Reagan administration's attitude toward SADCC states, 177; sanctions against South Africa debate, 175; transportation in, 170–172; U.S. relations, 176–178
Sahel, land conditions, 118
Salvador earthquake, U.S. relief efforts following, 196
sanctions, SADCC position on, 175
Sandinista National Liberation Front (FSLN), 184–190
Saudi Arabia, 69–73; gross domestic product of, 75–76; oil production and, 71–77. *See also* OPEC
security, as Third World objective, 83
Shuaib, B., 146
Shultz, G., 97
Sierre Leone: investment in, 131; Rokupr Rice Research Station, 133
socialist governments, revolutions and, 183–184

Somalia, U.S. aid and relations, 176–178
Somoza dynasty, (Nicaragua), 184–186
South Africa, 168, 170–172; destabilization efforts against SADCC, 173–175; SADCC and, 161–171; sanctions, 175
South America, foreign aid and debt, 16–17
Southern Africa, dualistic agricultural economies and, 111–115. *See also* Africa
Southern African Development Coordination Council (SADCC). *See* SADCC
South Korea, 200
Soviet Union: food production, 105; SADCC-Soviet relations, 176–178; SADCC support, 173
special drawing rights (SDR), 74
Sudan, 105
Sunnah. *See* Islam; Muslim fundamentalism; religion
Sunni fundamentalism, 58–59
Sunni traditionalists, 60–62
Swaziland, 161–178; energy development, 164–165; Lusaka Declaration, 161; size of, 163; transportation dependence on South Africa, 170. *See also* SADCC

tanning, in Nigeria, 155
Tanzania, 161–178; energy development, 164–165; food crop production, 108–109; industrial development, 169; Lusaka Declaration, 161; military expenditures, 173; per capita GNP, 163. *See also* SADCC
tawhid, definition of, 58
taxation, dualistic agricultural economies, 111–113
technological research, in Africa, 129–136

Tet offensive, 49

Third World: African foreign policy and U.S., 95–103; agricultural development in Nigeria, 147–151; agriculture in, 17, 141–157; Baker Plan for sustained growth, 197–198; Bandung Conference, 193–194; capital investment in, 198–202; communications technology, 168; definition of, 1–2; economic development perspectives, 26–29; economic growth strategy, 13–14; economic influences on, 28–30; energy development in, 164–165; family unit in, 15–16; flight capital and debt, 199–201; foreign aid, 16–18; foreign debt, 16–18, 193–203; foreign investment in, 195–196; government centralization, 16; human effects of oil economy on Arab Gulf States (AGS), 79–85; hunger in, 105–139; IB strategy, 19–20; index of state strength (1965), 30; Indian womens' changing role, 87–94; industrial development, 169–170; Islamic revivals in, 57–67; military budgets in Africa, 136–138; Muslim fundamentalism, 57–67; Nicaraguan revolution, 183–192; Nigeria, 141–156; OPEC and, 69–77; open economic index, 30–31; people-oriented strategy, 14–15; political instability (1958–1967), 30; population growth, 15–16; religion in, 47–54; repression in, 25–26; SADCC (Southern African Development Coordination Council), 161–178; strategies of, 13–22; traditional Muslims in, 60–62; United Nations and, 3; USAID (U.S. Agency for International Development) assistance, 134–136; U.S. commitment to market forces and,
202–203; U.S. exports to, 193; U.S. policy principles, 195–197

Thompson, C., 163

Tito (Marshall), 193–194

tobacco, in Nigeria, 154

training, for women in India, 87–94

TransAfrica lobby, 99

transportation: railway rehabilitation efforts, 171; SADCC nations and, 170–172

Treaty of Westphalia, 40

Turkey, Khilafat movement, 60

UNITA (National Union for the Total Indpendence of Angola), 171, 173

United Arab Emirates, gross domestic product of, 75–76

United Nations, 15; Conference on Trade and Development (1964), 194; Decade for Women, 87–88; Nigerian assistance, 150

United States: African assistance, 176–178; African foreign policy, 95–103; Baker Plan, 197–198; blacks' role in African policy, 95–103; cereal production, 105; commitment to market forces, 202–203; Contra attacks in Nicaragua and, 190–191; as creditor to Third World, 196–197; debt crisis of Third World nations and, 193–203; exports, 193; hostage crisis, 53; Iran and, 52–53; at Mbabane conference, 167; Nicaragua and, 185–192; OPEC and, 72–77; policy principles toward Third World, 195–197; prisoners of war (U.S.), 48–49; Reagan administration's attitude toward SADCC states, 177; relief efforts, 196; SADCC-U.S. relations, 176–178; Third World religion awareness, 47–49; USAID (U.S. Agency for International Development), 134–136

university education, in Africa, 129–
136
USAID (U.S. Agency for International
Development), 134–136
Usen, A., 144, 147
Usman, Y. B., 143, 157

Venezuela, 69; foreign debt crisis,
196–197
Vietnam, religion in, 49–52
Vietnam War, U.S. role in, 49–50
vitamin deficiencies, in Africa, 127
vocational training, for women in
India, 87–94

West Africa, ICRISAT in, 132
West African Rice Development Asso-
ciation (WARDA), 132
Western Africa, dualistic agricultural
economies and, 111–115. *See also*
Africa
Wiarda, H. J., 15

women: "Decade for Women", 87–88;
role of in India, 87–94; training
policy for increased role, 89–91
World Bank, 146; Baker Plan for sustained growth and, 197–198;
Nigerian assistance, 150–151
World War II, 95

Zaire, 161–178; SADCC rejection, 161.
See also SADCC
Zambia, 161–178; Lusaka Declaration,
161; military expenditures, 173;
mining in, 167–168. *See also*
SADCC
Zimbabwe, 161–178; energy develop-
ment, 164–165; food production
and distribution, 166–167; Lusaka
Declaration, 161; military expendi-
tures, 173; U.S. aid and relations,
176–178; U.S. aid to, 167;
Zimbabwe-Maputo railway, 171.
See also SADCC

About the Editor and Contributors

SHEIKH R. ALI is a professor of political science at North Carolina Central University, Durham, North Carolina, and a former diplomat in Washington, D.C.

PITA O. AGBESE is an assistant professor of political science at Grinnell College, Grinnell, Iowa.

JOHN G. BITZES is a university lecturer and a teacher in the public school system of Omaha, Nebraska.

ROBERT E. CLUTE is a professor and graduate coordinator of political science, and chairman of the Social Sciences Division, at the University of Georgia, Athens, Georgia.

ANDREW CONTEH is an associate professor of political science at Moorhead State University, Moorhead, Minnesota, and a former ambassador from Sierra Leone to the Soviet Union.

JACOB U. GORDON is an associate professor of African-American Studies and a research associate at the Institute for Public Policy and Business Research, University of Kansas, Lawrence, Kansas.

ZOHAIR HUSAIN is an assistant professor of political science at the University of South Alabama, Mobile, Alabama.

AMIN M. KAZAK is a Ph.D. candidate at the Graduate School of International Studies of the University of Denver.

JERRY KOLO is an assistant professor of political science and urban studies at Johnson C. Smith University, Charlotte, North Carolina.

THOMAS D. LOBE is an associate professor of political science, University of South Dakota, Vermillion, South Dakota.

SHAH M. MEHRABI is an associate professor of economics at Mary Washington College, Fredericksburg, Virginia.

MARY C. MULLER is a consultant in international human resources development and a member of the International Communications Consultants Cooperative, Sarasota, Florida.

STEVEN S. SALLIE is an associate professor of political science at Boise State University, Boise, Idaho.

MARC SILLS is a Ph.D. candidate at the Graduate School of International Studies of the University of Denver.